JEFF PANTANELLA

THE
FORGOTTEN
GODS

BOOK FOUR IN THE
EVER HERO SAGA

First Printing, 2021
Ever Hero Productions
Yorba Linda, CA 92886
United States of America

www.everheroproductions.com

ISBN: 978-1-7356025-9-2

Cover Design by Gene Mollica Studio, LLC

Author Photo by Asia Yen Productions and Design

Edit work by Wardog JoeV https://www.wardogjoev.com

To my mom, who is always close to my heart and never, ever forgotten. Love you!

Acknowledgments

To John S for giving me lots of amazing ideas for spin off stories and Brenda D for giving input on lots of rewrites.

Dramatis Personae

The Divine of the Seven Heavens

The Immortal Mother, creator of the Three Worlds

Illyria, ninth daughter of the Immortal Mother

Aetenos Sommai, 'The Divine Fist, The Great Monk', mortal, ascended to the rank of demigod

Lord Raguel, archangel, The Chancellor Pinnacle of the Seven Heavens, first of the True-borns

Lord Sonnalle, Equerry to the Chancellor Pinnacle, True-born

Zhao Houzi, animal spirit, monkey sage

The Wicked of the Abyss

Azrollorza, Supreme Devil, one of the 'Great Three', rules over the Mazzagratur, Sea of Terror, the fifth Layer in the Abyss

Morrdilliax, Supreme Devil, one of the 'Great Three', rules over Torremor, Plain of Infinite Decay, the sixth Layer in the Abyss

Xerthotha, 'The Chaos Devil', Supreme Devil, one of the 'Great Three', rules over the Stomoxys, The Land of Eternal Strife, the seventh Layer in the Abyss

Sekka, 'The Ice Queen', 'Mistress Sekka', prisoner of Xerthotha

Sess'thra, greater demon, succubus, infiltrator, commander of Sekka's agents in the Mortal Realm

Yanarothi, Lesser water demon

Monastery of Nu-Ordu, Kingdom of Baroqia
Kasai Ch'ou, 'The Divine Fist', The Ever Hero
Ninziz-zida, 'The Fire Serpent', sentient three sectioned staff
Brother Mando, junior monk
Brother Sando, junior monk

Lost Monastery of Symmetu, Kingdom of Baroqia
Cyrus Wraith, master monk

Forest Folk, Kingdom of Baroqia
Desdemonia Mishi, 'Nexus', daimus nexus
Pallo Katan, Kibo Gensai warrior, brother to Veers 'Run-Run' Katan
Veers Katan, 'Run-Run', Kibo Gensai warrior, brother to Pallo Katan

House Shiverrig, Kingdom of Baroqia
Gerun Shiverrig, 'The Barbarian Devil', Chaos Warlord
Hybrid Demons, 'Half-breeds', humans transformed into demons
Dai-Ko-Zior, Lich
Khalkoroth/Daku, 'The Pale Demon', shadow demon

Frona Tribe, Kingdom of Sunne
Ruith Zylris Faeharice, 'Gift', **Warrior Mage**

Isle of Yoru, Archipelago of Mith
Kazumi Hime, demon hunter, Yoru Ya-iba Clan

Contents

"You may not like it, you may not want it, but you embrace it. And you try your best to fix as many broken pieces as you can, because that is what heroes do."

~ Pallo Katan, Kibo Gensai

"Courage is earned by overcoming fear, and we all fear of something."
~ Gen Moll circa the First Frost War.

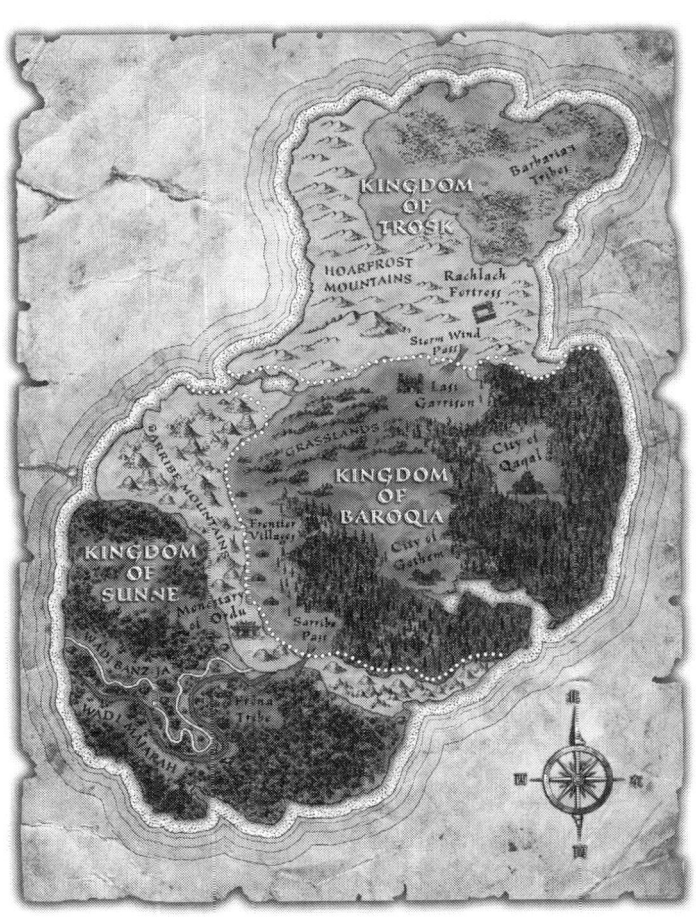

The Three Kingdoms of Hanna

Prologue

Kasai was a dead man walking. His sight blurred in and out of focus in time with the slow beat of his heart. There was blood everywhere — his blood. An eerie chill seeped through him even as his chest burned with throbbing pain. In disbelief and regret, he saw the awesomeness of Ninziz-zida's fiery form dissolve from reality and relit as a dim flicker along the three sectioned staff.

The dead weight of the staff lay heavy on his legs. Kasai felt the connection to the Boundless slip from his grasp as his blood bubbled out of him with each tortured breath. The battlefield faded away and blackness pushed in from the edges of his sight. He was finished.

"Kasai! Get up!" Desdemonia shouted. "You're not dead yet."

But it was over. Sekka was too strong, even against such a raw elemental force as Ninziz-zida. The archdevil would win this day, and the Three Kingdoms of Hanna would fall under her dominion.

+You finally see it now.+ Sekka's voice hissed like a viper directly into his mind. +You cannot defeat me.+

Then Desdemonia was standing protectively in front of him.

She shot a quick glance over her shoulder and shouted at him again. "I can't do this without you! Get up!"

Then she turned back to Sekka. "You will not touch him."

"Oh, I think I will," the archdevil said menacingly.

Sekka struck fast and Desdemonia was smashed aside in a blur of dark leather and black hair. She hit the ground hard and groaned in pain.

Then Sekka leered seductively at him. "Your essence will guarantee my place in the High Pantheon of Chaos."

"No, it won't," Desdemonia said in a frail voice.

Kasai saw the jungle colors of green, yellow, and blue bathe Desdemonia in a protective light. Sigils of power blossomed above her body as she raised a trembling hand and opened it toward the archdevil.

"Sek'Kiyohime!" she said and snatched at the air, closing her hand into a fist. "Weakness!"

Sekka stumbled a half step. She looked at Desdemonia with astonishment. "You dare!"

"She's vulnerable, Kasai. Fight," Desdemonia said in a strained voice. "I can't hold her forever."

Sekka spied the onyx ring on Desdemonia's finger. "Silly mortal. You had such potential." Her black within black eyes narrowed. "Break."

The onyx stone encased in the ring on Desdemonia's finger shattered in a cloud of black mist. Desdemonia cried out in pain but still managed to keep her fist closed, holding her debilitating magic over Sekka. Kasai could hear Desdemonia sucking in large gulps of air.

Somehow, he got to one knee. The pain in his chest was intense. But that was inconsequential now. He would die later.

Kasai searched for a strength that couldn't be found in muscle or bone. His heart would not let him quit, but that wouldn't be enough either. All that remained was his spirit and he would give that willingly to save Desdemonia.

"I give what remains to the Boundless and leave nothing for myself," he whispered in a hoarse voice.

And the Boundless accepted his gift. His spirit xindu opened into the ever-expanding space. He thought he was hallucinating as his view of the world around him shifted from one of physical things to elements of pure vibration. Desdemonia's magical command was siphoning layers of protection away from Sekka's human form. Darkness seeped from small holes across the archdevil's innate infernal armor, escaping into the air like billowing chimney smoke.

Sekka watched him with a bemused smile as he got to his feet. The Boundless was alive within him now and he filled his lungs with its invigorating air, then breathed it out slowly. He channeled white light into his fists. The energy was clean and pure, forcing Sekka to shield her eyes.

He walked purposefully toward the archdevil, without fear or caution, and commanded the Boundless to expand the openings across her body. On his third step he shot his fists into her chest, pulverizing Sekka's heart and lungs with the force of his blow.

Sekka gasped in shock and pain. Her mouth hung open, but she couldn't speak. Kasai withdrew his gory fists and stepped away. The archdevil's eyes were wide as she dropped to her knees, then fell forward, dead.

Kasai watched her body turn to cinders and then to chunks of ash, which rolled away in the wind. It was over. He immediately looked to where Desdemonia lay. Her hand was loosely clenched, but now rested on the ground. He stumbled forward and knelt at her side. She was cold and still.

Kasai pulled her body close to his, hoping to warm her. He

plucked wet strands of hair from her face and used the torn sleeve of his other arm to wipe away the tears streaming down his face.

His body felt numb and was covered in a patchwork of scratches and bruises. The horrible gashes across his chest had stopped bleeding. The Boundless was sustaining him now in a way he never thought possible.

It didn't matter. None of it mattered anymore. Kasai shifted Desdemonia's lifeless body across his own.

"Don't go, Des. We have more roads to travel together. I wanted to show you Ordu. I thought we could restore it, together." But there were no playful jabs from the frolicking gypsy or gruff words from the stoic druidess. He knew both were gone.

A thunderclap's deafening sound filled the battlefield. The heavy storm clouds vibrated, threatening to shatter like glass in the sky. Then came a second great boom. Everything stopped. Kasai stared into the heavens and saw a sight that could not be unseen. The sky was on fire.

The storm clouds evaporated from the heat of a second sun as a comet of light descended over the battlefield. Winged silhouettes numbering in the hundreds of thousands emerged from its center. The angels had arrived.

"They could have come anytime," he said and clutched Desdemonia's lifeless body to his own. "Anytime."

Kasai woke with a start and spit bits of grass and dirt from his mouth. He was on the ground. The air reeked of active fires and burnt things. Ash was everywhere, even here, high in the mountains. It clung to everything.

The dawn sun had risen long ago, and it was easily now past noon. He had missed or rather skipped another dawn meditation session. The heat of the day was collecting, and it was going to be another hot one.

Kasai raised his eyes to spy the edge of the chasm ahead of him. At this angle, the two sides merged into one. Maybe he would cross today, maybe he wouldn't. Though, avoiding what lay on the opposite side was preferable.

"Icy bones," he said, standing slowly and scowling at each new body ache.

Weeks ago, he had left behind the charred battlefield outside Winter Fury's walls. Before departing, he had said his farewells to Run-Run, who was busy nursing his wounded brother Pallo back to health. Though a seasoned warrior, Pallo would never be the same. He, like everyone else, had seen too many horrors for one lifetime.

Kasai did his best to shake off the memories of his last fight with Sekka. The archdevil had been the cause of such despair in his life. Her wickedness had scarred him deeply in mind, body, and soul. Even after her death, her legacy endured. He was broken and lost.

In his travels, Kasai met villagers and woodsmen who had suffered similar fates, loved ones gone, villages pillaged, lives destroyed. Kasai had saved the Three Kingdoms from Sekka's conquest, but now it was a desolate place, charred and ruined by the aftermath of the angels' heavenly fire.

It was a long journey home from the remains of the demon city aptly named Winter's Fury — Sekka's stronghold in the Mortal Realm, to the mountain peak that housed the Monastery of Ordu, or what was left of it.

"Damn Khalkoroth. Damn Daku, Shiverrig and all the rest of them," Kasai said bitterly. "What a mess. What a colossal mess. I should have been stronger."

It was said the capital city of Qaqal had been razed by whirlwinds of angelic fire. Kasai hoped the city of Gethem, and the corrupted Temple of Illumination had been exterminated in the same way.

"Fire cleanses everything," he said, tapping the ends of the three sectioned staff he had tucked in his sash.

We must rebuild what was lost, the sentient sanjiegun, Ninziz-zida, whispered in his mind. The ancient fire elemental's flame flickered along on the edges of the folded staff but didn't burn his robes or flesh.

"We will, Ninziz-zida, someday," he said. Though his words came out half-hearted and flat. He was too numb to care about anyone or anything. Kasai looked again to the chasm, which from this height, opened to a vast emptiness.

e was He "They could have come at any time, Des." He was prone to talking to her ghost as if she walked beside him. "Raguel could have come at any time and in a snap, destroyed Sekka, the Chaos Gate, and everything that came out of it. We should be eating honey cakes inside your cozy cottage. Wasn't that the plan?" He sighed. "But instead, I have the burnt remains of shattered dreams."

Kasai walked to the edge of the chasm. A frayed hemp rope was all that connected the sheer sides. Between them was an eternity of open space. He surveyed the chasm with a fair dose of foreboding, not sure if the line would hold his weight.

"I'm going to have to cross you sooner or later," he said with resignation.

Kasai grabbed the rope and lowered himself over the lip of the cliff. Hand over hand, he traversed the chasm. Midway across, he wished the rope would snap.

"It would be no more than I deserved."

Unfortunately, the rope held, and he reached the other

side where the trails leading to the Monastery of Ordu waited. He started up the winding path and worked his way up the side of the huge rock formation to the compound's outer walls. Fallen branches, leaves and assorted building debris greeted him when he reached the first steps.

"Master Choejor would've had my head if he saw this. But he's dead, isn't he. And you got him killed. Some hero you turned out to be."

Kasai looked longingly back towards the chasm. He could still turn back. *Just run and don't stop*, he thought. He noticed the distant sky was painted a faint orange glow from fires that still burned across northern Baroqia.

"They torched the cities and left the countryside to burn," Kasai said as he remembered the parting of storm clouds and the angels in their shining armor. Wave after wave of full battalions from the Heavenly Host appeared across the sky to smite Sekka's army.

They attacked like sea birds, diving from above and impaling demons like fish on their enchanted lances. The vast horde was decimated quickly, reduced to fleeing packs of monsters, attempting to escape the angels' fury.

But it was the holy fire that did the worst damage. Spinning columns of orange and yellow flames plunged from the sky and stretched to the ground, churning flaming madness through Winter's Fury. What didn't burn to ash, melted into slag. Nothing survived the firestorm that followed. How could it?

"The glorious angels and all their arrogance," he said, tasting the bitter dust floating in the air. "They could have saved the Three Kingdoms at any time. I hate them."

Kasai turned and walked toward his desolate home.

He picked up the stench of decay well before he reached the ruins. The remains of his dead brothers would need to be burned and the buildings purified.

The entrance to the monastery was wide open but for the remains of two smashed, wooden doors, hanging like limp flags on rusted hinges, creaking their lament whenever the wind blew. Like elsewhere, ash filled the courtyard like fallen snow and covered the surfaces of the broken buildings.

Kasai slowly entered the main courtyard and was appalled by the death and destruction he saw. A smokey aroma of charred wood clung to the air. The black ash of demon death rolled across the courtyard with the breeze. A handful of black crows perched on the skeletal frames of burnt buildings, squawked angrily as they leaped into the air. He saw the bodies of his brothers strewn across the yard, laying in awkward and unnatural positions.

What the mountain predators hadn't feasted on or dragged away, were now unrecognizable masses of withered flesh in tattered orange robes, blackened by decay. That was a crude blessing. It made moving the nameless ones from the monastery and out into the open hillside that much easier. If burning your friends was ever easy.

"Somewhere with a view," Kasai said as he opened the door to a tool shed that had miraculously survived the carnage. Inside were shovels, rakes, and an old wheel barrel. On the wall were smaller tools: hammers, hand saws, files, and blades for shaving rough surfaces smooth. Everything remained meticulously organized, as if nothing had happened.

"It's a start," Kasai said, then looked over his shoulder at the broken and black remains of the monastery. The building housing the master's chambers and Zazen Hall had suffered the most damage. They would need to be torn down and completely rebuilt.

"At least I'll have something to do."

He felt Ninziz-zida stir at his hip. She expressed a sensation of loss and sadness at the destruction of the home of Aetenos's monks.

"Let's see if anything else can be salvaged. It's doubtful, but worth a look," Kasai said aloud, and the Fire Serpent understood he was speaking to her.

As he had expected, the demon's taint was everywhere. Purplish filth covered the meager furnishings inside the sleeping chambers, the kitchen was trashed, the food storage spoiled, and the refectory tables and chairs had been smashed into broken pieces of wood. Thankfully, the demon invaders hadn't found the monastery's water basin reserve.

Lastly, Kasai came to the remains of the Hall of Artifacts. He avoided the wreckage of burned wooden beams and carefully stepped over the broken glass, covering the floor.

"You are the last surviving artifact of Ordu, Ninziz-zida. I shall honor your unrelenting fight against evil by rebuilding your new home first. There are no more battles I want to fight, and no more loved ones I want to lose. Thank you for accepting me, but our time together has come to an end."

Together we are strong. Separated, we are weak. We are nothing alone. Ninziz-zida whispered in Kasai's mind. *You will find your strength. I will guide you back to me.*

"One day, you will choose another wielder, one who will know better how to wield your power. I just want to be left in peace. Yes, a calm, stable, and peaceful life is all I want. That's all I ever wanted."

Kasai lifted a pedestal from the floor and brushed off the surface. He removed Ninziz-zida from his sash and held her in the air above his head. Her orange flame glided along the surface of her three segments. He bowed his head in reverence, then he placed the ancient staff on the pedestal and walked back to the courtyard.

There was much to do. He hoped rebuilding the monastery would act as a penance for the damage he had unwittingly caused by becoming the Ever Hero.

THE FORGOTTEN GODS

1

SEKKA

Swords clashed and shields clanged as Sekka's legions fought the last resistance to her rule. It would be over soon, and countless mortal souls would be hers. Oh, the power she would then control. Azrollorza would be the first she would make kneel before her.

The shrill cry of the dying rose until the shock of the boy-monk's arms were buried in her chest, filling her devilish mind with divine light. He was inside her, melting her from within. The pain was unbearable.

And then the brilliant light of a thousand suns lit the skies on fire. The angels had come and her war to claim the Mortal Realm was over. History had repeated itself, but this time it was a boy who defeated her, and not the Great Aetenos. The humiliation was worse than death.

Sekka stirred back to semi-consciousness as a wave of fierce heat wrapped around her, stealing the breath from her lungs. She gasped for more air and tasted ash on the tip of her tongue, then smoke filled her mouth, nose, and lungs

Fires flickered and crackled around her. Everything

was burning, metal, wood, ice, and flesh, her flesh. She was paralyzed from the neck down. Her arms and legs held fast. She panicked. But no, she could feel her body was still intact and had not melted from her bones.

Her eyes flashed open. She wasn't burning, though the air roasted her as if she were trapped in an outdoor clay oven that burned hot with too much fuel. As her sight cleared, she watched in horror as Gathos melted beneath her feet.

She was tied to a tall column in the barren wastelands outside of Furia Keep. Her wrists were bound tight on the back side of a stake. Shackles were snapped shut at her ankles and dug deep into her human flesh. She watched helplessly as newly formed rivers washed away centuries of her toil to build an everlasting empire of ice and snow.

A terrible crack shook her to her core. She craned her neck just enough to see Furia Keep explode from its center. Large slabs of black rock jettisoned into the sky and landed with great splashes into deep lakes and thudded into slushy ponds. The remainder of her tower sloughed open like a tired flower, soon to lose its petals.

She heard screaming laughter in her mind. Then her eyes caught a crimson comet streaking across the bright blue, cloudless sky.

"No, no, no! This cannot be!" she cried. "Dead and gone! Obliterated by Azrollorza! My gift to her. My protection. Where is my thrice-cursed protection!"

Zizphander, the Red Devil of Naraka banked in the sky. His bright red, feathered wings billowed in the hot air. He soared back to her position and then started a slow spiral down over her head. His pompous smirk was infuriating.

+*I will now take back what you stole from me.*+ His soft voice spoke in her mind. +*Gathos will be no more.*+

"I defeated you once. I will do so again. Free me and we will finish this," she said. The eerie laughter that followed brought a scowl to her face.

+*It is already ended. You are nothing. Defeated by a boy. The Abyss mocks you in your shame. Your alliances have abandoned you; sided with the Chaos Devil or destroyed by him. Either way, the outcome is the same. You are alone and I am your doom.*+

"No. I will survive. I will rebuild. It does not end here," Sekka said boastfully. She willed her infernal form to replace the frail human body she now possessed. Nothing.

Again, the sweet, high-pitched laughter. How she hated the sound of his voice.

+*I have a special treat for you today. Friends have come to wish you well and send you on your way to oblivion.*+

Sekka frantically looked left and right. The light of the blazing sun forced her to squint. In the distance, she saw the hazy form of two figures and one bulbous mass with hundreds of appendages tearing up the soft earth and coming at her fast. Her torturers had arrived.

She soon recognized the first with dreaded ease. "Kotto'gyges."

Behind him were other familiar demons. Lord Narthoth came next. His body was coal black, a walking shadow in the sunlight, except for the white mane of hair stretching down his back. Following the Valgothi warlord was Lord Oziax, the dead general of her once magnificent Frost Legions. He still wore his ice blue armor, covered in sharp coral barnacles.

"You are nothing but shades of another time. You

3

cannot harm me!" she shouted, willing herself to wake from what must be a nightmare.

Kotto'gyges's chitinous legs ended in sharp blades and stabbed into the ground, while the blueish, willowy stalks that ended in lidless eyes or gaping mouths, folded back into its body as it rolled. Then, the demon prince was before her.

Countless eyes and drooling mouths curled forward on their stalks to appraise the prisoner. He stared accusingly at her, while his mouths opened and closed, spraying spittle and screeching horrible curses.

Sekka paid his insults no mind. It was his raised appendages that held her attention. Each ended in sharp, dagger-like tips. Three flashed forward and sliced deeply into her flesh, leaving gashes in her thigh, abdomen and chest.

The many mouths of the demon prince squealed in delight. "Kotto'gyges will finally have his taste of Sekka's flesh. Long have I waited for my revenge."

"Revenge?" Sekka said as the wounds on her body seeped blue blood. "You were destroyed by Zizphander's horde. Your vengeance seeks the wrong target."

"No. It was Sekka who commanded Kotto'gyges to the front lines of an impossible battle against an endless horde. Kotto'gyges was sacrificed so Sekka could escape destruction."

"That's untrue," she said.

He struck again, this time with five thrusts, each one carved away more of her skin, muscle, and bone. Some of Kotto'gyges's mouths squealed like children, while others bit greedily at the fleshy morsels. Sekka could only watch as her body was ravaged and dissected by the bloated beast.

"Sekka's taste does not disappoint. Kotto'gyges will take his fill," he said as he stuffed more of her flesh down his eager mouths.

"Out of my way, beast," Narthoth said angrily. "You've had enough. I will not be denied my due."

"Lord Narthoth, free me now and I will double your territory on Vortexx. Together we will create a vast–"

"Shut your lying mouth," Narthoth said.

The thick mane of white hair along his back bristled and his bat-shaped face contorted in disgust. Beady black eyes bore into her as easily as Kotto'gyges's sharp tips. "You betrayed me and let the sorcerer cast me to oblivion."

"How Maugris came to possess a Pearl of Obliteration is anyone's guess. A device of that power was beyond him."

"Do you know what exists in oblivion? Nothing!"

Lord Narthoth's dark wings tensed behind his back and his hind legs contracted like a predator ready to spring. Powerful shoulders and arms flexed, raising oversized hands with claws meant for rending and tearing. Circling his torso were five smaller arms with crablike pinchers instead of hands.

He approached her slowly. A wicked smile broadened across his scrunched face.

She glared back defiantly. "Do it!" she yelled.

One hand wrapped around her throat while the other slapped her across the face. Then backhanded her in the same fashion. He brought his face inches from her own. "Who has the power now, eh?"

His hand wrapped tighter around her throat, and she was painfully aware of his crablike pinchers plucking and peeling at the flesh of her abdomen. Deeper and deeper they dug as his beady eyes held her own. She would not look away, no matter the agony or indignity.

She felt the movement of his probing pinchers as they ventured into her upper chest cavity. There was a sharp tug, and then a feeling of emptiness. Narthoth smiled with satisfaction.

"There it is," he said and stepped away. "I'm surprised I found it at all. Seems the boy monk missed his mark."

His pinchers had her beating heart within their grasp. One of his massive, five fingered hands took it and brought it to his mouth. "A kingly feast for your vacant throne."

Sekka slouched forward. Blue blood and bits of her flesh littered the ground at her feet. How she still lived was beyond her comprehension. Then the shine from polished, steel boots blinded her.

She raised her weary head and saw Lord Oziax standing before her. He wore no helmet and his long white hair billowed in the scorched wind. One hand gripped the fell blade, Eishorror. But instead of radiating a deep cold, the sword blazed with fire. Blue fire.

"Lord Oziax. Help me. Free me," she panted. "You were always loyal."

He looked back at her with contempt. "My loyalty was wasted on a fool. No longer will I be the whipping boy to your blind ambition; a dog to be beaten when your ill-planned schemes fail."

Sweat poured from what was left of her body, though the skin on Oziax's face remained dry. He shook his head in disappointment. "You were born to fail."

"I will survive. I will rebuild...again," she stammered.

"No. Never again."

Oziax drew back the flaming blade and thrust it deeply into the open wound caused by Narthoth's pinchers. She screamed as the flames cauterized her insides. He withdrew the weapon and still, she lived.

The bindings strapping her body upright to the stake were gone and she slid down the pole into a puddle of her own flesh and blood. Oziax glared down at her in disgust. "It will not be so easy as that."

The fingers of his free hand turned to five slithering tentacles that crawled across her face and wrapped around her head. The heat trapped in the air intensified, and the smell of burning wood became more pronounced. He forcefully lifted her back to a standing position. "You will watch," Oziax said.

She squinted through swollen eyes and looked out across the field. A lone column of fire swirled across the horizon. Circling the fiery whirlwind and flying in a perfect ring where thousands of armored warriors. The steel of their plate mail reflected the fiery light back at her like miniature stars.

"Angels," she hissed.

Then she saw another fire column farther to the left. Her eyes shifted right and three more appeared. No matter where she looked, everything was burning.

The fires collected and formed a giant wall of flames. Nothing was left untouched as the wind blew the inferno closer toward her. The heat hit her first and was harder than any blow she had ever received, until she felt the first licks of the flames on her skin.

Thankfully, her demon phantoms had vanished and could not relish in the humiliation of her death.

"I will be strong, until the end."

Then the flames engulfed her. As a wicked bonus, she remained conscious until the last of her flesh melted from her body.

Sekka's eyes flashed open and she gasped for breath. The ceiling above her was low and dripped with reddish muck. She tried to move and realized she was spread across an X-shaped rack with her wrists and ankles bound to the four ends.

She recalled using the same device on the demigod, Aetenos, and a similar one on the True-born angel, Artiya'il. Odd that she would recall such a memory so quickly.

Then a booming voice filled the small chamber.

"My dear Sekka. How are you feeling today? Vibrant and full of life?"

She closed her eyes and remembered. *All in my head.* Then, turned her head to the sound of the voice. "Xerthotha."

The Chaos Devil stood in the form of a small child against the far wall. He seemed disinterested in her and was preoccupied with something in his hands. She heard a snap and when he opened his hands whatever was there before was gone.

He shrugged his shoulders and picked up a wooden bucket at his feet, then walked towards her with a childish grin.

"I'm thrilled you have lived such a colorful and devious life. Even after a thousand years, I will not grow tired of spinning the deceptions of your existence against you."

"Angel fucker. How much more of Azrollorza's life debt is owed? When will I be free?"

"Ho, ho, ho!" Xerthotha bellowed in a voice far too deep

for his small frame. "Don't be hasty. We have so much more time together."

"I can be of use to you! I have skills!"

Xerthotha raised an interested eyebrow. "Skills? What skills could you possibly have that would replace the countless hours of amusement I would lose by freeing you?"

"Only I was capable enough to birth a Chaos Gate. Not since the beginning, when all things were created, has another been in existence."

"There are rules which cannot be broken," he said, and placed the wooden bucket at the side of the table. "Deep Chaos Magic has forever been forbidden for the likes of you. Ah, you little devils are always grabbing, grabbing, grabbing for the power reserved for your superiors. You were foolish," he said sternly, then with a wink and a playful smirk, "The Great Balance must remain after all."

Xerthotha walked to the rear of the room toward a table covered with small objects. He returned shortly with something shiny in his hand.

"You are wasting a great talent," Sekka said and cringed at hearing the desperation in her voice. "I have Azrollorza's trust. I infiltrate could her inner circle."

"Surely. Now, let us see what we can remove today," Xerthotha said.

"Just another dream," she said. "Not real. None of it. Only in my mind."

Xerthotha shrugged. "Say what you like," he said and came closer. "Now, this will hurt quite a bit."

The blade was dull. He meticulously took his time removing every inch of skin from her body and placing it in the wooden bucket. When it was over, someone or something peeled her off the rack and threw her over his shoulder like a heavy sack of unwanted goods.

A few moments later she was tossed back into her barren cell. Only the reeking straw welcomed her back. There was no solace there, only miserable brooding while waiting until the next time Xerthotha decided to take out his sadistic delight on her body and mind. He used whips and sharp things on her flesh and dragged mental barbs through her memories, warping them into nightmares.

Time moved on, though in this place, a day could be a year somewhere else, or only a split second. She wondered not for the first time how much of her soul debt belonging to Azrollorza she had worked off?

"What does it matter? There is no escape from this place," she said after one particularly grueling session. "There are no variables I can manipulate. One filthy cell. One windowless corridor. One painful rack. Then repeat in reverse. Even the dimwitted jailors are numb to my pleas or suggestive spells."

Remarkably, Xerthotha had not removed her ability to wield her magic. But she soon found out this seeming oversight was a double-edged sword. Her initial jailors were blasted to smithereens when they came to collect her for her private session with the Chaos Devil. That was a mistake. The punishment which followed was brutal.

Nonetheless, she repeatedly tried to escape. And each time her quest for freedom ended in dismal failure and painful repercussions.

"A thousand curses to that meddling monk, Aetenos. I'm sure he's enjoying every minute of this, laughing at me with his winged friends in the clouds. Angels, demigods, and Ever Heroes, I hate them all."

2

KASAI

Kasai wiped sweat from his brow before banging another tongue and groove joint together. The long edge was too fat for the opposite groove it fit into and splintered. He grabbed another board and forced it into place.

Not my best work, but good enough, he thought.

The lattice work of beams was mostly finished, and he figured the framing of the new Zazen Hall would be completed in a week...or two. The plank foundation for the new roof was coming slowly. He brushed off his sloppy craftsmanship thinking no one would know the difference once he laid the clay tiles down. Maybe he could finish the roof today.

"Or not. That's a hot sun," he said. It was mid-summer, and the morning was already a scorcher. It would only get worse as the day progressed. He wasn't in the mood to be on an open roof with such a sun overhead.

"I agree, Des. The shade would be cooler."

The ruins of Ordu had been cleaned of much of the loose debris. What he couldn't move on his own he left in place and worked around, thinking one day, others would join him and together they could clear away the bad memories. That was six years ago. No one had come, nor did he really want the company.

As the years went on, it was the lie he pounded into the truth, just like the faulty fit of the tongue and groove .

"Six years, and I still think about you every day. I wish you were here next to me, even though you were the biggest troublemaker. I don't know how many times I told you to be quiet." He chuckled to himself. "You never listened."

Kasai looked around to see what he had accomplished since arriving at the ruins. Sadly, not much. Most of the buildings remained charred to the studs. They would need to be torn down and rebuilt, eventually. But not today.

He was unshaven, unwashed, and was sure he had gotten used to a less than delicate body odor. But who cared? He had a supply of fresh water, fire, shelter, and food from the wilderness.

"It's enough. I don't need much anyways."

Kasai wiped a new line of dirty sweat from his forehead that threatened to drop into his eye. He could do without the sting. The back of his hand came away wet and smeared with moist dirt. He arched his stiff back to stretch.

"Weaving rope is sounding pretty good right now."

He reached the ladder leaning against the main header and climbed down. On a whim he jumped past the last two rungs and landed squarely on the ground. As he turned, he caught the sight of deep maroon robes worn by an old monk, cautiously entering the open gates of Ordu.

A frown creased Kasai's face and was mirrored in the sinking feeling in his gut.

"Should've barred those doors."

The old monk looked about Kasai's construction site with noted concerned. Loose boards and beams were strewn about with little to no care. Nothing was stacked with precision or any semblance of harmony.

"I see the discipline of Ordu has not been observed for quite some time," the old monk said.

"I'm working, Brother. What can I help you with?" Kasai said gruffly. He was in no mood to be lectured.

"I am looking for someone."

"I'm not him. Go away. Ordu is closed."

The old monk approached Kasai slowly, like a cat carefully placing its next step. "I seek the Ever Hero of Aetenos. I came to Ordu hoping to find him. If I'm not mistaken, I believe you are him."

"Mistakes happen all the time," Kasai said and turned to walk in the opposite direction. "There is rainwater in the barrel. You are welcome to your fill. Good day, Brother."

"A bit rough around the edges from how you are described in the stories. But that is to be expected, after what you endured."

Kasai stopped. His head drooped and he sighed. "I've done my time."

"And the world has been changed forever by your actions."

Kasai turned and narrowed his eyes at the smiling monk. He wasn't sure if he had just been complemented or insulted. "Listen, I never wanted any of it. I didn't ask to be Aetenos's puppet, and I'm not about to sign up for it again. Find someone else."

"Nor would anyone, if they knew beforehand of the awesome responsibility and sacrifice the role demanded."

"Who are you?" Kasai asked, his curiosity getting the better of him.

"My name is Master Cyrus Wraith. I am perhaps the last surviving member of the Order of Symmetu. I was on walkabout from the monastery when the world exploded. When I returned, I found my home destroyed. Everything was lost. Everything."

"Since then, I have wandered through the desolate kingdoms of Baroqia, Sunne, the extreme Northern Wastes of Trosk, and even ventured to the Yoru Isles, to speak with the famed demon hunters of the Yoru Ya-iba clan, each a formidable warrior and master of the silent blade. But nowhere could I find the answers I sought."

"A Master Monk, you say, yet you wear the robes of an initiate," Kasai said.

"There are times one must hide his purpose when raising delicate questions in a world devastated by our heroes."

"And Master Cyrus, what questions were so important to be answered that you would hide your honorable rank?" Kasai said. His curiosity evaporated and was replaced by suspicion laced with bitterness.

"They were numerous but eventually condensed down to one. I wondered how such calamity could befall a nation during the time of the Ever Hero. Though, I choose not to believe one man could make such a difference or cause such tragedy."

"You'd be surprised," Kasai said and walked over to a pail of hemp strands. He bent over, grabbed the handle and walked to the sunless side of a building.

"If you must continue talking, I'll be in the shade. It's getting hot."

Cyrus nodded politely and followed. "You must know, there is still a demon presence lurking in the shadows of the Three Kingdoms."

"Have at them, then."

"Of course, I destroyed the creatures where I could. But I suspect many remain in hiding, waiting for a new master to lead them."

"Lucky for me, none have bothered to venture into the peaks. Yet here you are."

"It is an odd and miraculous time. I have spoken to angels and otherworldly beings—"

"Let me stop you right there. I have no interest in conversations with angels or otherworldly beings, and the lies they spew."

"You misunderstand. Hope is needed. From the most divine being to the lowest peasant, they all seek hope for a new beginning, one which rises from the ashes of the past."

"I'm quite certain the divine, as you say, need nothing from me."

"The people, they need you. Who else but the Ever Hero has the power to restore hope, regardless of the far-fetched stories that multiply faster than forest rabbits?"

"Stories?" Kasai said.

"Oh yes, there are many. For instance, there are whole villages that condemn you as a heretic and deceiver. Others say you were seduced by the wicked powers of a wood witch and coupled with dem—"

"Are you purposefully trying to provoke me?"

"Oh no, not at all. I beg your forgiveness. I would never

believe that a devote follower of Aetenos would lower himself to such depravity. I have been long without company and have been told I have a long tongue."

"Longer than a green moss chameleon's, I'd say," Kasai said, picking through the strands of hemp.

"But one story remained consistent throughout the Three Kingdoms and is partly why I am here."

"Whatever you've heard, I'm sure it's been highly exaggerated."

Master Cyrus continued, "All agree, the Ever Hero wielded the ancient Fire Serpent, Ninziz-zida against the archdevil, Sekka, and smote her back to the Abyss."

Kasai selected three strands of hemp and sat on the ground. He then deftly wove the strands together. Cyrus bent over the bucket and selected three as well. Kasai didn't know if the old monk did it to be polite or just out of habit.

"Why are you here?" Kasai said.

"As I said, everything was destroyed at the Monastery of Symmetu. Buildings, livestock, scrolls, books, weapons. Our Hall of Artifacts was leveled to the ground. What the demons did not defile, the fires took. I came to Ordu to see—"

"To see what, if we had anything worth stealing?"

"I am here as a friend and fellow follower of the Great Monk," Cyrus said, taking offense of Kasai's blunt statement.

"I'm sorry, I meant no disrespect. I have a hard time trusting anything these days, or anyone. Wolves come in all shapes and sizes."

"I can understand your feelings of reservation. I too have been alone for a long time and carry the woe of these last six years on my shoulders. It's a difficult journey for anyone."

"Yes, it is."

The two remained quiet for a time. Each lost in their own thoughts while adding more lengths to their ropes. Eventually, Cyrus broke the silence.

"Did you truly wield the venerable Fire Serpent against the archdevil?"

"Yes."

"Is she here? Can I see her?"

Kasai was instantly apprehensive. He didn't trust the monk, not yet. But maybe it would do him some good to reconnect with Ninziz-zida. He had to admit, having some company after all these years wasn't half bad.

Kasai stood and brushed himself off. "Come with me. But be warned, Ninziz-zida does not take kindly to strangers."

Soon the two monks reached the basic structure that served as the Hall of Artifacts. It was the most finished of the buildings in the courtyard, though far from complete. At least the seasonal elements were kept at bay.

"Ah, yes, immense power housed in the most modest structure. It is a perfect metaphor for the Four Orders of Light. You have built a very fitting home for the Fire Serpent But why Gen Moll brought her here instead of Symmetu has always been a mystery and point of contention between our two Orders."

The two monks walked inside to where Ninziz-zida rested on a central pedestal. Cyrus reached out his hand tentatively to touch the three wooden sections.

"You may want to reconsider," Kasai said, half-jokingly. "She's very particular."

Cyrus brought his hand back quickly and gave Kasai a nervous smile. "Perhaps another time."

"She's not for everyone," Kasai said and smoothed his hand across the polished, black wood. A yellow flame rippled to life along the surface at his touch. He watched Cyrus's eyes light up at the uncanny nature of the artifact.

"You must be tired from your journey. Please, take some refreshment and a rest. You're welcome to stay the night and continue your walkabout in the morning. As you can see, Ordu is far from complete and there is much I must rebuild before she is ready for initiates or trained Masters."

"Thank you for your hospitality, Master Ever Hero. I would enjoy a respite from the wilderness."

"Call me Kasai."

"Certainly, Master Kasai," Cyrus gave a polite nod. "I will take a brief rest and then join you in the evening when the temperatures have cooled. If we are diligent, we should be able to finish covering that incomplete roof before nightfall. Perhaps during my stay, we can learn from one another."

"You're staying?"

"Of course. We may be the only two Masters left of our respective Orders. It's our duty to rebuild what was lost and train the next generation of Brothers in the Way of Aetenos. In time, the Four Orders will grow strong enough to influence the shape of the Three Kingdoms of Hanna."

Kasai peered into Cyrus's aura. The monk was covered in a neutral red glow with sparks of orange, darting back and forth in an erratic dance. He didn't detect a demonic influence or otherwise unfriendly hostility nestled within the older monk's personal energy. Though he had to admit, the ability of his inner sight had dulled with lack of use over the years.

One thing was unmistakable though, Cyrus was filled with fire xindu. Daku had the same aura, but that was long ago, when they were friends, and he was still human.

"You possess an abundance of fire energy," Kasai said. He hoped he didn't sound overly concerned, but the accusation was there, nonetheless.

"Yes, it's the Way of Symmetu. We focus our studies on developing our fire xindu into a powerful reservoir of strength. I will teach you our ways, if you are open to learning. And I would be honored to learn the techniques of Ordu from Aetenos's chosen one in return."

Kasai clenched his jaw and was hesitant to say anything more. His connection with the Boundless had grown stale over the years, like so many other things. The loss of Desdemonia still filled him with guilt and remorse so much so that he doubted he would ever find the sure path to the Boundless again. *Funny how one person, who I knew for such a short period of time could have such an everlasting effect on me.*

"We can discuss it later," Kasai said eventually.

"Fine then. First, we rest, and then we rebuild," Cyrus said with a smile, then added, "And not just the monastery."

"Thank you, Master Cyrus. Your help is appreciated."

The morning sky was bright blue as Kasai strolled across the neat and orderly courtyard. He heard birds chirping in the trees outside the monastery walls. The autumn season had brought warm winds from the south and this part of the Sarribe Mountains was experiencing an extended summer. Kasai didn't mind. He wasn't overly fond of winter, the snow, or the cold.

The addition of Cyrus to Ordu proved to be a blessing

for Kasai. The older monk enforced a rigid schedule that included rebuilding the structures of Ordu, sparring, and deep meditation, all of which kept Kasai's mind busy and not dwelling on the past. The buildings took shape, albeit slowly and his eagerness to test his skill against a worthy opponent returned.

Kasai felt the greatest sense of accomplishment after a hard day's work or an intensive sparring session. He didn't mind how sore his muscles were and he rarely complained, because for the first time in a long time, he felt alive.

Unfortunately, his meditation sessions weren't as satisfying. Dark visions of his past, and the lives lost from his ill-fated actions still clouded his thoughts. The path to the Boundless remained hidden, and only with the help of Ninziz-zida could he even come close to a proper connection.

Cyrus told him it would come in time and to be patient. Kasai had his doubts. He stretched his sore back from side to side. Yesterday, Cyrus had given him a taste of a secret fighting technique used only by the monks of Symmetu. Kasai had found himself flat on his back after the quick demonstration of a focused fire xindu speed attack.

"Your fire xindu can be used to increase all of your mundane abilities," Cyrus had said.

Kasai had to agree, though he still held to the notion that raising the levels of his four basic xindu energies, fire, air, water, and earth, and then using his spirit xindu to control them, was a more balanced way to fight. His musing was interrupted by a pounding on the front wooded gates.

Someone else had found him.

"Friends of yours?" Kasai said to Cyrus.

For a hopeful moment, he thought Desdemonia had found him. It was an impossible wish. The dead did not visit the living. He walked hesitantly to the gates and peered through the spyhole. Ten, orange robed monks of various ages stood on the other side of the closed doors.

Accompanying them were three, dear friends. Kasai immediately unbarred the gates to grant entry to the outside party. Pallo and Run-Run were first to push through the group and embrace Kasai.

"You've aged!" Pallo said, grabbing him by his broad shoulders. "Goddess above, just look at you. You're a grown man."

Run-Run stood back with his fist on his hips and gave Kasai an approving smile.

"How did you find me? This place is supposed to be hidden from the sight and thought of all outsiders."

"Outsiders are we now? Some thanks we get, eh, Run-Run?"

"That's not what I meant."

"I know. Luckily we came across this motley crew." Pallo pointed over his shoulder to the group of monks patiently waiting at the entrance. "Apparently, my bold actions at saving your arse countless times didn't go unnoticed."

Run-Run got Kasai's attention and pointed to himself eagerly and gestured with his hands in quick succession.

"Yes, yes, Run-Run, you brought the Miko Nuna and her followers. Without them, we never would have gained the middle ground."

"You look well. Master Kasai," Gift said as she joined the two brothers.

"Gift!" Kasai said excitedly. "How are you here?"

"And why wouldn't I be here? We are of one tribe, are we not? The three of us have met on the anniversary of Sekka's demise at the remains of the old Frona village to honor those that took the long sleep. You have been missed."

"Run-Run decided it was high-time we came to you," Pallo said.

"But you are not an easy hero to find," Gift said.

"You could have chosen an easier place to reach if you were set on building a new monastery," Pallo said. "Maybe one without so many cliffs?"

"I was thinking it be best if I was unfindable."

"Too bad. You needed to be found and he can find anyone, anywhere," Pallo said, nodding to his brother.

Run-Run smiled broadly, then clasped his nose together with his fingers.

"We followed the path of demon filth. I will never forget the stench of their kind. It still clings to the air and fouls the sweet smells of the jungle," Gift said.

"The same was true across the Sarribe Pass. I fear no matter how hard you scrub the stones, they will always reek of demonkind," Pallo said.

"Yes, that will take some time to cleanse, from stone and memory alike," Kasai said.

"Well, we've come to help. Plus, what kind of shields to the Ever Hero would we be if we were hundreds of miles away?"

"Ugh, that time has passed. Just Kasai with you, ok?"

"Ho-ho! Listen to him, Run-Run. It appears the kid's balls have finally dropped."

Run-Run grabbed his crotch with both hands.

"That's not what I meant."

"You look good, healthy. Stronger in the flesh than before," Gift said, ignoring the two brothers' comments.

"It's the food. Turns out, Master Cyrus is an excellent cook. Sticks to your ribs, if you know what I mean."

"No, I do not. Though, this new flesh, it suits you. You have the stature of a warrior. I find it pleasing."

Run-Run and Pallo exchanged looks and both raised their eyebrows at Gift's blunt flirtation.

"What's this? What's this?" Cyrus said as he approached with raised hands. "You will stop right there."

"Speak of the devil, here's Master Cyrus now." The friends' laughter dwindled to a few isolated chuckles.

Cyrus looked unfavorably at Gift and the two Kibo Gensai warriors. "You must leave. Ordu is closed. In another time, you would have been struck down before crossing the first bridge."

"Pleasant fellow," Pallo said to his brother who gave a high-pitched whistle.

"Master Cyrus, meet Pallo Katan and his brother, Run-Run. No two brothers from the same mother could be closer to me or share my trust. And this is Gift of the Frona Tribe. She is from the jungles of \Sunne."

"Clearly."

"Without their help, Sekka would have surely won control of the Three Kingdoms. I owe them much. We all do."

Kasai scanned the ten monks that now surrounded the small group. All but one was unfamiliar to him. "Brother Mando!"

"Master Ever Hero," Mando bowed low.

"I barely recognized you. You grew tall," Kasai said in astonishment. "Come in, come in! You are all welcome."

23

"Master Kasai, perhaps we should discuss this first. The monks are permitted to stay, after they have been properly vetted, but the admission of strangers to the hallowed grounds of a monastery of Aetenos—"

"Master Cyrus, I said they are welcome," Kasai said sternly. "Agreed?"

"As you wish," Cyrus said in a huff, contrary to how he obviously felt.

"Come, come, let's get some breakfast in you. You must be hungry," Kasai said and led the way to the refectory.

"Sorry, we only have three chairs," Kasai said sheepishly. "We haven't had time to make more."

"Nothing to worry about, Ever Hero. Run-Run is handy when it comes to chairs and tables. He'll have plenty made for everyone's arse before the week is up," Pallo said. "And we discovered young Mando here is an excellent cook as well. Meaning no offense, Master Cyrus. I'm sure he can lend a hand in the kitchen."

Mando bowed. "It would be an honor, Ever Hero."

"Well, get to it then. And please, just Kasai." But Mando was already on his way to the food locker and ingredients for the meal."

"Have you found peace in your Boundless?" Gift asked.

"His studies are coming along nicely, thank you," Cyrus said. A look of consternation crossed his face. "Though I fear your intrusion will cause him to lose what little focus he has regained and set him back weeks if not months in his training."

"Don't listen to him, Gift. He is overly fond of worrying," Kasai said.

"If not for me, and my worrying, you and the sacred

monastery would still be in a shambles," Cyrus interjected, still fuming over outsiders being admitted within the gates.

Kasai raised his hand and nodded. Cyrus was right, of course, but now was not the time for embarrassing stories. "It's a difficult path and I mostly feel like I am wandering aimlessly in the dark. My meditation sessions are distracted and filled with barriers. But Master Cyrus is instructing me on the Way of Symmetu. And for all his worrying, he is a needful mentor."

Master Cyrus' back straightened, and his chin protruded in a superior manner.

"I'm hoping a new approach will help me establish a more fluid connection to the Boundless. It's a long road, but I'll get there," Kasai said.

"And where is the great Fire Serpent? It is odd for me to see your waist so bare," Gift said.

"Ninziz-zida is here, resting. She is a weapon of war, but I am no longer the champion she needs. I doubt I ever really was. We are no longer connected as Weapon and Wielder."

"Bah, who fills your head with this nonsense?" Gift said. "The staff was always more than a weapon to you, and you more than a wielder. That is what made your bond so special."

"Until he can master his fire xindu, the Fire Serpent will always be a distraction. I suspect it is the staff, who prevents Master Kasai from reaching his true potential. We must not rely on relics or talismans to enhance our abilities, for when they are taken away from us, we find ourselves lost in the darkness."

"Is that so?" Gift's brows knitted together. "And who is this man who claims the right to tell the Ever Hero what is right and what is wrong? Where were you when the devil's horde rampaged across the kingdoms?" She pointed an accusatory finger at Cyrus. "Where were any of your Order?"

Kasai stepped forward. "Easy, Gift. I have asked Master Cyrus for help. What good is the power if it cannot save those we love?"

"It was love that saved you. Which is another reason why we came to you. Have *they* been here yet?"

"Who?"

"The winged warriors."

Kasai's stomach rushed to his throat. "Why would angels come here? The Challenge of Righteousness has been fulfilled. I owe them nothing. I've paid my debt. We all have."

"They have been seen sneaking through the jungles, asking questions."

"About?"

"Desdemonia," Gift said in a hushed voice, looking distrustfully at Cyrus. "Fear not, Master Kasai, we have hidden her well. She sleeps peacefully until her time of reawakening."

"Why do they care? They don't care about anything."

"I'm not sure. I was hoping you might have some answers. You knew her best."

Kasai noticed Cyrus hovering close, adding an interested ear to their conversation without being part of it.

"Let's talk about this later. It's a worrisome thought."

Gift glared at Cyrus. "Yes, it's a family matter and not for outsiders."

3

SHIVERRIG

Another stinging wind whipped across the northern tundra and burned Gerun Shiverrig's exposed cheeks. A thick beard had grown over much of his face and strong chin, but it helped little when the icy winds blew. His eyes watered in the crisp air then quickly froze at the corners.

The bleak landscape made his usual foul mood worse. When the wind passed, he raised his eyes to the sky. Even the sun looked cold. Its pale light pressed through thin clouds, churning in a maddening morass of multi-colored currents.

"I hate this place," he grumbled.

"You're no picnic either," Daku said from Shiverrig's side.

"Must every otherworldly power be found in a glacial hell?"

Daku gave him a sideways glance, wondering if he was serious, then lowered his snout and trudged onward.

As his small warband traveled farther north, the sightings of migrating elk or the lone moose was a rare and

27

precious thing. Luckily, fuel for fire on the permafrost was less important, provided the sorcerer survived. As frail as he appeared in body and health, his ability to endure the hardships of the wastelands was impressive.

Shiverrig's stomach ached from days-old hunger. The meager rations of frozen meat they acquired weeks ago from ice nomads barely sustained him. It was a penance for his failure, so raw or cooked, he ate it without complaint.

But that food was long gone. He tried to swallow Dai-Ko-Zior's magically conjured food, but more times than not, it came back up worse than when it went down.

Daku, however, took to the harsh climate like a fish in water. The colder it became, the more at home he seemed. This disconcerting detail was not lost on Shiverrig, due to the heritage of the shadow demon, Khalkoroth, whose body Daku now inhabited.

"I had the Three Kingdoms in my grasp," Shiverrig mumbled. "A united land from which my everlasting empire would grow, until it turned to ash."

He scanned the bleak horizon. Somehow, people managed to survive here, mostly camped on the ice flow, hunting fish and seal. Though Shiverrig couldn't fathom why. *They're all insane, just like me.*

When the natural food supplies had dwindled or became too troublesome to hunt under the ice, his warband of followers had to adapt. Luckily for the few horses in his troop, they encountered a wandering tribe of barbarian nomads who had mistakenly decided to attack rather than join or flee.

Unfortunately, after the slaughter, Shiverrig's men didn't find much meat or bread to appropriate. But food was food and the flesh of one animal was just as good as another, if you could keep it down.

"We'll make frozen meat sticks out of them," Daku said with a feral grin. "Food supply problem solved."

The pale demon kept the fell blade, Eishorror sheathed across his back. This type of wet work was more suitable using teeth and claw. Shiverrig had had enough of warped magic, food or otherwise, infecting his body and reckoned this was the lesser of two evils. He feigned disinterest and ate his fill.

Uncounted years passed and the search for Dai-Ko-Zior's mysterious Northern Vortex, which the sorcerer had promised would grant Shiverrig the favor of ancient gods, had turned into a mind-numbing odyssey. Not for the first time, the would-be ruler of a usurped throne and then destroyed kingdom, sank into looping thoughts of ruin and defeat.

Wiped out like an afterthought by fire from the sky. Bloody angels. Obliterated everything, Shiverrig thought. He sat stoically in his saddle as his horse plodded though shin-high snow. His bearskin cloak, leathers, and gloves had practically frozen into a mold of his stooped posture.

Gone was his ancient armor. The family heirloom had been cast aside for warmer, more practical clothing. The sword he kept. Holding it made him feel more human.

He squinted through the unbearable glare of sharp sunlight against a brilliant white landscape. "I hate ice. I hate snow. This place is insufferable," he mumbled more than spoke for his mind was crammed with other voices that dominated his thoughts.

+There is no escape. Blood of legions flow as Circles of power

29

collide. Drip, drip, drip. Trapped! Spinning helplessly. Nothing escapes. Push through the breach. Squeeze everything through the breach. A devious and delicious mind. There is no escape for you, Shiverrig!+

Abyssal voices spoke in spoke in queer and foreign tongues, rambling endlessly in his head. If they had remained undecipherable, he might have been able to cast them aside as ambient noise. But sadly, he understood them all.

One last, parting gift from that blasted Chaos Devil, he thought.

Sometimes the voices came as a whisper, not louder than the aggravating buzz of a gnat in one's ear. Other times, his head rang for days from the booming shouts of Xerthotha's endless, pontifications. And through it all, he was a helpless bystander, forced to endure the thoughts of the Supreme Devil's chaotic mind.

Shiverrig had hoped to be free of Xerthotha's influence when the angels split open the sky and set fire to the world. For a time, he enjoyed a glorious reprieve from the devil's boastful arrogance and impossible demands. Though, with the absence of possession, so too went the many gifts Xerthotha had bestowed upon him.

His extraordinary sight and inhuman strength waned as the connection to Xerthotha was stretched thin. By all rights, he should be dead in his saddle, but whether through sheer will or an extended life force granted him by the possession, he survived.

Unfortunately, there was no escape from Xerthotha's influence and the Chaos Devil's eerie presence rose from the ashes of memory to become a throbbing beat of murmured thoughts echoing in Shiverrig's mind. The dribbling of constant yet incoherent diatribes was maddening.

"Shut. Up," Shiverrig said after another failed attempt to exert some form of control over the voices. His head throbbed endlessly. From time to time, he pressed the heel of his hand into his left eye. *Maybe it would hurt less if it popped,* he thought. *I'm sure I could survive with just the one.*

The sharp pain dulled momentarily but came back more acutely when he relieved the pressure from his hand. Shiverrig had learned to live with the headaches. Some days were better than others. Today was a bad day.

The top layer of yesterday's snowfall had frozen overnight and was now a blinding sea of light, reflecting directly into his throbbing eye as if it were magnified by an alchemist's lens. Spikes of pain filled his skull. *The point of a dagger is not so sharp. Bloody demons and devils. A thousand curses to Maugris and his stupidity.*

Shiverrig sighed and tried once more to piece together the disjointed bits of information he was receiving from his fickle patron. Something was happening in the Abyss. Something awesome and terrible.

"Blood of the Abyss, shut up and let me think!"

Daku kept pace with Shiverrig's horse. The pale demon was a white shadow to Shiverrig's black fur cloak and dark-skinned steed. Standing upright, Daku stood almost eye-level to Shiverrig and glanced at his master in concern, then scowled at Dai-Ko-Zior. The cloaked sorcerer rocked silently in his saddle three horse-lengths behind the pair.

"The voices again? I've told you before, it's the death wizard trying to control your mind. Let me slay him and we'll return to Baroqia. There is nothing here worth our time," Daku said, then nodded back to the ragtag group that followed them like a haphazard herd of cattle. "We would move faster without them, too."

Shiverrig grunted his indifference. The warriors who now followed him were outcasts, deserters or wanderers from insignificant barbarian tribes that had proclaimed him their promised savior. Shiverrig suspected any hero would do in these wastelands.

I was born to rule. And yet, the events of my life have led me here, an aimless vagabond, wandering through the northern wastelands with a handful of barbarian riffraff, following the delusions of a mad sorcerer. How had it come to this?

Shiverrig knew exactly where mistakes had been made. He had assumed logical results would follow precise planning, and even through the chaos of war, he was sure he could control the outcome. But his deeds were undone when vengeful sorcerers and devils brewed from the depths of the Abyss added their own special blend of madness to the mix. Too late he learned the insane did not follow the rules of the sane.

But greatness was reserved only for those who would sacrifice everything to attain it, and where they perished, he survived.

"Shadows are few and far between here, at least until nightfall, but we could start making the jumps tonight," Daku said.

"You'd be just as lost as the wizard," Shiverrig replied.

Daku grunted. "At least we would know when we reached our goal." He peered over his muscular shoulder. "And have less mouths to feed."

Shiverrig didn't bother turning in his saddle. The riffraff that followed was there, trailing behind in a long, thin line. The moment the warband stopped moving, they would gather around him to fawn and boast of their valor in previous battles. What glory was there in slaughtering defenseless nomads and ice farmers?

These outcasts reminded him of the spineless nobles of Baroqia. *Bloody sycophants and worthless turncoats when their honor was called due.* But, as he had said before, flesh was flesh, and he had no intention of starving to death in the wastelands.

"I will not squander precious resources needlessly," Shiverrig said.

"That's right. Each one is a potential meat locker," Daku said. His sarcastic laugh quickly turned mean and guttural.

Shiverrig cocked his eyebrow toward the pale demon. The golden circlet, holding Khalkoroth a prisoner within Daku's mind, was still in place on his beastly head.

"How are you feeling, Daku? Everything handled?" Shiverrig said. His sword was strapped behind his saddle and his joints were stiff. Getting to it in time would be problematic if things went bad.

Daku swiveled his head back slowly toward Shiverrig, almost menacingly.

"I'm fine. Stop nagging me like a worried mother."

"I just don't care to slay you out of hand is all. Though it would be a welcome break from the nothingness of this land."

Shiverrig felt the eyes of Dai-Ko-Zior on his back. He was used to it. The sorcerer studied him endlessly, asking questions and prying out irrelevant information. He maintained Shiverrig walked a preordained path, one that would usher in a new beginning for the Three Worlds. Shiverrig was special, a true Champion of Chaos.

I hate sorcerers. He rubbed his full beard, breaking away bits of snot ice from around his nose and mouth. *I hate the bloody cold worse.*

"I never knew Trosk went so far north," Daku said. "The maps I studied at Ordu must have been flawed. Why am I not surprised?"

"The maps were true, demon, to the best of what your masters knew of the physical realm. We have walked along paths of Chaos for some time. These lands are commanded by powers beyond the material."

"Isn't that just lovely," Shiverrig said in a less than enthusiastic tone.

"You said you knew the location of the Northern Vortex. It seems *your* masters have led you astray or more likely, abandoned you," Daku said. "Look around you, wizard. What do you see besides ice and snow? Nothing, lots and lots of nothing."

Dai-Ko-Zior merely shrugged. "I see the consequences of the Heavenly Host's invasion into the Mortal Realm. It would be the same if a Supreme Devil of the Abyss walked the kingdoms of men.

"And so, as the Circles of the Abyss churn and collide, so too do the Lands of Chaos shift in the Mortal Realm. Such a great imbalance must be righted and equaled. Therefore, the location of the Northern Vortex has moved accordingly to where it remains hidden from righteous eyes. Its whereabouts have become shrouded in the unknown. That should be obvious by now."

"You're lost. Admit it," Daku said.

"Quite, but I feel we are close. I can sense the power of the Ancients."

"I was a fool to follow you this far," Shiverrig said and pulled hard on his reins, drawing an indignant snort from his steed. He had heard the sorcerer's excuses too many times in the past.

"For once, the demon is right. This odyssey of yours is over. There's nothing here. I'll reclaim my birthright without the help of your gods. Angels be damned, I'll cut them down too if they get in my way again.

"Daku, get the mongrels together. We're turning south."

"Would you leave such a bounty untouched when it is in your grasp? Our search is over. We have arrived," Dai-Ko-Zior said and pointed toward the horizon. The whistling winds took a moment to breathe, and the landscape cleared of swirling snow.

Shiverrig squinted his eyes and there in the distance were a gathering of primitive huts, barely perceivable, standing above the snow-covered ground.

"This had better be the last time," Shiverrig said.

"Lucky for you, wizard," Daku said with a sneer. His purple lips curled back, revealing needle-sharp teeth. "Mongrels! We have more food to gather."

Shiverrig's warband spread out in a long line before the village. He sighed with disappointment. There was nothing here that he hadn't seen before. A handful of nomadic families brought together for survival and clinging to the belief that they were safer in numbers. Somehow, they managed to eke out an existence on the permafrost of a desolate tundra.

The villagers shambled from their ice homes to stare at the warband, though not in awe or fear, but as expected visitors. Their movements were slow and weak, like slaves who had not been fed for days.

Some wore thick fur, which did nothing to hide their exposed heads and emaciated faces. Thin, blueish skin was drawn tight against the sharp bones of their skulls. Then, Shiverrig spotted the protrusions on their heads. *Were those fucking horns?*

"I don't see our mysterious vortex or anything else of value here. What do we do with them?" Daku said.

"Kill them all," Shiverrig said. "And leave their bodies where they fall. Their flesh is tainted."

"I agree, there's not much left on the bone, but food supplies are low and it's better than nothing," Daku said in protest. "Maybe the sorcerer can neutralize the—"

"I said leave it!" Shiverrig barked.

"Shall I melt their ice huts, too?" Daku said with a sneer.

"You would be wise to reconsider," Dai-Ko-Zior said as he brought his steed parallel to Shiverrig's horse. "As I have said, we have arrived. My masters are here."

"And I said, kill them all. Not another word to the contrary from either of you, or you'll be added to the numbers of dead. Now move!"

Daku waved the barbarians forward. "You heard him. They die."

The pale demon shook his head in disappointment and shuffled off after them. He left Eishorror strapped to his back. The sorcerer said nothing, but Shiverrig sensed the arrogant amusement hidden under Dai-Ko-Zior's heavy cowl.

4

RAGUEL

"Come," Raguel commanded.

"More boxes have arrived, my lord," Ja'el said at the entrance to Lord Raguel's office. The tall True-born was responsible for keeping Lord Raguel's schedule and was loath to bother him with disruption. Standing behind him were sixteen couriers, eight pair holding a large box between them.

"Put them there, with the rest," Raguel said without looking up. He pointed to ten large, open containers filled with golden tiles. Three smaller boxes had been opened, and their contents spilled unceremoniously across the smooth marble floor like discarded treasure. The smooth ceiling reflected the light and bathed the room in amber.

"They contain more petitions, my lord," the lead courier said.

"I know damn well what they contain!" Raguel shouted. "Now put them with the rest and leave me in peace."

"Yes, my lord. Right away," the courier said and directed his assistants to do as the Chancellor Pinnacle demanded.

When they left, eight additional boxes sat in the middle of the room, staring at him. Judging him.

"Their lack of vision is astounding," Raguel sighed.

"Who, sir?" Ja'el said.

"Everyone."

"Shall I fetch you an elixir for your troubles, lord? Something to sooth your mind?"

Raguel was about to reply when an itch crept up his neck and drilled into his mind. The springtime fragrance of the room turned sour. *What is it now?* he thought.

But Raguel knew. He had been expecting this "conversation" the moment Illyria forced him to destroy the Chaos Gate prematurely. If he had just stood his ground with her, and finally said, "No," then things would now be on the other side of cursed and ruined.

"No, just leave me to my work," Raguel said.

+What do you want?+ Raguel sent his thoughts into the void when Ja'el had departed.

+I want what was promised, *partner*.+ Xerthotha's voice boomed like thunder in Raguel's mind. +Sadly, I have yet to see one of your famed golden birds materialize in the Abyss to smite Azrollorza's forces.+

+Must you be so loud. The Chaos Gate is no more. Time-tables have changed.+

+Not for me they haven't. I have committed whole worlds to the war effort against Azrollorza. However, based on your inaction to tip the balance in my favor, I find I am bleeding troops when I should be claiming victories. Do you have any idea of the soul energy I have had to expend just to hold the borders of the Outer Circles under my control?+

+I'm sure it's staggering.+

+Do not mock me or treat me like a worm you would swallow whole, little bird!+

+Please, settle down. I have not forgotten you. The promise will be honored. It will simply take more time.+

+Shifting timetables are not my concern, nor were they part of our deal. Do you know what happens to those who attempt to break a blood contract with a Supreme Devil?+

+Do not attempt to strengthen or pact with assumed ties. No blood has been shared, nor will it be. Know our goals remain mutual and that is enough. The Heavenly Host will fly while the Amaranthine Barrier is weak.+

+Power and influence are fickle mistresses. Do not betray me, older brother, or you will find this worm's bite sharper and deeper than you know. Now, send your warriors!+

The connection faded, though Raguel still felt the itchy sensation of small, biting things on his skin.

He walked across the room and kicked over one of the eight, neatly stacked boxes. It burst on impact with the floor, sending tens of thousands of identical golden tiles spinning and ricocheting into the walls. Each one was inscribed with flowery, calligraphic letters, and held the same request, "Free the witch."

"I need some air," Raguel said, unconsciously brushing off the invisible pests covering his arms.

He called to Ja'el. "This room stinks. Have someone scour every surface. Replace the furniture if you must but make it clean. And get those boxes out of my sight."

"Right away, my lord," Ja'el said.

Raguel then stepped out onto the balcony overlooking the city of Asher. The city sparkled in the warm sunlight. From this height, everything beneath him was perfect.

"I know what I am doing," he said and leaped into the cloudless sky.

Raguel soared over the colossal administration buildings with ease. His majestic wings splayed wide as he caught another updraft giving him lift and speed. Soon, beneath him were the sky-scraping residential complexes that housed the celestials fortunate enough to work in Asher.

Neat rows of mile high buildings stretch out across vast city blocks in spiraling designs. Pure silver and gold were fused into the outer building materials, creating a shimmering effect as the sun transitioned across the sky.

When seen from this height, the sea of rooftops composed a flawless mosaic of overlapping symmetrical patterns, while each individual residential cluster created the shape of a unique snowflake crystal. The juxtaposition of macro and micro elements pleased him. After all, it was his design.

He caught the smell of burning wood and turned to his left to see dirty, yellow smoke rising in the air, curling like a living thing over the horizon.

"And now it begins in Tanalum," Raguel said. He flapped his great, multi-colored wings and darted to the source of the blemish on his once perfect city.

Within moments, he descended over a large group of celestials gathered around a wooden totem, protruding from a bed of lit kindling. Strapped to the post was a woman with long, black hair. Raguel carelessly fanned the flames as he landed, and the fire leaped up the post and covered the woman.

"Burn! Burn! Burn!" the crowd chanted in unison.

He grabbed one of the celestials roughly, turning

the startled angel to face him. "What is the meaning of this? Who sanctioned an execution? Get her off that post, immediately," he commanded.

He looked again at the woman tied to the post and realized, thankfully, it was not the witch and only a stuffed dummy. Then the dry hay wrapped under tightly bound clothing, ignited in a bright flash of orange and red flames.

"Evil has returned to lowly Elysian. The taint and corruption the witch possesses must not be allowed to infect the Seven Heavens. She burns as a symbol of our love for you and support for your edict," the celestial said.

Raguel frowned. This would not be well received by the governors and directors of the lower levels. "Clean this up immediately. Your support is noted, but I will not see Tanalum in flames."

"But?" the celestial said.

"Now!" Raguel leaped into the air without turning back. He didn't care if the pyre continued to burn. He assumed it would.

Raguel drifted to the sixth, Heavenly Level of Paradise. Puffy, white clouds dotted the sky, birds flew, but the airways were absent of celestial bodies. An eerie quiet had fallen over the land. He glided over the capital city of Vibrance. It was a virtual ghost town. The streets were empty. The buildings were closed. Duties were being neglected. The cogs of his flawless machine were stalled.

"I ordered no such lockdown," he said and immediately compiled a short list of angels that would be called to his office for explanation. "I should have removed them long ago."

Then it dawned on him. *Aetenos was popular among the philosophers and meditators in Paradise. This is a protest.*

41

"Unacceptable!"

A foreboding crept into his thoughts and Raguel darted to the city of Principia, a smaller, but influential city also on the sixth Level. The city's wide streets were filled with protestors heading for the Sacred Libraries and Archival Halls. Banners of red, gold, and purple waved in the wind.

"Save Artiya'il" was stitched in bold letters on some, while others bore the slogan, "Bring the angel home."

He sent a mental message to Sonnalle. +Where is the Praetor Guard on Paradise? There is an uprising occurring in the Archive District in Principia.+

+My lord, the Praetor have been called to Arcadia.+ Sonnalle answered immediately.

+Arcadia, why?+

+The warrior casts have splintered into violent gangs. Rioters destroyed a monument. It was an unremarkable sculpture of an unimportant mortal. But it offended many and offered enough of a spark for brawling to ensued. Now, things are worse.+

+Handle it, Sonnalle. Then bring the witch to me.+

+Yes, my lord.+

Raguel flew back to Tanalum. His clothing stunk of smoke and he still felt the foul touch of things from the Abyss. His mood darkened with each beat of his great wings. "All of this could have been avoided. All of it."

The day was bright and warm when he reached the Heavenly Hall, though Raguel's mood remained glum. He quickly refreshed with clean robes and pondered the actions he would take against prominent appointments in the hierarchy of his administration.

Animals. They are behaving like animals, he thought as he

brooded in silence, pacing the austere yet bare floor of the suite he often referred to as his Chamber of Reflection. *This madness starts and ends with Aetenos and his brood.*

He rubbed the bridge of his nose and massaged his inner eyelids. No matter how calm he endeavored to remain, he still burned with humiliation over the destruction of the Chaos Gate. In one fell swoop, his plans for extending the influence of the Seven Heavens were thwarted.

And as a further insult to his pride, the destruction of the portal freed the souls of Aetenos and his brat Ever Hero back to their corporal bodies. His thoughts drifted to Illyria as they always did, and with them came more insult and more shame.

My Great Work suffers due to her interference, all directed by him. How dare she usurp my authority, enforcing her will over mine as if she were the Immortal Mother herself? That blasted, one-eyed monk muddles her mind. If not for him, she would be mine and everything would be perfect. Everything.

"And now this unrest. Has everyone gone mad?" he said aloud just as his equerry entered the room. Sonnalle's blonde hair was platinum-colored in the bright light. His white-plumed wings were tightly folded across his back with thin golden ribbons woven between the long primary feathers.

"My lord, the disturbance on Arcadia has been settled."

"Good, good. Sonnalle, it seems we are approaching a tipping point."

"Indeed sir. The angel, the monk, and now the witch seem to act as multipliers to the unrest. They are catalysts for dissent."

"The Seven Heavens have become a circus."

"Yes, my lord. She has gathered quite a following of supporters since her return. I have numerous petitions granting her asylum on two different Heavenly Levels."

"Will this insanity never end? I am the most powerful being in the Three Worlds and I am vexed by a simple wood witch. Everything that monk touches is a plague upon me."

"There are ways to make her disappear."

"I will not make the same mistake as with Artiya'il's banishment. This will be done quietly," Raguel said. "But I want to see her first."

A malicious grin broadened across Sonnalle's face. "As you wish, my lord," he said. "Bring her in."

Desdemonia was held, struggling between two angels of the Praetor Guard. Their silver armor shined brightly and the black feathers on their helm were immaculately groomed.

"What is the meaning of this? Let me go!" she said, then looked straight at Lord Raguel. "Why have I been imprisoned? I did as you commanded. If not for me, that ice bitch would still be stealing your souls."

Raguel gave her a bemused smile. "I see the horns are gone, but the tongue is twice as sharp." He gave a short gesture to each guard. "That will be all. You may return to your duties."

"Yes, my lord," they said in unison and left the room.

"So rude," Desdemonia said and rubbed the sides of her arms.

"I'm sure you are wondering why you've been brought here."

"Dragged is more like it." She gave Sonnalle a mean, sideways glance, then looked back to Raguel. "I have no idea, nor do I care. Listen, I don't know what you're up to, but you're definitely not my type, if that is what you're after."

"Hardly. You are the cause of an intolerable disturbance in the Seven Heavens, which is about to be put to rest," Raguel said.

"Not everything in its proper place in your perfect world anymore?" Desdemonia chuckled.

"You will speak to the Chancellor Pinnacle with respect, or you will never speak again," Sonnalle said.

"Alright, alright. Geez, learn to take a joke already."

Raguel frowned. "The Three Worlds are set on a cosmic scale. The Abyss is filled with malice and corruption and seeks only to throw all creation into disarray. Its lifeblood is the death of all things.

"The Seven Heavens is the counterweight. Only through the discipline of law and order is the Mortal Realm kept safe. Yes, we are extreme in our pursuit of perfection, but it is a necessity, for the Great Balance must remain."

"Thank you for the history lesson, but—"

"But the scale has been tipped. An element has been added to the Seven Heavens that does not belong. You."

"Me? You're crazy. You can't blame me for your precious world turning upside down. Sekka's ring was destroyed. I'm free of her influence."

"Are you? Perhaps. But whether that is physically true or not, you still infect the harmony of paradise. Simply put, you must leave."

"To go where?"

"Isn't it obvious?"

"No. Not there. You can't. I did everything I was asked to do and more."

"Sonnalle will guide you, most of the way. You're path will be swift and direct."

"You're a fiend."

Raguel smirked. "You can discuss my merits with your kind when you arrive."

The room brightened as if a solar flare shone through the windows.

"Raguel, what do you think you are doing?" Illyria's clear and melodic voice came from over his shoulder."

Raguel turned as she materialized before his eyes. Aetenos appeared next wearing a disappointed expression on his face.

"Do not interfere again, Illyria. This time it will take the hand of the Immortal Mother to stop me. The witch must leave."

"You speak eloquently of the Great Balance and yet, continue to add weights to one side, hoping to offset the scale," Aetenos said.

"You are not welcome here, monk. Because of you there is great unrest throughout the Seven Heavens. You bring nothing but sorrow and strife wherever you go."

"Change is never easy," Aetenos said. "But this one here, she's not a villain."

"The Challenge of Righteousness proves otherwise. She did not pass the test, yet somehow she arrived here after her death," Sonnalle chimed in.

"Dear, obedient Sonnalle. The girl is a hero. She saved us all. Who knows who would be on Heaven's doorstep if not for her sacrifice?" Aetenos said and gave Raguel a questioning look.

"Unknown and irrelevant. Her friends have been proven

innocent, though with more time, those still living will continue to blunder. But this one," Raguel said and pointed directly at Desdemonia, "She still has the blood of the devil flowing through her veins. The smell follows her wherever she goes and has now infected the righteous souls of Heaven."

"The blood, no. But the essence, maybe. That malady may never completely vanish. Nonetheless, a pardon is in order."

"She cannot remain in the Seven Heavens. I will not allow her to corrupt my paradise."

"Yours?" Aetenos said with astonishment. He looked to Illyria in amazement. "You see? It's worse than I thought. He must not be allowed to sentence her again."

"But sentence her, he will, as is his right." Illyria sighed and approached Desdemonia. "He has been given the authority to make such decisions as the first among the True-borns." She turned to hold Raguel's gaze. "And be held accountable for the outcomes of those decisions."

"No, no, no," Desdemonia pleaded. "You can't."

"Do not fear, young one. You will not be forsaken," Illyria said kindly.

Desdemonia's panic-stricken face turned red and angry. "What? Forsaken? I'm not going anywhere. I've earned my right to peace. Just let me sleep and reawaken when my time arrives."

"Young one, your trials have yet to begin," Illyria said. She leaned in close, "I know of the light in your heart and the darkness that still burns through your veins. That is why I have chosen you to be the one."

"The one? The one for what? I don't want to be chosen for anything."

"I give you this kiss, and with it the air of life that I breathe."

"No, stop. Keep your kisses to yourself. Get away from me."

Illyria took the sides of Desdemonia's face in her hands and kissed her squarely on the lips. "May it sustain you as you grow with new purpose."

Desdemonia drew back and wiped her mouth with her sleeve. "What have you done?"

"Touching," Raguel said. "Sonnalle take her away. If Illyria or the monk get in the way, imprison them."

"Yes, my lord," Sonnalle said, then turned his head to Aetenos. "You should learn obedience. It would keep you out of trouble."

"What a dull existence that would be," Aetenos said.

"Aetenos! Illyria! You must stop them. I belong here. I can change! Please don't let them banish me," Desdemonia shouted as she was dragged away.

"Raguel, be mindful of your steps. The fate of the Mortal Realm sways in the balance," Illyria said. "Destroy the middle and both ends crumble with it."

"Your worry is unfounded. I am aware the birth of the Chaos Gate awakened the Ancients. The portal is gone and with it, their means to by-pass the barrier. They cannot harm us now."

"Anything is possible," Illyria said. "You don't know them like I do."

5

KASAI

Kasai watched his breath form in a light cloud before his face. He enjoyed this time of year, when the musky scent of fallen leaves filled the monastery courtyard. Outside the newly repaired walls of Ordu, the deciduous trees had changed color from green to bright yellow, red and purple.

The northern winds had grown stronger and blew their cold breath across the Sarribe Mountains, another sure sign of an early winter. Kasai watched the treetops outside the monastery walls sway in a stiff breeze. A parade of multicolored leaves tumbled into the courtyard and swirled into a mini tempest across the raked ground.

"Someone is going to be sweeping a lot of steps soon," he said and gave Brother Sondru a knowing look. The youngster had been late to the morning meditation session in the reconstructed Zazen Hall.

Kasai raised one brow, then scrutinized the group that stood in a line before him. Gift, Pallo, Run-Run, and the younger monks had gathered for morning exercises.

"Maybe not just Brother Sondru by the looks of this bunch."

Kasai watched the distracted eyes of his students look over his shoulder and soon heard the huffing approach of Master Cyrus. He was sure the older monk wore his customary scowl of disapproval.

"I will say one last time, this is a mistake." Cyrus focused his attention on Gift, and then the two brothers. "I cannot condone the sacred xindu teachings to outsiders."

"We gain strength by learning from each other. Ordu can benefit from their skills," Kasai said. "And again, they are my friends and are welcome here."

Cyrus's mouth formed a straight line, and he folded his arms across his chest. "Stubborn as you are disrespectful of the old ways. Must I remind you of the sacred text prohibiting the exchange of secrets?"

"Look around you, Master Cyrus. Do you see a thriving monastery filled with a hundred initiates? Your precious secrets were ill kept at the highest level of our Orders. Trust me, they have no use to us now."

Master Cyrus sighed in resignation. "We will speak of this in private."

"I have made my decision. There is nothing more to discuss."

Kasai turned back to the line of trainees. "Now that's settled, we will begin our lesson today by reviewing the introductory principles of the fighting techniques of Ordu," Kasai said.

He immediately heard a few groans from the older monks. Some of them where rubbing their arms to keep out the morning chill.

"Some of this may seem tedious for the older brothers, though based on our initial sparring sessions, I can see you have not been keeping up with your exercises over the last six years."

"Will you be demonstrating using the Fire Serpent?" Brother Mando said. Kasai saw the eyes of the other younger monks open wider in eager anticipation.

"Not today, Mando. Ninziz-zida possesses an awesome power and I relied on it too much in battle. Too many times the wielder failed when he was without the weapon. Master Cyrus is teaching me a different way."

"Sekka died by your hands, not Ninziz-zida's fire," Gift said. The look of confusion on her face deepened. "You did just fine without the staff when it mattered the most."

"The road to enlightenment is beset by distraction," Cyrus said. "Veer too far to either side and you will become lost in the wilds of chaos. The closer you approach the doors to infinite abundance, the narrower the path becomes until it is but the edge of a thin blade of grass. Only the worthy may enter, for those who are not fall to the side and into darkness."

"Like Brother Daku," Mando said.

"Don't say his name," Sondru said, and looked around nervously, worried that the shadow demon would appear.

"Exactly. Here is a perfect example of how the path of ease can lead to despair. Brother Daku was a promising member of this fine Order, with a deep reservoir of fire xindu. But Ordu taught Daku a different way, one that failed him."

"Perhaps, if he had been groomed at Symmetu and been taught to harness his fire xindu effectively, things may have been different. And so, because of lack of proper guidance from his masters, he became reckless and was led astray to become an agent of evil. His treachery was inevitable."

Cyrus turned to Kasai to make his point. "This is why you must resist the Fire Serpent's call. She will be your doom until you can master the deep fire xindu within you."

Gift's eyes narrowed at the older monk. "I know of a different story. One where a humble monk took the long sleep so the Ever Hero could awaken and save the world. I have seen extraordinary things during this waking period, and none have compared to the bond I witnessed between Master Kasai and the Fire Serpent. The harmony between this wielder and that weapon cannot be denied or distorted. All things created by Nayche are this way."

"If you please, Gift, we prefer not to worship the lesser fragments of the Immortal Mother while on hallowed grounds," Cyrus said, looking down his nose at her, but arching his back due to her height.

"I am Ruith Zylris Faeharice of the Frona Tribe," Gift said. She proudly stepped forward and the cool, morning light accentuated her high cheekbones. The dark tone of her skin was as vibrant as the fierceness in her eyes.

"I have been named, Gift, by Master Kasai. But perhaps you should use the formal name given to me by my elders, as is fitting for outsiders of my tribe. And I will worship my goddess how I please, where I please."

"Master Cyrus, the Sunnese are great wielders of Elemenati magic. My late Master Choejor said they draw from the same elemental energy as the xindu mysteries," Kasai said. "I believe Nayche is their version of the Boundless. If you look closely, you will recognize the design tattooed across the side of her head. She, too, bears the Mark of Aetenos."

Cyrus glanced briefly at the design across Gift's head. He looked to the sky, shook his head once, then nodded as if he was having a conversation with himself.

"It's time you knew the truth. The Master Monks of Ordu have long held an odd devotion to their concept of the Boundless. The idea of a sacred place where limitless power can be exploited to deceive the laws of nature is quite fascinating."

Master Cyrus turned to Kasai with an air of superiority. "But you must now know, the Boundless is a myth and impossible to achieve by mere mortals. Whatever you think you achieved on your own was merely a temporary extension of power granted to you by Aetenos, or more likely, the staff. I suspect you suffered from a severe form of possession and nothing more."

Kasai stood dumbfounded. "That's not true."

"I am sorry to be the one to inform you of such matters," Cyrus said, then smirked at Gift. "Forgive me for being blunt, but the jungle lore of the Sunnese, and the following of a primitive nature spirit wielding Elemenati magic is but a drop of enchantment in the sea of wonder held by the xindu mysteries."

Gift's eyes widened and her nostrils flared. "Shall we test your theory?" A slight ripple of orange flame circled around both of Gift's writs.

"Let's all take a breath," Kasai said, stepping between the two.

"Never before has an outsider—" Cyrus said, brows furrowed and red flashing across his face. A flicker of fire shimmered across his body.

53

Kasai stood fast next to Gift. "Yes, I know. You disapprove. I don't care. If you wish to remain at Ordu, you will follow my lead. I am the master here, not you."

A sharp silence hung in the air. Kasai saw the anxious expression on some of the younger initiates. Cyrus had said the unthinkable. The Boundless was fake. It was tantamount to heresy.

Gift was fuming. She shifted into an attack position. This was not how he envisioned rebuilding the monastery and passing on the teachings of Aetenos to the next generation of monks. Master Cyrus took a ready stance to defend himself, but then, with a stiff smile, he straightened and bowed to Kasai.

"That's right. You are the master here, and I will honor your wishes, for now," Cyrus said. "You must see with your own eyes that which is hidden from you in plain sight. Wisdom comes in all forms, and you will one day see the folly of your path to achieve the unachievable. For now, I will return to my chambers and study.

"Just yesterday, I found a crate of books and scrolls in the lower catacombs. Miraculously, they were not degraded by demon filth or scorched by fire. I will clean them and add them to Ordu's woefully stocked library. Though what use is knowledge to the man who clings to fairy tales?"

Cyrus bowed again to Kasai and headed for the dormitory where a crude version of the Masters' Chambers had been rebuilt. Kasai watched him until he entered the dormitory building.

"Master Kasai?" Mondo said hesitantly.

"It's ok, Mondo. Master Cyrus is entitled to his beliefs," Kasai said. "We must be tolerant of other's opinions no matter how different they are from our own. Now, beginning stance. Sondru, get your elbow up. That's better."

Kasai led the initiates through the basic movements, though his mind was elsewhere. He understood the fighting techniques of the Monasteries of Aetenos had been shrouded in mystery for centuries to protect the Orders and by teaching outsiders he was breaking a sacred vow of noble silence.

But was that any reason for Cyrus to discredit the teachings of Ordu? Kasai thought. *I hope this isn't a mistake.* And he didn't mean teaching his friends how to use xindu energy to fight.

The musky-sweet aroma of late Autumn wafted over the monastery walls and into the courtyard below. Kasai was pleased with the progress of the revived monastery, and the modified name it had been given, Nu-Ordu.

The name had originated with the younger monks almost as a playful joke but seemed apt to Kasai's thinking. All things change, no matter how much one wills it to be otherwise, or for how many thousands of years it seemed to stay the same. Ordu was no different.

The call of a wild beast echoed through the mountains. Kasai heard another shriek, this time closer. The vargru were on the hunt. Kasai hoped they were after deer, and not a band of hapless merchants.

It happened too often now. The fires had displaced too many people throughout the Three Kingdoms and the brave or desperate assumed life would be easier elsewhere. Most lost their way searching for the Sarribe Pass and became prey.

"The territory of the vargru has grown over the years,"

Kasai said. "They were never this bold when I was first at Ordu. But then, I wasn't permitted to travel far outside the walls, and certainly not past the last bridge."

Cyrus stood at his side. They used this time for early-evening meditation and discussion as they walked the highest wall encompassing the monastery grounds. They could talk together quietly, while appreciating the mountain landscape at sunset.

An uneasy truce had formed between the two masters. Kasai allowed Cyrus to remain at the monastery provided he ceased provoking the others by discrediting their faith. The two masters would speak of the merits of the Boundless in private, but Cyrus was not to conduct sermons dedicated to deconstructing the foundation of the Order. That would only serve to confuse the younger initiates and keep them from diving deeper into the xindu mysteries.

"And more numerous, at least in the wilds surrounding Ordu," Cyrus said. "My brothers and I completely eliminated their existence for hundreds of miles outside the walls of Symmetu.

"The vargru are loathsome creatures. It was a chore dispatching the handful of them I encountered on my way here. Such a bother."

Kasai found Cyrus's first statement hard to believe. It was true the vargru were hostile beasts and needed to be culled for the safety of the frontier villages, but hunting the beasts was a job for the King's Rangers, or skilled hunting parties and not a service the monks were asked to perform. The local lords were responsible for keeping the hamlets in their territory safe.

According to the long-lost textbooks he studied growing

up, the monasteries of Aetenos were only emptied during times of great need across the Three Kingdoms of Hanna. Famine, war, or natural disaster would be likely events to cause the monks to venture from their hidden homes.

Or the birth of a Chaos Gate that emptied hordes of demons into the land of men, Kasai thought miserably.

Only the Travelling Masters were permitted to venture beyond the last bridge connecting the monasteries to the outside world. But, after journeying abroad, and beyond, Kasai knew firsthand that things were not always as he was led to believe.

Cyrus was a strange fellow, and certainly didn't sound like any of the Three Masters he had trained under at Ordu. His mentors all spoke in mysterious ways filled with riddles, especially Master Choejor. But Cyrus tended to express himself more bluntly like Daku.

He uses derisive, boastful words and tries to smother his insecurities with accolades that can hardly matter when seeking the Boundless, which he doesn't believe is real. He's eager to express the differences between the two Orders, as if one is better than the other.

And then there's his obsession with Ninziz-zida. He feels robbed that Gen Moli determined Ordu would be the resting place of the Fire Serpent rather than Symmetu.

"We will destroy them together," Cyrus said, slapping his hand on the wall shelf and interrupting Kasai's musing.

Kasai gave him a sideways glance. "I will organize a tournament tomorrow with the higher-ranking brothers. We'll rate their fighting technique using basic xindu enhancements. It will be an adequate demonstration to see what they have learned. The winner and runner-up will join us on an expedition outside the monastery walls. I'm sure Gift, Pallo and Run-Run would also enjoy the hunt."

"Hmm... the vargru present us with a unique opportunity to determine which of the two Orders is more effective in life-or-death combat, something a tournament cannot duplicate. We will eliminate the vargru menace and have a clear understanding of the other's skill, for teaching purposes of course," Cyrus said. "We will kill two birds with one stone, so to speak."

Exactly like Daku.

Kasai stared out at the setting sun. *If he's going to be a problem, it'll be better to find out before the winter months close off the trails.* "I agree, the packs of vargru need to be thinned. The demon taint they carry cannot be allowed to multiple." *And now I sound like one of those callous angels.*

"Then it's decided. Tomorrow we will hunt the chaos beasts. Obviously, you will need to leave behind the sanjiegun. The Fire Serpent provides an unfair advantage, and undoubtably will keep you from finding your path to self-mastery of the xindu mysteries."

Kasai nodded his acceptance of the rules of the contest. "I will leave her behind this time."

"Good, that is a courageous first step." Cyrus breathed in a deep draught of Autumn air, appreciating the scents, then turned to Kasai. "I am surprised anyone other than a chosen Master of Symmetu, and the Great Monk, Aetenos, of course, could wield the staff in battle. It's an affront to the Fire Serpent to be held by anyone less than an equal to her majesty, or with a poor supply of fire xindu."

There it is again. He's obsessed with her. "You mean like you?"

"Me? Oh no. I would not dare to presume I am worthy." Cyrus thoughtfully turned back to appreciate the landscape. His nose had the profile of a raptor's hooked beak. "My humble hands are not meant for such power. I only meant the staff will hinder your progress.

"Think of your failure wielding the staff against Sekka. When the Fire Serpent called for you to lend her your fire xindu, you could not, and she faded back into the staff, defeated. Is this not what you have told me?"

"Ninziz-zida wasn't to blame for my lack of knowledge of fire xindu. I did not fail. Sekka was destroyed by me. She fell when I was one with the Boundless."

"Yes, of course. Unfortunately, Aetenos no longer needs you and the way to the Boundless is closed. But now, it's the Fire Serpent who clouds your reasoning and draws your attention away from higher learning. She sees you as a pawn to carry out her will, like Aetenos did in the past. Perhaps the two were working together, in some cosmic way."

Kasai rounded on the older monk. "Master Cyrus, I respect your rank and your age, but do not presume to know anything of my connection to Ninziz-zida. As I have said, we have a bond that is impossible for you to understand."

Cyrus craned his head upwards, taking in the first stars that appeared in the evening sky. "Trust me, she is manipulating you. I fear your path to enlightenment may forever be hidden if you stay your present course."

"No, she isn't."

"Time will tell. But let's not quarrel. I'm famished and the smell of Brother Mando's rabbit stew in making my mouth water, though I'm positive he's added too much garlic again, for my tastes at least."

Cyrus put his hand on Kasai's shoulder. "Do not worry, young man. As we have rebuilt the monastery, so too, shall we rebuild you. When you are stronger in mind and spirit, your fire xindu will dominate the will of the Fire Serpent, as is proper for the Ever Hero of Aetenos."

Kasai saw past Cyrus's lying. *He's going to be a problem.*

6

SHIVERRIG

"Horns," Shiverrig said in disgust as Daku and his loose flock of barbarian warriors raced toward the helpless nomads. "They've been altered by the chaos change."

"It would appear that way," Dai-Ko-Zior said, bemused at the obvious remark.

Shiverrig noted the nomads resembled more the beasts of the forest and plains, rather than the bird-like appearance of the half-breeds born from his seed and the taint of Xerthotha's essence.

But that was a different time when he commanded legions and the world was his to conquer. *Now look at me. I'm a hollow man wandering a frozen waste searching for something that cannot be found.*

"Xerthotha?"

"The Chaos Devil's reach does not affect those who worshipper the Ancients," Dai-Ko-Zior said. "These are my masters' brood. Command your warriors to heed."

The nomads didn't flee as his barbarians advanced.

Instead, they danced and jumped in wild agitation. Shiverrig could hear them bleating like so many goats, screaming what could only be obscenities in their native tongue.

"Kill them all," Shiverrig shouted. He reached to gain his sword and then spurred his reluctant horse forward to join in the melee.

The nomads opened their arms wide in supplication as the first wave of Shiverrig's men crashed into them. Blue blood the color of a cloudless sky, splashed into the snow. The slaughter was welcomed, as if the nomads were overzealous participants to a sacred rite, throwing themselves on bare blades.

"Stop! Stop!" Dai-Ko-Zior shouted. "The vortex is here. My masters are here!"

Shiverrig soon understood what the sorcerer meant. He spotted a deep depression behind the wall of sacrificial beast men. Another group of wild things danced around the edges of the pit. Their hair was styled in long manes, braided with small bones.

"Stop! Withdraw. Now," Dai-Ko-Zior said and with uncanny speed, the sorcerer's steed was at Daku's side. He mumbled cryptic words and Daku froze mid-step and tumbled into the snow.

Only with great effort did he manage to lift his face at Dai-Ko-Zior. The icy snarl across his muzzle was enough to tell Shiverrig the pale demon would strike the sorcerer dead the moment he was freed.

But as quickly as it began, the melee was over. Shiverrig watched as the last beast man beyond the vortex was chopped down, his arms willingly flung out wide. They had died without a fight or attempting to defend themselves in any way. Not one ran away.

Shiverrig observed the carnage. The pungent smell of otherworldly sorcery was in the air, but it wasn't one of Dai-Ko-Zior's spells or Xerthotha's Abyssal magic that lingered like sulfur and rotten eggs whenever the Chaos Devil invaded his mind. This was something different. A feeling of foreboding crept up his spine.

"Sorcerer, release him."

Dai-Ko-Zior nodded and with a flick of his wrist, Daku was freed. The pale demon sprang to his feet and meant to rush the sorcerer.

"Enough," Shiverrig said. "Leave the wizard alone until I know what's going on here."

He looked to where the nomads circling the pit continued their bizarre dance. They were seemingly oblivious to the slaughter wrought by his barbarian troops. Shiverrig noticed their eyes never left the center of the pit as they moved faster around the edge, caught up in a perverse ecstasy. They danced with fervor and soon their arms moved as if they were beckoning spirits to come forth from the pit.

Shiverrig moved his mount closer to Dai-Ko-Zior and nodding in the direction of the wild things.

"Sorcerer, what's this?"

"My masters are close now. They will see I have served my purpose by bringing you here. All has transpired as they foretold. The snow, the ice, the portal, and the means to carry out their will. My reward shall be limitless!" A wild ecstasy lit Dai-Ko-Zior's eyes.

"Well, get on with it then. Open the portal. Call them. Do whatever you were meant to do so we can leave this wretched place."

"The sorcerer's task was not to open a portal," said an eerie voice that carried with it the itch of static friction.

Dai-Ko-Zior's eyes shifted past Shiverrig's shoulder and went wide in awe. He dropped from his horse and knelt in the snow. "Get off your horse, you fool. Do it now."

Shiverrig twisted in his saddle and saw two, naked figures hovering above the snow. One was male, the other female with facial traits similar enough to make them twins. The observation of their sex made obvious by their exposed bodies.

Somehow, they had gained his unprotected side undetected. He turned his steed to face them and raised his sword, but they did not attack. Instead, they stared at him with hungry eyes.

"Daku, to me," Shiverrig said needlessly. Daku had already joined his side.

Their long hair was a cloak of purplish-blue behind their backs, whipping like thick banners as the wind shrieked across the plain. They were as tall as Daku standing upright, but willowy and emaciated, with translucent skin that did little to hide their organs, muscles, or bones. They had the same sunken cheeks and withered skin as the beast men his troops had slaughtered.

"Specters in the snow," Daku mumbled.

"Can you speak?" Shiverrig called out.

"Get down I said!" Dai-Ko-Zior cried.

The female turned to the sorcerer. "You," she said in a commanding tone. The resonance of her voice was in sharp contrast to the high-pitched wail of the wind.

Shiverrig's horse shied a few feet away and he kicked it hard to bring it back around. The twins had moved with preternatural speed, and planted themselves on either side of Dai-Ko-Zior. His head was still low enough to touch the snow.

"Whatever happens next, do not interfere. Am I understood?" Dai-Ko-Zior said.

"Whatever you say, sorcerer," Shiverrig said. He heard the milling of the barbarians under his command forming a loose line behind him.

Then the male spoke. "You have brought us what was demanded?" His eyes lingered on Shiverrig for a moment, then returned to the prostrate form of the sorcerer.

"I have, my masters. He shall be the hammer to shatter the barrier."

The woman's gaze shifted to Shiverrig. "Why are you not kneeling before your gods."

Shiverrig raised his eyebrows.

"I said, kneel."

In the blink of an eye, she was at his side. She touched his horse and the animal crumpled under him. His movements were slow due to the cold and fatigue, though he still managed to push himself free and roll awkwardly with his sword in the snow.

When he rose, he saw the grisly remains of the horse sinking into the melting snow. Daku bounded next to him and crouched, ready to strike.

"I have had enough of this," Shiverrig said.

"The mortal has failed us, Damiano. This one is not the daimus nexus," she said with a sneer and twisted her head to the male. "He tries to trick us with an imposter."

"Impossible. The visions—everything has happened according to your instructions," Dai-Ko-Zior said. His head was raised now, and he looked with bewildered eyes at the twins. "I have delivered what was demanded."

"Silence!" the female shouted.

"The worlds have shifted, and destinies have been altered," the one called Damiano said. "The Chaos Devil failed to hold open the breech and the barrier still protects this world. The warlord is no longer the one we seek. But you may still serve us."

"I am yours to take. The promise holds," Dai-Ko-Zior said with resignation. He rose to an upright, kneeling position with his arms held wide to either side.

The female was on him, ripping through his fur cloak with ease, and leaving him bare to the elements. Shiverrig watched as each bit deeply into the sides of Dai-Ko-Zior's neck. Then he heard thick, slurping sounds of liquid sucked through meat. The heat of Dai-Ko-Zior's blood steamed in the cold air.

Vampires. Why am I not surprised? Shiverrig thought and readied his sword.

Through it all, and it was messy, Dai-Ko-Zior remained silent and let the twins take their fill. Finally, the otherworldly creatures stepped away.

"It is done. I will ascend," Dai-Ko-Zior wheezed and fell over into the snow. His dissected body was a husk of withered flesh and soft bone. Deep gashes covered his colorless flesh, though no blood drained from them. The skin of the twins gained a rosy complexion and a bit of vibrancy, but then it was gone.

"I thirst for more, brother," the female said, leering at Shiverrig as she moved in his direction. "This one has something special inside. Something tasty."

"You'll get none from me, leech, or whatever foul thing you are," Shiverrig said, pointing his sword at her as she advanced.

"Daku, find us some shadows!" Shiverrig said, thinking of a fast retreat. His men would be left behind and slow any quick pursuit. He'd done it before. They were expendable.

"Daku?" Shiverrig glanced to the ground. It revealed what he already knew. The snow and ice of the tundra created a permanent white out. The sun was a blurred disc in the sky that gave no heat and emitted a pale, ambient light. Shadows did not exist in the chaos wastelands.

"I heard you. It's going to have to be the hard way this time," Daku said and unsheathed Eishorror. "Protect the Aj-Kahun!"

"Baast hold. I smell it too, though the Chaos Devil's reek is faint. This is one of his mortal slaves," Damiano said pointing at Shiverrig. He didn't bother wiping away the blood covering his mouth and chin. "He can be of use to us."

"I am slave to no one," Shiverrig said, keeping his sword level on Baast. "Or meal ticket. I was promised many things. I'll have my due before I die."

"But you are only half of the whole that is needed. You are filled with chaos but hold none of the purity required," Damiano said.

"He is flawed, brother, and I hunger," Baast said, licking the sorcerer's blood from her fingers. "This form will soon perish feeding only on the human beasts."

"I am the favored by the Chaos Devil. If you harm me, you will face his wrath," Shiverrig boasted. It was a losing gamble, and he knew it.

"You dare threaten the will of a god?" she said.

Damiano squinted his dark eyes at Shiverrig. "I sense your connection to the Chaos Devil is waning, yet, it will be enough," he said, while Baast levitated above the snowy ground and glided closer.

"A god? Ha! You're no god, bloodsucker," Shiverrig countered, sizing up his opponent.

Baast's wicked smiled extended across her face farther than humanly possible. "Oh, is that so?"

"Sister, hold. We will use this one until we can be made whole."

Baast growled but relented. "You must bring us the daimus nexus paradox," she hissed.

"I say, fuck you and your whatever nexus. There isn't a devil, angel, or the Immortal Mother that pissed them out, that can be trusted. I was promised the means to conquer the Three Kingdoms and beyond. And this time, I will have my empire first before I agree to any demands."

Baast spread her arms out wide. "You will have nothing. This world is ours and you will do our bidding or be sucked dry!" Her eyes held a sinister look, but an enigmatic smile played across her lips. It was almost sexual.

Shiverrig smirked. "Keep it. Come on, Daku. Gather the troops. We're leaving."

"Sister be calm. The mortal can be an asset, like the others who willingly advance our goal."

Baast drew air deeply through her nose, taking in Shiverrig's scent. "The Chaos Devil has abandoned this one. He will not survive the trials to come."

Her gaze drifted to Daku and the rest of Shiverrig's troops. "None of them will. There is barely enough soul energy here to satiate my hunger for a moment."

"Then he must be altered. The sorcerer did not fail completely when he brought you to us. You have something we can use. But not in this raw form," Damiano said.

"I'm fine just the way I am. Others greater than you have tried, and failed, to control me. I have taken their power and turned it against them. What makes you think you will be any different?" Shiverrig said. He moved a half step backward, though without a horse he doubted he could outrun the preternatural speed of the vampires.

"You see only a fraction of our true selves. With the daimus nexus at our side, we will be made whole, and this world will tremble," Damiano said.

"And why would I want that?" Shiverrig took another step back, as did Daku.

"Because you will finally have the empire you crave, Gerun Shiverrig. Not only on this world, but countless others we can show you," Baast chimed in. Her disposition became more inviting, almost alluring.

"Do not look so surprised, son of Gareth Shiverrig, and great grandsire to Baroq Shiverrig. We have watched this world from the cosmic shadows for what would seem like ages to your primitive mind."

"I've heard these types of promises before," Shiverrig said. "They were all lies."

"The Chaos Devil has a twisted tongue. He will be dealt with for failing us, as will his siblings. Not even your Immortal Mother will stand in our way once the daimus nexus is ours."

"And the sorcerer? What of him? His deal with you went sour rather quickly."

"He has served his purpose," Baast said indifferently. "And has been rewarded."

Daku laughed but his smile instantly faded, and a wary expression took its place. "So much for delusions of power and grandeur," he said. "I guess you sent him the wrong visions."

Baast snarled at Daku.

"Can you imagine a more wretched way to die? I thought sorcerers were supposed to be smart."

"The boy brings up an interesting point. If you're so powerful, and ready to offer me my heart's desire on a silver platter, why not just find this magical being yourself? Should be an easy enough task for a cosmic god."

"We cannot attract unwanted attention while we are in this incomplete form," Damiano said matter-of-factly.

Shiverrig understood. The vampires, like all foul things, feared the angels' wrath and the retribution that followed. He knew how they felt.

"It seems you have quite a predicament. I'd wager you're shackled here for reasons beyond having a good hiding place, which means you can't help me, even if you wanted to. And I really doubt you do."

"If you refuse to help us, then we have but one use for you," Baast said.

"We abandon the barbarians and with some luck, get far enough away from that pit so they can't follow," Daku mumbled quietly.

"It's not like you to back down from of a good fight," Shiverrig said from the corner of his mouth.

"Call it a demon's sense. They're not right. There's something about them that says this is a time for flight, not fight." Daku gave the twins a hard stare. "I'm sure of it."

"We will have your answer, mortal," Baast said.

"My answer is no," Shiverrig said.

"Good," Baast said and licked the frosty blood from her lips.

Damiano sighed. "Nonetheless. We have a need that cannot wait, and the essence of Xerthotha you already possess will make you an apt vessel. Baast, take him."

Baast leaped at Shiverrig. In a smooth motion, Daku stepped forward and drove Eishorror through her mid-section. The pointed ice blade came out the back as clean as it went in.

Daku gasped for breath as she grabbed him by the throat and lifted him effortlessly into the air.

"Now you see it, don't you, ape?" she said.

"What are you waiting for? Help him!" Shiverrig yelled to his warriors.

The barbarians rushed forward. Some jumped on Baast's back, jabbing her with daggers, while others grappled with her legs, trying to bring her down into the snow. A second, more cautious group stayed outside her reach and repeatedly stuck her with their spears.

She just laughed.

Shiverrig watched Damiano slowly approach. "I told you, we cannot wait," he said. "Whether you agree willingly or not, is irrelevant to our need."

"I told you, others greater than—" Shiverrig's voice faltered. He felt the pain of unseen worms squirming under his skin and burrowing into his body.

"You see, the Chaos Devil filled you but left you incomplete. I will begin where his influence ends," Damiano said.

Shiverrig heard the horrible shouts of the dying rising

above Baast's maniacal laughter. His men were being butchered, but there was something more, like the shrieks of war horses aflame on the battlefield. Somehow, his eyes focused enough to watch the bestial shamans surrounding the pit burst into explosions of gore.

"All I need are more parts." Damiano's hands and arms moved as if he was sculpting a large piece of organic matter.

"No, you will not have me!" Shiverrig growled, holding his body tight, fearing it would burst. "I refuse you."

"But you are already mine," Damiano said and came closer. He reached out his translucent hand and placed his palm on Shiverrig's forehead.

Shiverrig screamed and dropped feebly into the snow. His arms and legs were useless, but that did not stop them from moving, and changing. His chest heaved and he vomited warm bile. He felt as if nails were being driven into the back of his skull and escaping out his forehead.

The wails of the dying subsided and Shiverrig heard only the moan of the wind. His body was numb and wet as he lay in deep snow. The snow hugged his sides. It was almost comforting.

How long he had been there was unknown. Shiverrig was aware of footsteps crunching in the snow. Then he heard voices.

"This one takes the pain like a stone," Baast said, approvingly.

"There, that's better. Now you are a true Warlord of Chaos," Damiano said.

Shiverrig tried to rise to his knees. Snow and ice blurred his vision. His back spasmed and his head was thrown forward into the snow. He managed to roll over and wiped the debris from his face. The pale sun was a bright disc in the sky that offered no warmth or comfort.

He removed an unrecognizable hand, covered in course, black hair from his face. The pain subsided and his vision cleared.

"What have you done?" Shiverrig said, panting.

7
RAGUEL

"A thousand damnations on that monk and his constant meddling into the affairs of mortals. He should never have been given the divine spark. Illyria's games have gone too far. She humiliates me with every move, thinking I am powerless to stop her."

Raguel fumed while standing at an open window overlooking the city of Asher. The golden sun was bright in a cloudless sky. He recalled a sonnet he had written to Illyria, years ago, comparing her flaxen hair to the rays of that brilliant orb. He pounded his fist on the windowsill.

"I am the one true power in the Heavenly Realm. How dare she usurp my authority. I could have achieved much while the Chaos Gate remained open. Our territory would have doubled if not tripled. The soul power would be near incalculable, even for Lord Metatron. But now, I am laughed at for being weak. Damn him to oblivion."

Even as he said the words, a queasy feeling of apprehension overcame him. He quickly pushed it aside. "She is nothing. I allow her to much latitude."

The more he recounted the events following the destruction of the archdevil, Sekka, the more infuriated he became. In the blink of an eye, the Seven Heavens had become a realm of rioting and insubordination. Mini revolts erupted across the six lower levels. The dissidents were eventually put down, but force was often needed to quell the uprising. Only Tanalum remained stable. His control of Asher remained undisputed.

"It's high time I ended this folly. I will set things right."

Raguel leaped out of the window and plummeted toward the roofs of hundreds of thousands of buildings. Wind rippled through his rainbow-colored wings as they unfurled. He soared across the city on warm thermals, searching for the one man who had vexed him for what seemed like an eternity.

It took little time to find the half-blind monk. As usual, he sat in mindful contemplation under a single tree on an isolated hill overlooking the city. Seeing him so peaceful infuriated Raguel even more.

"Aetenos!" Raguel growled as he set down to the grass covered ground.

"Hello, my old friend. Have you come to enjoy the view?"

"You must leave," Raguel said, stomping forward.

"Is this your favorite spot, too?" Aetenos asked. He scooted over a few feet and patted the grass. "There we are. Come, there's plenty of room for us both."

"Leave now or you will find yourself in chains before officially being banished forever. You are no longer welcome in paradise."

"I see. What have I done now, hmm?" Aetenos looked thoughtful, then raised his finger. "Wait, I know. This is the blame game. You need someone to be responsible for causing your perfect world to come unhinged, and I'm the perfect candidate. Am I right?" Aetenos said eagerly.

"If not for you, I would—"

"I am right! I knew it! Dear Raguel, you can't control everything. And that is the nature of your dilemma. Be at peace. Sit with me and enjoy the view. It's a wonderful day, and the breeze is exceptionally pleasant."

Raguel glared at Aetenos. "Then it will be chains."

"You cannot banish everyone who disagrees with your view of the Laws of Heaven. Eventually, the Seven Heavens would be a barren place. Come, sit."

"You dare to insult me with your patronizing remarks? I am the Chancellor Pinnacle. I *am* the Law of Heaven."

"No one doubts that you are Chancellor Pinnacle, Lord Raguel," Aetenos sighed.

Raguel's fists clenched.

The monk continued, "A wise woman once told me, pay attention to how someone acts when they don't get their way. Look to your actions and see if they are just. Was Artiya'il's banishment needed? You condemned him to a cold and lonely death. Oblivion would have been more merciful than the torture he endured under Sekka's wickedness.

"And for what, to show everyone you were in control? That you held power in the Seven Heavens? When has anyone said something of the contrary?"

Raguel was sure he heard condescension in the tone in the monk's words. "Artiya'il willingly defied me. As you do at every opportunity. If not for Illyria's interference, you would not enjoy such liberties."

"I do no such thing." Aetenos waved his hands, mirroring

his words. "But in truth, you were wrong, old friend. You cannot blame me for something I did not do. You have been too preoccupied with your fantasies of reshaping the Three Worlds, that you failed to see the pot of the Seven Heavens boiling over. What is happening now took root long ago and well before my time."

The monk was always a shambles. He seemed but a child against the stature of the True-born. How could Illyria see anything but a dirty animal in this mortal?

No, not a mortal, not anymore. Not since she begged Raguel to place within Aetenos a sliver of the divine spark and ascend him to the rank of demigod. Raguel had foolishly agreed.

Aetenos stood and did his best to brush out the wrinkles of his robes, an impossible task.

Now he's going to preach, Raguel thought.

"You must understand, the Great Balance is constantly in motion. It's fluid, malleable and follows the natural law, which was set in harmony by the Immortal Mother at the creation of all things. But you want to change that.

"No one can tell the rainstorm to leave the ground dry once it has fallen from the clouds, or insist the fire not burn the paper after it's lit. You command the law of nature to be otherwise and are perplexed when it cannot."

"I can command you to be gone from this place," Raguel said, narrowing his eyes. "This time, your banishment will be eternal. Go and trudge through the mud of the Mortal World since you are so fond of helping those primitive souls."

"No, that's not going to happen. I will no longer appease your false sense of honor. I allowed it once when you sent the boy and his companions against the devil. It's a miracle they survived."

"But they did, unfortunately."

"And have you thought of the consequences of those actions? Have you wondered at the damage you caused?"

"The Heavenly Host saved the Mortal Realm. Our fires cleansed the lands of demonkind," Raguel said, smugly. "I saved the mortals."

"Did you? Have you thought of the bitterness you left behind? Hmm? How many innocent and unformed souls have now turned from the path of righteousness to march down a darker trail?"

"I cleansed—"

"You burnt everything! Cities, forest, animals, people, everything. The heat of the angelic fires melted rock. It was a bitter abuse of power. All for what, to abate your wounded pride?"

"You had best be careful. My mood is foul enough already, and I will not think twice about throwing you into shackles."

"Oh Raguel. It's not only me. The Lady Illyria has said the same. Your methods have become unsound. How many pure hearts have you ruined by your callous ways? How many horrors will be born from the soul energy that should have fed into the divine host, especially now, with a terrible war coming?"

Raguel felt his face flush with anger. "If it wasn't for you and your meddling, that boy would never have brought us to this point. He's the one responsible for countless deaths, and by implication, so are you. And now, now, things are worse. You have brought chaos to paradise."

"It's so much more than that, and you know it. The visions can no longer be denied. The avatars of the Ancients have taken shape and now walk upon the Mortal Realm.

"Somehow, they slipped through the breach caused by the Chaos Gate. You should have closed the portal the moment it was born."

"They will fall to the Heavenly Host as easily did the she-devil. I am not worried about such phantoms," Raguel said with a confidence he did not feel. "I'm sure your so called Ever Hero will—"

Aetenos raised his eyebrows. "Did you know your eyes change color when you lie? No, this time, the challenge will be too much for my boy, and I dare say your fine warriors will do no better against them once they have taken their true form. Your short-sightedness has cast the Three Worlds in peril."

Raguel backhanded Aetenos across the face. Quick as the old monk was, he was not fast enough to dodge the blow. He spun in a loose pirouette through the air and coughed out a spray of blood when he hit the ground.

"You look surprised, *monk*," Raguel said with distain as Aetenos stared at him in shock. "I have endured the embarrassment of your rise through the upper echelon of the Seven Heavens for long enough. Illyria will not save you this time. She should never have been yours."

"It is the wounded heart that clings to memories that were never real. You must let her go. She does not love you."

Raguel gave Aetenos a broad smile. "Paradise can soften the hardest heart given time and attention. I have an eternity to give her both. One day, she will see me in the same glorious light as she once did, one brought about from the ascendance of the Heavenly Realm over the other two, lesser worlds. Sadly, you will never see that day."

Aetenos lifted himself off the ground and stood on unsteady legs. Raguel saw he was hurt as he wiped the blood from his mouth.

"I suspect it's madness that waits for us all at the end of so much life. I pity you, old friend, for you have lived the longest by far. But if this is the only way your soul may be at peace, then come, let us put an end to your bitterness."

Raguel watched the one-eyed monk curl his fingers together to form hooked fists. He swayed from side to side as if still reeling from Raguel's first blow. Raguel scoffed at the absurdity of the gesture.

"The divine spark should never have been yours. Today I take back what you stole," Raguel said. His hands glowed with multi-colored light then his left fist flashed at Aetenos's head.

The monk moved in a blur to dodge the blow. When he stopped, his head swayed like that of a befuddled fool. Raguel was astonished that he missed his mark, until the monk's foot hit him across the cheek. The strike barely caused any pain on his perfect face, but then the humiliation registered in his perfect mind. *He struck me!*

Aetenos wobbled backward and created some distance between the two. His one eye looked glazed and distant. Raguel snarled and rushed forward to grab the monk's robe. Jagged lines of lightning swarmed around his right hand as he struck Aetenos in the chest.

The monk's face froze in an awful grimace as powerful currents of energy squirmed and crackled through his body. His agony was intoxicating to watch. Then Aetenos closed his eye and his face softened as white light blossomed from his body.

Raguel's smirking expression turned to curiosity as he felt the air shift around him. Then the currents of energy flowing from him reversed direction. The resounding BOOM knocked Raguel back. He hit the ground and screamed as the lightning of his own attack flooded back through him. No, not his lightning, but something raw and different.

Raguel gritted his teeth until the destructive energy dissipated. Aetenos had shuffled back again. His body bobbed and weaved in an irregular fashion.

"You are nothing but a drunken monkey," Raguel said. He felt the effects of divine healing rejuvenate his body.

"Perhaps," Aetenos said as he stumbled a few steps forward before coming up fast and rigid. "The tiniest of monkeys can deliver the most powerful blow when timed correctly."

"You cannot hurt me. I am the first and greatest immortal." Raguel's broad rainbow wings fanned out behind his back.

"My desire is not to hurt you, old friend, but to teach you, before it's too late."

More preaching. The arrogance of this monk!

"Stop calling me that!" Raguel shouted. "We have never been friends. I was begged to save you. You do not belong here. You are imperfect in every way."

"And this is my strength. It's the imperfections of all living things which allows for growth. And growth is power."

Raguel saw every flaw in Aetenos and hated the demigod for his inability to see he was inferior. "No more lies. No more compromises. No more of you and all your troublesome creations. After I'm finished with you, I'll make sure your boy suffers the same fate. And that will be the end of it. The line of Aetenos and his Ever Heroes dies this day."

Aetenos's calm demeanor turned cold and serious. "You will leave him be."

A wicked smile curled on Raguel's face. "I will end him in the most painful way."

Aetenos came at him fast, no longer as a drunken fool, but with the precise speed of a viper and the powerful fury of a tiger. This time, the strikes hit hard and deep. Raguel saw blue flames trailing the punches and kicks before they struck him. The blows connected like heavy war hammers, pounding across his body.

The resounding cracks and a bright pain flooded his senses. The monk had broken two of his ribs. Raguel gasped for air. He was losing. Aetenos came at him again. A fist connected with Raguel's mouth and the True-born tasted blood on his lip. The monk fought with the strength of a legion. *Impossible!*

"This cannot be," Raguel stammered as he backpedaled from the attack.

"Anything is possible when one surrenders to the Boundless," Aetenos replied in a determined voice.

Raguel leaped into the air. His insides were mending, but the pain to his pride would not subside. He watched Aetenos push his open palms through an intricate dance around his body.

Raguel narrowed his eyes. *What is that fool up to now?*

Then the air under Raguel's wings shifted, and he was buffeted by strong winds, forcing him back to the ground.

Raguel saw red. He gathered into his hands the divine

power reserved for the damnation of tainted souls. "You brought this fate onto yourself," he said as he unleashed a blast of ethereal energy into Aetenos.

Miraculously, the monk withstood the searing energy, but only for a moment. Aetenos dropped to his knees, then collapsed to the ground. Raguel knew the monk's body was shattered, yet somehow, he managed to crawl back to the tree with the view of the city.

"You should not have come back to the Seven Heavens. You should have known this would be your fate."

"I knew," Aetenos said and coughed up blood. "But it was the right thing to do. The boy needed guidance."

Aetenos righted himself and put his back to the tree. Raguel was perplexed at how content the monk seemed. He must know his soul was already gone. Aetenos caught his gaze and smiled warmly back at him but with distant eyes. He coughed up more blood.

"This is such a wonderful view of the city, and I am happy to see it will be the last one I look upon in this time. Leave the boy alone, Raguel. He is innocent of the crimes of your jealousy."

"Shut your mouth, monk."

"But this too will come to an end, someday. The buildings gone; the sun burned out of the sky. Nothing but memories for lost spirits trying to find their way home." Aetenos shifted his weight ever so slightly. "Yes, yes, everything changes, and nothing lasts forever."

Raguel wore a smug expression as he circled Aetenos to stand proudly before him, victorious at last.

"Not even you, old friend," Aetenos said. "But there is still time to set things right, old friend, and to save yourself."

Raguel despised the pity he heard in Aetenos's last words and was about to strike him again when the monk closed his remaining eye and slumped to the side. The archangel gave Aetenos's side a tap with his sandaled foot and his body fell over to the ground, lifeless.

"Finally, it's finished."

He expected to feel a burst of euphoria, but instead the realization that in his blind rage, he had torn asunder the soul of the one man who had captured Illyria's heart. She would be furious. He felt no remorse for the monk, but the ramifications of his deed filled him with dread.

Raguel knew without a shred of doubt that she would hate him forever. He screamed in frustration. "He must be brought back!" Raguel said in desperation and reached into the ether for the monk's soul, but it was gone.

Even in death, the monk plagues me.

Raguel panicked. "This time, there will be nothing for Illyria to mourn. No one for her to watch between worlds. I send your remains to oblivion, where not even she can find you."

Raguel drew down a mighty column of fire from the sky. "You will burn like the filth that dwells in the lower worlds. You deserve no better for the grief your existence has caused me."

Raguel had left long before the fire burned itself out. Now, only a charred depression remained where a lone tree once grew on a solitary hill. A warm breeze lifted from the city and blew away the cooling ashes of the legendary monk.

8

KASAI

Kasai heard the unmistakable screech of a vargru to his left, then moments later, a second to his right, howling in what sounded like gibbering laughter. The ground trembled underfoot, and saplings swayed, cracked, and snapped ahead of him. But instead of fleeing, he and Master Cyrus ran after the chaos beasts.

"We're gaining on them," Kasai shouted as they dashed past another charred tree.

The angelic fires had spread to this part of the Sarribe Mountains six years prior. The hilly terrain had leveled out and the remaining trees were spaced farther apart, looking like stoic, blackened idols.

But life carried on. With most of the canopy burned away, the undergrowth grew in abundance and saplings now competed with fast growing ferns and mountain scrub for sunlight.

"If we are lucky, these two will lead us to their den," Cyrus shouted back.

Lucky, lucky, lucky, Kasai thought, thinking just the opposite.

"Look, there they are!" Cyrus said, pointing ahead.

Two adolescent vargru darted into the open from clumps of thick fern patches. While only three or four years old, the creatures were easily the size of large, wild boars. Their bodies were thick and muscular and hadn't grown overly bulky with age.

One was covered in a brownish shag coat while the other was wrapped in greyish-green fur. Young antlers sprouted from their heads, which transitioned into lines of sharp, singular horns that traveled down their body and double tails.

The greyish-green vargru turned fast and held its ground. It had five rolling eyes and a wolfish snout. The brown leaped ahead into another patch of ferns, shrieking while it ran.

"We take this one together," Cyrus said.

Kasai heard deeper howls coming from the direction where the brown had escaped.

"We've found the pack."

Master Cyrus nodded. "Or they have found us."

The two masters slowed their pace.

"Now, remember your lessons. You are in control of your xindu energy, not the staff. Give your fire xindu its lead and it will guide you."

Kasai's fire xindu was eager to rise. They had been tracking this evasive pack for three days through the lower mountain forest and he was ready to be back to his daily routine at the monastery. *Some time away from Master Cyrus wouldn't be bad either.*

Cyrus had a tendency to turn every conversation back to Ninziz-zida. He ceaselessly prattled on of how the three-sectioned staff kept Kasai from developing his fire xindu into a powerful weapon, since it syphoned away most if his energy for its own use, or that one who knew only the teachings of Ordu could never wield the true power of the Fire Serpent.

Kasai just wanted him to shut up. He was beginning to dread every time Cyrus opened his mouth to speak, even the sound of his breathing was irritating. Six years in solitude would do that to a person.

Kasai steadied himself and channeled his fire xindu energy into his palms. He immediately felt the heat shooting into his hands as he clenched and unclenched them. It was the opposite from the cool sensation of white energy Kasai typically felt when he activated his xindu power.

Instead of bringing up his air xindu for speed, and his earth xindu to anchor him, he gave more emphasis to the fire xindu already burning through his body. His fists glowed like hot coals. Without a second thought, he bounded forward and smashed his fist through the skull of the greyish-green adolescent. The vargru's five eyes widened in shock, then boiled. Three bursts, spewing liquid pulp over Kasai's auburn vest. Maybe not the smartest strike given the messy consequences.

Kasai withdrew his hand and let the creature slump to the forest floor. He gritted his teeth, letting the fire xindu energize his body. Adrenaline pumped through his veins, and he wanted something else to smash.

"You see? The power is substantial," Cyrus said from some distance behind him.

"Yes. But it is demanding and reckless," Kasai said and shook out his hands. "Fire is only one quarter of the elements we can harness. Why forsake the other three mysteries? It seems…wasteful."

"At Symmetu, we learn to focus our fire xindu into whatever weapons or salves we need. Fire is the spark of life. It propels our actions and commands the other xindu energies to obey."

Multiple shrieks and screeches erupted around them.

"And everything burns. The vargru have come," Cyrus said.

"Let them," Kasai said and squeezed his hands back into fists. The molten glow returned effortlessly.

The vargru obliged Kasai's invitation. Three colossal chaos beasts bounded from the tall ferns. Each stood six feet at the shoulder and another five from their heads to the tips of their gnarled antlers.

Two had the bodies of bears with long, heavy fur. The third boasted a mane of tangled hair with shorter, reddish fur covering the rest of its muscular frame. It snorted and stomped the leafy forest floor, then charged like a mad bull at Kasai. The other two were quick to follow.

"Are you planning on assisting?" Kasai shouted back to Cyrus.

"Let's see what you have learned," Cyrus replied from a safe distance. "You are the Ever Hero, after all."

"Lucky me," Kasai said and concentrated on his charging foes.

The ground shook from their weight. Like the pack's youngsters, the vargru had multiple eyes but the gnashing jaws on the adults were horrifying. Nonetheless, Kasai held his ground. He balanced on the balls of his feet, waiting for the right moment to strike. The long mane of the lead beast rippled in the air as it drove into him.

The vargru lowered its head, attempting to gouge Kasai. Long trails of slobber sprayed from its mouth. The other two howled in frustration that their brother would draw first blood, if not the kill.

Against Cyrus's teaching, Kasai lowered his fire xindu and tapped into his air xindu instead. He stepped like the wind to the side, wide enough for the vargru to pass him by, but close enough to grab a section of antler.

Kasai was pulled along as the chaos beast continued to run while shaking its head, trying to dislodge him. Kasai grabbed thick tufts of hair and pulled himself up the vargru's neck, then activated his fire xindu. Once more, his hands glowed like hot embers.

Instead of forming a full fist, Kasai curled his fingers into a tight hook, then struck fast to the side of the vargru's skull with the sharp points of his knuckles. The loud crack of bone was impressive.

Kasai saw the eyes of the beast roll back into its head as it plunged forward into the leaves and dirt. He rolled with it and let his momentum carry him back to his feet and right into the second and third vargru.

The first to hit him, caught Kasai in its antlers and tossed him in the air. The second leaped after him like a ferocious dog. Its jaws opened wide and tongue lolling to the side. Kasai twisted in the air and barely avoided being bitten in half.

He landed hands first and back flipped twice to gain some distance from the wheeling chaos beasts. They came at him again, spraying dead leaves and dirt as they locked on his position. Kasai ran towards the one to the right, veering to the side to create a better angle of attack.

The left most vargru knocked into its brother and snapped at its ear, pushing both towards Kasai. While running, Kasai loaded up his hands with more fire xindu. *And a little zip for good measure,* he thought, adding more air xindu to the attack.

Kasai's hands flashed in a flurry of blows across the unprotected side of the right vargru, ending with a crushing strike to its knee. Happily, he heard ribs break along the way as the monster wailed in agony. His fire xindu grew in strength and his anger followed.

Now for the last, he thought, sliding to a stop. *I'll kill them all.*

A dark shadow appeared over the top of the hurt and hobbled vargru. Kasai looked up with wide eyes and moved too slowly to avoid being buried under the last chaos beast. Its jaws snapped at his face as he squirmed in a desperate attempt to escape. The vargru's weight was overbearing and the stench of its breath was suffocating.

"A little help here," Kasai yelled from his back. "Cyrus!" He was being pounded by the superior strength of the beast while rear claws dug through his pants and found flesh.

Kasai was reminded of another time when his life was threatened by the vargru. It was Master Choejor who had pushed the vargru back long enough for...Desdemonia to save them.

But she can't save you now, can she? You failed her, just like you failed the people of the Three Kingdoms after the war.

Kasai's anger grew. His fire xindu spiked like a pillar of flame through his inner spirit. He brought his forearms together over his chest and then pushed up with the burning palms of his hands.

His arms were lost up to his forearms in vargru's chest

cavity. He smelled burnt fur and charred flesh. The vargru yelped and gasped for air. Its eyes blazed into him and with one last effort, the beast's mouth clamped down over Kasai's head.

But the momentum of the beast's death strike ended as the last bit of life faded away. The vargru's powerful front limbs locked in place as its rear quarters sank into the ground. Kasai pushed the head away and scrambled out from underneath. He was soaked in foul, greasy blood.

Kasai quickly scanned for Cyrus, worried the older monk had been taken unaware by an unseen vargru, but he saw only dead and dying beasts littering the ground. Then, he felt the hair on his neck rising and he spun to his backside.

Cyrus was there, less than an arm's length away. The monk hit him hard in the chest with a fist loaded with fire xindu. Kasai flew backward, hit the ground, and rolled to an upright position. He struggled to catch his breath.

"What's wrong with you?" Kasai said in a wheezing voice.

But instead of answering, Cyrus marched forward. His hands gripped in tight fists, glowing molten orange.

Kasai took an unsteady step backward, unsure what was happening. His left leg was on fire, and he saw blood pooling by his foot. "I'm injured. The competition is over."

"We had agreed to test our skills in a life-or-death arena." Cyrus smiled without mirth. "It's a wonder the Fire Serpent chose you as wielder when you resist using the power of fire xindu and instead, pamper yourself with the lesser xindu energies."

He lunged forward, throwing one fist, and then swinging the other in a wider arc. Kasai dodged both, then swept Cyrus's leg with his right foot. The leg moved no more than if Kasai had hit an oak tree.

Cyrus grabbed him by the upper vest with one hand, lifting him up and struck him in the face with the other, catching the side of his jaw. Kasai saw light flash before his eyes.

He's really trying to hurt me, Kasai realized.

"And you are not even a Master Monk," Cyrus said. "It's a perplexing riddle."

Kasai chopped down with both hands over Cyrus's forearm to free himself. Backpedaling on one leg, he called his xindu forces together. "Cyrus, this is insane. Enough. I will not warn you again."

Though the Boundless would not answer his call as it had done in the past, he could still coil his xindu energies together into a churning force. He delved into his earth xindu and undammed the currents of his water xindu. The burning sensation in his hands was replaced by a cool, soothing vibration as white light seeped from his palms.

Cyrus cusped his hands together and let the fire between them grow.

"Don't make me do this, Cyrus. Just relax," Kasai said, then saw the missing youngster had crept up behind Cyrus and was ready to pounce.

"Cyrus! Behind you!" Kasai shouted.

Cyrus turned fast as the vargru leaped. He batted away its head and then shot his knife-shaped hand into the beast's neck. With a twist of his wrist, he broke its spine, then tossed it unceremoniously to the ground.

Kasai was amazed at the fluidity of Cyrus' deadly strike and remained on guard. Cyrus became calm, slowing his breathing and smiling peacefully.

"You see, fire xindu consumes the other xindu energies as a fire burns wood for fuel. This is what you must learn to be worthy of the Fire Serpent." He lowered his hands and the orange glow softened.

Kasai just watched him, thinking this must be a trick.

"Come, let's finish the vargru you left crippled and return to the monastery. It was a productive hunt and we have learned a valuable lesson today," Cyrus said and started walking back the direction they had come.

Kasai took a deep breath and whipped the sweat from his shaven head. "I learned a few things as well," he said to himself and walked after Cyrus, who was already at the lame vargru.

Cyrus casually laid his hand on the wounded beast's head. It whimpered once then lay still as smoke rose from its eyes and ears. Kasai assumed Cyrus has sizzled the creature's brains.

"We will mount the heads. The vargru will think twice before coming back into this territory," Cyrus said and took out a long skinning knife from his pack. "It will be messy work, but worth it."

"Master Cyrus, I'd like an explanation. Your actions were uncalled for and dangerous."

"You seem surprised. My intent was not to permanently harm you."

Kasai merely shook his head. *Next time, I'll be ready.*

"You should mind that wound. The vargru can smell blood from miles away. It will attract more of them if you don't tend to it now."

The trek back to the monastery was uneventful and Kasai and Cyrus spent much of their time debating the merits of their respective Orders.

"Why do you think the Three Masters taught you to rely

so heavily on the three lesser xindu energies?" Cyrus said. "At Symmetu, we build our fire xindu reserves by sacrificing the others."

"Yes, you mentioned that. You treat them as fuel."

"You must learn to let loose your fire xindu," Cyrus said. He raised a hand in the air and Kasai watched it glow bright yellow, red, and orange.

Then, Kasai looked deeper into Cyrus's aura. Dark and foreboding colors swirled around pastel blues and violets. He shifted into a defensive posture. "You're hiding something. Reveal yourself, now."

Cyrus continued walking at a leisurely pace. "What you see is the chaos portion of fire xindu. Surely you were taught the energy of the world is neutral. There is no good or bad, only vibrations that are attracted to their likeness. It is balanced. Therefore, we all carry an amount of deep chaos within us, just as we soar through the heights of lawfulness. This was the truth of the Wood Witch. Once you understand this, you will be one step closer to enlightenment."

Her name was Desdemonia. Kasai knew Cyrus had heard the stories of his last stand against Sekka, when Desdemonia broke through the archdevil's charm spell and helped him destroy her, though he doubted Cyrus knew what she meant to him.

Kasai started walking, following Cyrus, albeit hesitantly.

"I'm sorry. I've seen too much treachery and I distrust quickly. Plus, the separation from the Boundless is difficult to endure. It's like experiencing bliss, and then having the source of that euphoria ripped from your soul. I know it's there, but I can't reach it. Every time I try, I just graze it with my fingertips."

"You describe the Boundless as a drug to use to quell your unsettled spirit, and sound like an addict that yearns for more of his debilitating habit. You must let go of your fantasy that this all-encompassing, abundant power source exists, just as you must let go of your more material and emotional crutches."

Kasai wondered if Cyrus meant Desdemonia. Her image lurked in the shadows of his thoughts and along with it came the feeling of guilt and loss.

Did none of the Master Monks ever experience hardship and feel like their heart was torn out and stomped on? Did none of them experience love?

"The staff holds you back," Cyrus said, breaking Kasai's pondering. "The Fire Serpent demands your fire xindu and that you keep none for yourself. Your connection to her is like a son suckling to his mother's breast. But when will the son grow up and become a man?"

Again, with the staff. I should just let him hold it. She would enjoy explaining the Boundless to him, Kasai thought.

"Tell me of Aetenos. I would have liked to meet him and talk to him about his Way. You certainly are the luckiest man alive. I envy you."

Kasai looked at Cyrus sideways. "Hardly. He was an odd bird, and mostly spoke in riddles. I barely understood anything he said."

"The genius of the divine is often hard to understand by mere mortals. Yet, there are other masters we can learn from, which are more direct and to the point, so to speak. They are still out there. We must find them." Cyrus waved outwards and above his head.

"I'll pass. I have no desire to learn of the lofty ways of

angels. They're not what you think. If you'd met one, you'd know what I mean. No one meets an angel without being scarred."

"Oh, but I have met angels. And I agree, they are somewhat difficult to converse with as equals. I am speaking of another, well to be fair, two others. You could call them siblings."

"And what mysteries have they unveiled to you? What challenges must you endure to prove yourself worthy of their praise or powers?" Kasai said with no small amount of bitterness.

"They will bring back balance to the Three Worlds on a cosmic scale."

"Then I'm definitely not interested," Kasai said, feeling a pending doom take shape in his gut.

"But you are the Ever Hero. This is your calling."

Kasai kept walking in silence. New plant growth was covering the charred landscape, but the scars across the land ran deep.

"I've done my time."

9

RAGUEL

Lord Raguel walked purposefully through the great hall leading to the Cloud Court's amphitheater. It was an exceptionally bright day and broad bands of sunlight streamed through the tinted glass of clerestory windows, bathing the vast area in a rainbow of vibrant colors.

Four-legged, animal spirit couriers sprinted down long hallways on their way to other sections of the vast administration complex, while those with wings flew to the upper office levels, bringing important documents to True-born directors. Celestials came and went through lower office doors, according to their station or duties. Each bowed respectfully to Raguel as they passed by. It was business as usual in his pristine building.

The Chancellor Pinnacle was pleased. He was fond of this hall and the colorful open space gave him peace of mind. This was often where he contemplated creative ways to expand the influence of the Seven Heavens over the Mortal Realm, and of course, the three bothersome devils controlling the Abyss.

However, today was not a day for enjoyable daydreams. Sonnalle was at his side giving yet another account of insurrection within the city of Haven, one of the major cities on Canaan, the Fifth Heavenly Level.

"Have they been caught?" Raguel said.

"Yes, my lord. Though, with every band of dissenters we incarcerate, another three splinter groups emerge on different Levels. The Praetor Guard cannot be everywhere at once, and Elysian and Eden have required intervention from the Heavenly Host stationed at Arcadia."

"There are protestors gathering at crucial administration facilities, demanding to be heard," Sonnalle said as he rolled three pages of his report over the thick pad of parchment he held.

"Yes, here it is. Districts twenty-four-eighteen, and fifty-five-thirty-nine, on Eden, and nine more districts, four on Elysian. He rolled through more pages. Their numbers are growing. I have the exact locations written down."

"Which one are they crying about now?" Raguel interrupted. "The angel or the monk?"

"Mostly the monk."

Raguel nodded his understanding. "I assume Aetenos is championing their cause and stoking the rabble into a frenzy."

"Actually, sir, the demigod has not been seen in days."

A tight smile formed on Raguel's lips. "Maybe he has returned to the Mortal Realm where he belongs."

"I thought you might want to know his exact whereabouts and took it upon myself to find him. But not even the Far Seers on Erewhon can pinpoint his current location."

"Let it be, Sonnalle. Soon, he will be a forgotten memory, and everything will be back to normal," Raguel said.

"Certainly, my lord," Sonnalle said and glanced at his data pad again. If we diverted a small number of troops from the invasion expedition we could—"

Raguel stopped short, his head arched back, and eyes were drawn to the ceiling of the Hall. "The Immortal Mother summons me."

A look of worry came over Sonnalle's face. "Trouble?"

"Fear not, my friend. I'm sure she's curious about the new hierarchy of the Three Worlds and possibly wishes to give her blessing. Continue extinguishing this tiresome revolt and round up the rest of the agitators. Explain to them that their time in the Seven Heavens was a privilege and one they have squandered."

"More banishments, lord?"

Raguel clenched his jaw. "I trust you to do it quietly. You shall be my velvet hammer."

"Your will be done, my lord." Sonnalle bowed and took to the air.

Raguel watched him go and then turned his attention to the summons. He was commanded to return to the spot where but a few days earlier he had cast the soul essence of Aetenos into oblivion.

What's this about? he wondered. *The Immortal Mother had never interfered with his plans before. The monk certainly means nothing to her unless Illyria has cried on her lap because she cannot find her toy. I will not be commanded to fetch him a second time.*

He unfurled his great wings and flew off in the opposite direction, smirking. *Not that I could, anyways.*

The hilltop was bare of tree or stump. He had made sure the landscape was quickly repaired and looked as if nothing had ever grown there but long grass. Maybe in a hundred years he'd cover the hill with a copse of birch. He's always liked the black and white design of their bark.

He landed gracefully. A dark sense of foreboding gripped him as a sensation of heat warmed his back. He looked over his shoulder to see Illyria materializing in a blossoming sphere of light.

"You had no right!" Illyria screamed.

"Illyria? What are you doing here? I have pressing business with—"

"You had no right to send him away. You knew I loved him," she said as tears rolled down her cheeks.

Raguel's flash temper erupted. "And what of the love you took from me, or should I say, shunned? I did everything you asked from the beginning. I saved that wretch's soul and brought him here as something akin to an equal. Where is the love you owe me?"

"He was everything to me," Illyria sobbed. "He was perfect. Oh, I shall never love again."

Raguel rolled his eyes. He didn't have time for her childish behavior. His attempt at consoling her was blunt and harsh. "I warned you this would happen. I told you he would betray you again. He was never one of us and belonged with his own."

"Did you think there wouldn't be consequences to your actions, Raguel?" She glared at him, her mood quickly turning serious. "Or did you think I would fall into your arms now that he was gone?"

"Maybe, over time." His voice softened but then hardened when he saw the look of disgust on her face. "And why not? Why not me?"

"Oh Raguel, when will you understand? You were made

to be a means to an end; a tool I used to craft my will. But you have proven to be no better than the devils of the Abyss with their wild desires and inflated egos."

"You view of my worth is disconcerting. But now you must leave. I don't want you here when the Immortal Mother arrives. Now is the time for my great work to begin and I am sure she will want to discuss the finer points with me."

Illyria's eyes narrowed, then she slowly shook her head side to side. "You will be stripped of your role as Chancellor Pinnacle."

"Silly child. You have no say in the matter. The Immortal Mother has entrusted me with the evolution of this world. Never has there been an opportunity to place the Seven Heaven at the apex of control. We will remove one, if not two Supreme Devils with one fell swoop."

"You dare break that which is sacred. The Great Balance must remain."

"Oh, yes. I intend to make full use of the blunder that insipid monk forced upon us." His words now carried the anger of his bruised pride. "Now, leave me. I cannot have you whining at my heels like a spoiled brat and distracting the Immortal Mother from what is truly important."

He brushed past her, scanning the heavens for the Immortal Mother. "I'm sure this was the intended spot."

"He was everything to me!" Illyria screamed behind his back.

"Find another's shoulder to cry on. I will no longer be swayed by one of your dramatic tantrums."

"I forbid you to rally the Heavenly Host," she said, her voice growing bolder.

"You have no authority over me," Raguel said over his

shoulder while still gazing skyward. "Only the Immortal Mother may command me."

"I said, the Heavenly Host will not fly," Illyria's thunderous voice boomed with the sound of a thousand angels and demons shouting out as one.

"Illyria?" A cold sweat covered Raguel's body. He turned slowly.

Illyria's body was the same, but now radiated with great power. Raguel shielded his eyes from countless bright sparks popping and sizzling around her.

"You? You cannot be her," he said at last, squinting.

"I am," her voice boomed again, shaking the ground like the tremor of a quake.

"How is this possible? After all these years. H–how could I not know?" Raguel's eyes looked to the flowing grass, searching for answers. "I don't understand. You have always been...her?"

Then, a dreadful reality dawned on him. *She knows I killed him.*

"Raguel, why can I not see Aetenos? I have searched the three worlds of my making and still he is lost to me. What have you done? Where is he?" She asked. Her innocent voice had returned but each sentence was more menacing than the last.

Raguel's legs turned to jelly, and he fell to his knees. "No, no, oh no," he said, shaking his head. "How could this be?" Tears blurred his vision. "Why him?"

"Does there need to be a reason? I am she and I am all. My decisions are final and not to be questioned or debated. Now, where is he?"

"Gone," Raguel whispered.

"Bring him back."

"I cannot. No one can, not even you. He has been cast into oblivion." He looked up at her with watery eyes. All I wanted was—"

"Your needs and desires have never been my concern. You were created to be the pinnacle of law and order. Your role was to build the counterweight. Now look at you. You have let your ego rise above my desires and devolved into a jealous man-child."

"I am ruined," Raguel said. "Have mercy."

"I will not destroy you, nor will I interfere again to redirect the folly of your decisions. You are on your own against what is coming. Your actions have tipped the sides of the scale to a dangerous level."

Raguel dropped to the ground and pushed his forehead into the grass. The cool blades poked like needles into his feverish skin. *How could this be? Aetenos? Him?*

Then, he felt a profound sense of betrayal. "You created me to be perfect in every way, then mocked me by giving your heart to a lesser being."

"It matters not now. But before I leave you, I will part with dire news. My siblings have found me."

Raguel raised his head, recovering from his self-pity and anger. "The Ancients cannot breach your barrier."

"I was foolish to think I could hide these worlds from them, their hunger is too great. The way was easily enough to follow from the fresh scent of souls leaking from the Chaos Gate."

"You must allow me to send our warriors against them." Raguel raised himself up and stood proudly once more. "Let me redeem myself in your eyes. I will lead the Heavenly Host myself and destroy them in whatever form they have taken. This, I vow to you."

"No."

"Whom else? Aetenos's boy cannot stand against the might of the Ancients!"

A look of deep sadness came over her face, and he immediately regretted speaking the demigod's name.

"Dear Raguel, my first born and most beautiful child," she said and cupped his face in her hands. "You are not the champion I had hoped you'd become. Another has been chosen."

"Who but me can save your creation?"

Illyria's form shimmered and began to fade. "These worlds may not be worth saving. Their fate will be decided by the one you condemned," she said.

"The boy will fail on his own without my help," Raguel pleaded.

"His role will become clear in time. But it will be she who determines the fate of the Three Worlds. Pray that she is more in death than you ever allowed her to be in life. Good-bye, Raguel."

Then the Immortal Mother was gone.

10

DESDEMONIA

esdemonia was tossed unceremoniously into a dank and dark cell. This one had no windows, much like every other cell she had occupied in the Abyss. She had expected more from the Chaos Devil. *A shifting change of scenery would be nice,* she thought.

Her jailors snorted and snickered at her as they shut the iron door. It locked with an echoing clunk. The clang of iron bells tolled in the distance, how far away or near was impossible to tell. Desdemonia got up and brushed herself off. The shift she wore was paper thin and did little to hide most of her body.

"Typical," she scoffed and looked around the cell for a place to sit.

The room was sparse with furniture, but at least there was a bed of sorts. A long box was tucked in one corner with a dirty blanket draped over it.

"This looks vaguely familiar," she said. "At least it's not as cold."

Hanging from the ceiling was an iron canister filled

with hot coals and cut with mismatched holes. The glowing embers from the canister's lazy spin threw moving shadows into darker corners of the cell. Desdemonia's eyes swept the room as she adjusted to the dim light.

"Hello, Desdemonia," a sultry voice came out of the darkness.

Desdemonia was startled to see another prisoner sitting quietly at the end of a second long box in the opposite corner of the room. A tangle of white hair hung across her beaten face. The prisoner had been given a shift, like Desdemonia's, though hers was ripped, tattered, and stained.

"You!" The magic in Desdemonia's soul boiled and her hands flared with blue fire. She shot three, shimmering magic missiles at the mangy prisoner. Each one found their mark, or so she thought. Ice blue sparks twinkled momentarily as they drifted upwards against the far wall, then were snuffed out. The prisoner sighed and rose from the box, unharmed, as if the shots had flown through a ghost.

The prisoner slowly came into the meager light with her face coming in and out of shadow as she approached. She did her best to make herself presentable by straightening the wrinkles on her ragged clothing and tucking long strands of white hair behind her ears.

"Put those away, child. I'm in no mood for a fight," Sekka said.

"Fuck you! I'm not your little bitch any longer," Desdemonia shouted and raised her hands again, but Sekka remained calm and then disappeared from sight.

"Where are you! Show yourself, you fiend. Let's finish this!" Desdemonia shouted into the cascading shadows.

"Oh hush. Be thankful you're still alive. Whether by

accident, coincidence or intention, we find ourselves together again. How fortunate we are."

The voice was all around her. Desdemonia spun in a low crouch, ready to fight. But there was no one there. She was alone in the cell. Eventually, she stood up straight, eyes wide and mouth closed tight. Then she laughed out loud at the absurdity of it all.

"Welcome to Hell, Desdemonia," she said jokingly. "And by the way, you're insane."

"Insanity has its benefits," Sekka said. She was back on her box, sitting relaxed.

"You're not real," Desdemonia said, though she wondered if that were true.

"You're probably right, but for the moment, let's pretend I am. Come, sit with me child. Let us talk once more as mother and daughter," Sekka said and tapped the open surface beside her.

"This is a special torture to be sure," Desdemonia said. She crossed her arms across her chest. "Something Raguel, or his platinum-haired lapdog, Sonnalle, concocted to make my stay here uniquely unpleasant."

"Raguel? No, I don't think so. But I believe Xerthotha has something special planned for you," Sekka said. "And if that's true, you may find that accepting his gift will be a greater boon than mine by a thousandfold. Yes, this is quite an exciting time for you."

"Are you mad? I'm not accepting anything from him. Look what happened last time I played that game with you. I wound up here *just because*," Desdemonia said. "And why would you tell me such a thing? Wait, why am I even talking to you? You're not real."

"Why? Oh child, didn't you learn anything while you were my daughter? I'm telling you this so we can use it against him of course."

"Him who, Raguel or Xerthotha? Ugh, shut up. I hate you."

"Of course, you do. Now, let's see how we can turn this to our advantage." Sekka paced the floor, tapping her long fingers to her chin.

Desdemonia shook her head in disbelief, watching Sekka pace. Then she turned to the door, searching for a latch that wasn't there. "I guess having someone to talk to in the joint is better than nothing. I just wish it wasn't you," Desdemonia said as she examined the door. She assumed the guards were gone because the snickering had stopped.

"Yes, yes, something special and...creative," Sekka continued.

Desdemonia gave Sekka an incredulous look over her shoulder. "What is wrong with you? He has nothing special planned for me. He's going to hurt me. Forever. If I'm lucky he will forget I exist."

"He, she, it, whatever you want to call the Chaos Devil, it doesn't matter. You are being saved for a special purpose. But why you, I wonder?"

Desdemonia pulled on the small window bars of the cell door. She shook back and forth, but the door remained unmoved. "Don't be a fool. He will gloat, intimidate me, and laugh when I piss from fear all over the floor. Then I'll be tortured in some cruel and horrible way. Oh, I never should have left my little cottage in the woods. Gauldumor was right. I never should have gotten involved."

"You are a lucky one."

"Would you shut up already? Oh, I'm real lucky alright. I'm stuck here with you and your idiotic ramblings for all eternity. Why couldn't I have someone cuter as my imaginary friend?"

Desdemonia gave up shaking the bars and looked for a door handle. She turned and huffed. "This is miserable."

"Haven't you wondered why you are still in one piece? Why you were not tortured the moment you arrived?"

"What are you talking about? I just got here. I think," Desdemonia brushed her black hair from her eyes and looked up to the ceiling. She couldn't recall arriving. It was like the shifting moments in a dream that slid from one event to another.

Sekka chuckled. "It's good that's all you remember. No matter how long you think you've been here, and it has been longer than you think, you remain without a blemish. Not even a scratch."

Desdemonia couldn't argue with that. She had hoped beyond hope that she had simply been overlooked and forgotten, until today, and this cell, and *her.*

"How long have you been here?" Desdemonia said, noting Sekka's weightless appearance. The archdevil seemed too light to be filled with meat and bones, which was a good thing. Desdemonia would hate to be sharing her cell with the real Sekka.

"Since the boy found his courage and his power. You remember that day, don't you? I should have known that cursed Aeteros would have one more trick up his sleeve. He even told me how it would end, but I didn't listen. I was too busy watching the angels shatter my dreams and torch my glorious Frost Legion." Sekka's expression turned sour.

"Oh, you poor dear. Do you need a tissue?" Desdemonia laughed, then rubbed her eyes with the heels of her hands. "Come on Desdemonia, get yourself together. This is just a bad dream. I'm not here. She's not here. Just wake up and this will be over."

Sekka shook her head slowly. "Sorry. You're dead. I should know. I killed you."

"You're horrible."

Sekka gave Desdemonia an amused smile. "Quite."

There was no marker for when day changed to night, or back again. There was only the gonging of the droning bells. Dong. Dong. Dong. When sleep came, which was rare, Desdemonia's dreams were filled with disturbing images of dark things to come. Great battles erupted on open plains of shifting rock. Steam vented from yawning chasms. The faces of demons and devils raced towards her, snarling and gnashing their teeth, and then vanished before her eyes.

She would wake with a start and scan the cell. It would always be empty, then just as she looked away, she would spot the archdevil sitting motionless in the opposite corner, waiting for her.

Most days, Desdemonia attacked her immediately, sending blue missiles or red-hot fireballs at the archdevil. First it was by instinct, then just for fun. The wall behind Sekka's box-bed became pock-marked and blackened with soot.

But no matter how hard she tried, Desdemonia couldn't hurt Sekka. Her attacks would strike their mark and engulf the devil in flames or wrap crackling lightning around her body, singeing her skin and hair and leaving her a smoking husk, or simply passing through her as if she were a phantom.

For unfathomable reasons, Sekka never once retaliated. Instead, she'd smile blandly and wait patiently for the effects of whatever elemental spell was cast at her to pass, which frustrated Desdemonia to no end. At least a good fight would relieve the boredom.

Desdemonia wondered if Sekka had somehow discovered a latent altruistic side to her awful demeanor. However, after much prodding and begging for an answer, the reason was revealed to be much more basic—Sekka said she didn't want to anger the Chaos Devil.

She had related numerous times how she had flayed the skins from the guards that came to claim her or had ripped out their spines or froze them into blocks of ice. Unfortunately, new jailors respawned a short time later, ones that were unaffected by her magic, and dragged her to Xerthotha.

"Trust me when I say, the Chaos Devil does not like to wait. The more damage I did to his miserable minions, the more pain he would inflict on me. So, I pleaded for a truce.

"If I came willingly, Xerthotha would leave my punishment up to chance. Some days it was mild, the random broken bone, or an eye removed, or we would talk as old friends. On other days, however, it was more severe.

"Often was the day, or night, that I would lay semi-conscious in a pool of sticky muck, watching my torn-out heart spit the last fizzle of my blood on the floor. Then, I'd wake back in this cell, regenerating lost body parts until the next day when it began again."

"Do you really expect me to believe such an outrageous story?" Desdemonia said. "You made a deal with the Chaos Devil to go easy or hard on you, depending on his mood?"

"Of course. I was merely appealing to his appetite for chance and change. He in turn was impressed with my cleverness and originality."

"Sure, he was. I bet he let you know how much he appreciated your wit, each time he did some new and terrible thing to you."

Sekka merely frowned, then launched into another long account of her failed campaign to steal the souls of the Mortal Realm and take her place on the High Pantheon of the Abyss, next to Azrollorza as a Supreme Devil. Her hatred of Aetenos was palpable, as were all things associated with him.

"The Great Monk thwarted my plans at every turn. It was as if he was made to make me suffer. Oh, how I wish I had destroyed him when I had the chance."

"Ya, I know. I was there, remember?" Desdemonia interjected.

The jailors never came at the same time of day to collect Sekka. The only consistent part was that they came. Desdemonia called the warden Mister Shlub for lack of any formal introduction. Mister Shlub had a sickly-looking assistant; a fiend she called Hench. He was a ghoulish thing with glutinous lips and a gooey smile.

The fiend loved to talk and told all sorts of wonderfully demented tales of life in Xerthotha's palace. Desdemonia would take whatever current events she could get, since conversations with Sekka tended to be one-sided.

"What a chirper!" Desdemonia would say to herself after Hench was called to Mister Shlub's side and scoffed across the head for dallying too long at the cell door.

Mister Shlub was a cruel hobgoblin, covered in greasy

ooze and reeked of something rotten. He enjoyed taunting Sekka to the point where she'd tear him to shreds. And true to her story, something different would respawn in his place and drag her by the wrist, ankle, or hair to the rack. Mister Shlub would respawned soon after, just to add insult to injury.

"That was unwise. My lord and master will not be as nice today as he usually is with your flesh. And maybe afterwards, when you are weak and more pliable, he will let me take you."

Mister Shlub giggled, coughed, and then spit out something fleshy. "Come, Sekka, Ice Queen of Gathos, your special session with my lord awaits."

Desdemonia wondered why he let himself be killed in such a way. *Fuck, it's the Abyss. Maybe he likes it.*

Desdemonia listened to the sounds coming from the nearby chamber. She heard shrieks, groans, and grunts of passion. It was repulsive to think of having the hobgoblin's hands, mouth, and other parts inside her.

Ugh. Disgusting. Still, better her than me, Desdemonia thought as she stared up at the ceiling and the slowly spinning canister filled with hot coals. The chains connecting the canister to the ceiling spun it in one direction, then reversed it when the coils became tight.

Oddly, the coals never needed to be replaced, nor did the jailors ever came for her and take her to Sekka's rack. On good days, Desdemonia encouraged Hench to stay and talk.

He'd look over his shoulder with the eyes of a conspirator, then whisper rumors to her from the upper dungeon levels. The jailors and torturers all said the same thing; a Great War for the Abyss had begun.

What else is new? Desdemonia thought. She listened to it all and hoped that the Supreme Devils would annihilate each other and destroy the Abyss in the process. *Ha, fat chance of that ever happening.*

The day finally came when Desdemonia was brought before Xerthotha. He sat high on a throne of small, writhing things that looked more like fingers than worms. He wore a simple, blood-red robe, tied by a golden cord at the waist and cut at the shoulders. His body was toned and slender of frame.

Xerthotha's head was hidden behind a multi-faced helm, which spun and randomly stopped on one of its eight sides. A stylized jackal's head was the first to appear, then a snarling lion's snout with blazing eyes. Next came the maniacal face of a laughing man, followed by something that could only be described as melting ooze.

A fifth plate shifted into place showing the mask of a doll-faced child with three porcelain eyes and circular blush to emphasize her rosy cheeks. Next came a grotesque visage of organic parts; eleven eyes, three mouths, slithering feelers for whiskers and a fan of colorful horns, which then melted into small sacks, dropping to the ground, and bursting into a thousand blue butterflies, allowing the final side to revolve into place with a click.

Desdemonia gasped when she saw Kasai's face smiling back at her.

"That's just cruel," she said and looked away.

"I thought you might like to see a familiar face," Xerthotha said.

"Another one? Ha, ha, that's funny. Yes, we are getting

along famously well, thank you," Desdemonia said.

Xerthotha raised an eyebrow at the remark. He then stood from the throne, which collapsed into a bubbling puddle beneath his feet. The room folded like a complex paper animal and then was gone.

The two faced one another on an open plain. Xerthotha's helm was gone and now he sported a long mane of black hair and a handsome face with chiseled features. Long grass brushed up against her skin. It itched. She scratched.

"You know who I am?" he said. His voice sounded romantic and soothing.

"Yes," Desdemonia said with her chin held high.

"And yet, you are not afraid."

Of course, I am afraid. I'm terrified, Desdemonia thought, but said otherwise. "I've stood against a horde of fiery fiends, swatted your red-faced champion out of the sky with my magic, crippled a mighty archdevil with the power of my voice, and cursed out *the* archangel to his face. Who are you to me?"

Xerthotha's deep laughter rolled like thunder across the darkening sky. "And now you are here for eternity with me," he said.

"Clearly, mistakes have been made. I don't belong here. Eventually, one of those snooty, white-winged bookkeepers will discover that I am in the wrong place and, whoosh, quicker than you can blink, I'll be gone."

"Such are the hopes of all who enter here. You must know, you are worth nothing to the little birds in their cloudless sky."

"Trust me, I won't be forgotten. They'll come for me. And then you'll be sorry," Desdemonia said, boldly pointing her finger at him.

She watched in disbelief as the grass around her feet dissolved and the earth began to bubble and foam. Then she felt a tremor running under ground and farther away, the fields opened to a lava-filled fissure.

"Will I?" Xerthotha said. "You know as well as I that they have forsaken you."

Desdemonia looked at him and tried to be strong. But then the tears came. "I know," she said, crestfallen. "I'm a witch with black blood running through my veins."

"Black blood, how appropriate. The angels see everything in terms of black and white. They have no appreciation for endless shades of grey in between," Xerthotha scoffed. "Now, let's see what's so horrible inside of you that gave Raguel such a fit."

Desdemonia blinked and Xerthotha was intimately close, as if he was already inside her. A wave of heat slammed against her and choked the air from her lungs. Her throat burned when she tried and failed to swallow.

"What will you do?" Desdemonia said, quavering.

There was a discomforting glint in his eyes. "I'm not sure. I'll have to find it first, and then we'll decide."

This is it, Desdemonia thought. She vaguely heard the shrieks of demons fighting in the fields. A fragrant, lavender mist rose from the ground and she felt sleepy. Her head lolled back, and she felt herself falling, but never reaching the ground.

The distant sounds of chaos were replaced by the thunderous thumping of her heart in her ears. Her entire body throbbed as it kept pace with each beat. Something inside of her was being tugged on, pushed aside, grabbed again, and jerked harder. She wondered if she was being disassembled one piece at a time.

Absentmindedly, she tried to wet her dry lips. They tasted metallic. Then, she heard a voice. It sounded like a whisper at first but then grew deep and gravelly.

"Could this be true?" Xerthotha said. His booming laughter echoed over the barren field. "Ho, ho! Raguel, you fool! You have sent me the greatest prize."

11

RAGUEL

Raguel grabbed another golden-laced parchment from the mountainous piles crowding his desk. Every line of the report he now held told the same story across the mega-cities of the Seven Heavens, there was more insurrection, more destruction of monuments, and more duties being neglected. The unrest was everywhere, and it seemed there was no end in sight.

"One problem is solved and ten more erupt," he said. His disappointment in the citizens of the Seven Heavens deepened by the moment. "What shall I do? They leave me no choice but to declare martial law."

A rap on the thick oak door leading to his study alerted him to Sonnalle's return from the waypoint between the Seven Heavens and the Abyss. He shook his head, still flabbergasted at the unfolding events across his perfect world.

"Enter."

"The task is completed, my lord. The witch, Desdemonia Mishi has been condemned to the Abyss. Curiously, I was greeted by Xerthotha's agents, who collected her with great haste."

"Yes, well, anywhere but here," Raguel said but didn't bother looking up. He put one report down and pick up another with a sigh. "What has gotten into their heads? They saw that I gave the mortals the chance to prove themselves. Curse all those who survived the Challenge of Righteousness."

"How she escaped judgment—" Sonnalle said.

Raguel looked up fast. "You said Xerthotha claimed her. She was not directed by normal means?"

"Yes, my lord. The Chaos Devil has her, though I gave no word to any of the Great Three of her departure from the Seven Heavens. I thought secrecy best, though word travels fast along the nether ways between realms. Is there a problem?"

"Condemned," Raguel said, mostly to himself. "Illyria said...never mind."

Raguel pushed his chair away and stood from his desk. He had not forgotten the Immortal Mother's threat, depriving him of authority as the Chancellor Pinnacle. This wasn't the first time he had pushed her boundaries and sparked her displeasure. Her temper would cool off over time. After all, he was her first born and brightest star. She would forgive him.

He moved to the windows and gazed out over the sea of golden rooftops. *Why Aetenos? Why that awkward, imperfect, thing and not me?* he wondered.

"My lord, are you well?"

"Yes, I'm fine. Thank you, Sonnalle. That will be all. Continue with the purge of dissidents."

Sonnalle bowed and left the study. Raguel's thoughts turned to Xerthotha.

"What's he up to? Why would he go through all that trouble to secure her soul? Unless he knew ahead of time she was—."

Raguel established a mental connection with Xerthotha. Horrid sounds flooded into his mind. Shrieks, moans, and incoherent gibberish echoed in his opulent chamber. The floral fragrances floating through his study were replaced by fetid, gamy odors.

+Xerthotha. Attend to me.+ Raguel sent his mind to the Abyssal Layer of Stomoxys, The Land of Eternal Strife, Xerthotha's realm.

The connection was stale. Was the Immortal Mother's threat real? He tried again.

+Xerthotha!+

+Blood of the Abyss, what do you want? Unless the Heavenly Host is in need of refreshments from their long journey to my world, assume I am busy.+

+The Ancients have arrived,+ Raguel fought through the astral static to create a fluid connection, already feeling his patience thinning.

+You're late to that party. The twins were hiding among the mortals long before the boy monk broke Sekka's heart, so to speak. By the way, nice touch with the columns of fire. Though I would've thought you'd want to clean up the mess, rather than make it worse.+

+They must be stopped.+

+Then deal with it. I have other, more pressing matters before me since you reneged on our deal. And they call me the Great Deceiver.+

+Shut up you twit and listen to me. The twins will cause irreparable damage to the Amaranthine Barrier.+

+And why should I care? I have been devouring stockpiles of soul-slaves to fund this miserable war, unaided as I am by my feathery friends. Easy access to the Mortal Realm would serve my immediate needs nicely,+ Xerthotha thought, sending his message with a growl.

+Because the destruction of the barrier allows their true form to enter. The Three Worlds would be at their mercy. Only with our combined forces will we prevail.+

Raguel heard echoing laughter in his mind. He gritted his teeth. *I will kill him slowly when it's time.*

+The Abyss and the Seven Heavens united at last! Ho, that's rich! Should I send a flowery invitation to Azrollorza requesting her to cease hostilities and ask her nicely to join the resistance? Maybe you could put some hugs and kisses at the bottom next to your signature.+

+Do not mock me, devil.+

+And then there is the hundred-headed beast to consider. Which of us should ask Morrdilliax? Perhaps we both go and take turns convincing each head of the merits of our campaign.+

+They are destroyers of worlds and will devour everything. You, me, everything the Immortal Mother has created will be consumed.+ Raguel realized he sounded desperate and regained his composure.

+Stop your fretting. The Immortal Mother would prevent it.+

+She no longer cares!+ Raguel's flash temper erupted, and he immediately regretted the outburst.

+My dear Raguel, what is it? Is mommy upset with you?

Or is it something else?+ Xerthotha's thoughts turned sly and slippery. +I can't recall the last time you were so unhinged.+

+You're mistaken.+

+And you worry too much. I have a plan to deal with the twins. But first you must honor your word and send the Heavenly Host to destroy Azrollorza.+

+The Heavenly Host will fly when I say it will.+

+Are you sure? Your arrogance reeks of desperation and despair. By the way, you wouldn't believe the prize that fell into my lap,+ Xerthotha sent.

+You were told you would receive Sekka upon her defeat at the hands of the Ever Hero. That should hardly be a surprise.+

+Sekka, yes. She's such a treat. But I speak of the Ever Hero's love, the wood witch, Desdemonia.+

+Ah yes, the witch. She must be returned. There was a mistake in her processing. She belongs in the Seven Heavens. I'm sending my equerry, Sonnalle to collect her.+

+Ho, ho! But you're quick to take back your gifts. She's tainted now and not much good to you.+

+I assume as much. Nonetheless, have her ready for transport back to the Heavenly Realm. Sonnalle will meet your emissaries at the waypoint.+

+Oh, she was full of surprises, that one. I gave her a quite a deadly dose of deep chaos magic, something to really stir things up, if you know what I mean. And guess what happened? She drank it in like a hungry babe, thirsting at her mother's breast for more warm milk.+

+What of it? I suppose you have changed her into something sordid and terrible.+

+She will make an excellent addition to your collection

of freaks once the change has fully taken hold. Which is a beautiful thing. Though, I must warn you, the change produced something unexpected, even for me.+

+Be clear. I haven't much time or desire to maintain this loathsome connection.+

+I'm sure you don't. Nonetheless, a true master doesn't reveal his best move until the endgame.+

+As I said, she is to be returned. I want her back.+

+I'm sure you do. But she is my property now, although, I'm willing to make a trade. Let's say the Heavenly Host descends on Azrollorza *and* Morrdilliax, and I rule the whole show when the ashes settle. In return, I'll send you back the delightful Desdemonia. I'll even put a bow in her hair for you.+

+Impossible. Such an expedition would never be authorized.+

+Ho, ho, ho, Raguel, you are so easy to read. You've lost your luster. The Heavenly Host cannot fly because you can no longer command it to muster.+

+Nonsense. I will show you how wrong you are by eliminating you first.+

+Do it then. I dare you. And if that sniveling sycophant you call an equerry steps one foot in my realm, I will send him back in the dung of the beetles that devoured him.+

Raguel severed the connection and stood in silence. He had been outmaneuvered by being rash. One more misstep would bring ruin to his great work.

Who can I trust beyond my loyal, Sonnalle? he wondered, then nodded with certainty. It would begin with the warlords of Arcadia.

The Stables of Helios were a vast complex of interconnected stalls, oat dispensaries, water towers, and gated pens, extending in orderly lines beyond the horizon of the Third Heavenly Level of Arcadia. Their gates opened to a sea of grass and wildflowers. A gentle wind blew across the plains, swaying the greenery like rippling waves.

Raguel dropped down from the sky. The booming sound wave followed shortly after. Sonnalle materialized beside him with a flow of static electricity traveling across his body. The warhorses in nearby stalls tossed their heads happily. Pegasi and kirin pranced across the way in open pens, neighing with excitement at the approach of the First Lord.

Raguel heard the combined screeches of griffons, giant eagles, and hippogriffs tethered within towering aviaries. The beat of their wings filled the air with a mixture of pollen, hay, manure, and adrenaline. They knew as well as he, that the smell of war was in the air.

A True-born in riding gear, tending to a magnificent white unicorn with speckles of sky blue on its rump, turned to acknowledge the arrival of the First Lord and his equerry. The spirit animal snorted eagerly and raised up on its hind legs. The True-born then directed the stable hands to fetch more golden hay for the warhorses in an adjacent structure.

"Lord Raguel, Lord Sonnalle," Lord Malik said and bowed respectfully. "My lord, Samal spoke of your interest in meeting, though I wonder why it must be done in such a clandestine manner and not among the council members."

"Our intentions are pure," Sonnalle said. "However, now is certainly a time for caution. The True-born and celestials under your command, can they be trusted?"

Malik gave Raguel a worried look, then nodded. "I am aware the unrest grows. Many fear that you will turn the Heavenly Host on the citizens of the Seven. Are we meeting to discuss such a mistake?"

"No, of course not. But precautions must be in place should a few groups of unruly dissenters grow into a formal uprising," Raguel said. "My great work is at hand. If the Abyss is to be tamed, then I must have unconditional support from the generals of the Heavenly Host."

"Lord Malik, you are held in high respect by your men and those you have served with over the millennium. The Chancellor Pinnacle needs you by his side if the Seven Heavens are to know peace," Sonnalle said. "Lord Raguel asks for your assurance that if the need calls, you will fight the enemies of Heaven, wherever they may be. These countless distractions in the Seven do nothing more but drain resources that should be better spent quelling the chaos in the Abyss."

Malik raised his bushy eyebrows. Raguel knew the veteran of the Mystic Calvary was no fool. Countless campaigns had not only weathered his appearance, but also gave him the experienced wisdom to see a real threat, no matter how hidden it may seem.

"You have clever words, Sonnalle. Distractions, uprisings, unrest, call it what you will. It is a weak dam which holds back the flood of rebellion that flows. The moment arms are raised against our own is the moment that dam bursts," Malik said.

"Then we must make sure the dam holds," Raguel said. "I am merely asking for assistance in keeping the foundation of Law and Order stable while we are abroad."

Raguel brought his hand to the unicorn's muzzle. The animal spirit didn't flinch away, but instead nuzzled in closer.

"This is a fine steed. What's her name?" Raguel asked.

"Qalidon, my lord," Malik answered.

"Qalidon. A proud name for a fearless warrior. Sadly, she will not know the sweet taste of victory against the Abyss."

Raguel looked to the other stables and sighed. "It's a shame really. Just think what we could do against the minions of evil but will never know because we will not be permitted to go."

Malik tilted his head slightly. "What exactly are we talking about here, my lord Raguel? Quelling the unrest of a few citizens is not the same thing as overriding the will of the council.

"And without the council's backing, you cannot unilaterally command the Heavenly Host to leave our realm, unless you have the blessing of the Immortal Mother, which I suspect you don't or we would not be having this discussion. And then there is the mere idea of invading the Abyss. That borders on heresy against the Great Balance."

Sonnalle was quick to interject, but Malik immediately put his hand up. "Please, equerry, do not insult me with whatever retort you were about to utter. I haven't said no, yet. I assume you have a plan."

12

SHIVERRIG

Shiverrig stood on uncertain legs as his body shuddered like a pending avalanche before the fall. The sensation was incredible. His perspective had changed when he glanced at Daku, he realized he was seeing him at eye level. The pale demon held a wary expression.

"That was a colossal mistake," Daku said. "But what do I know of accepting gifts from strangers?" He nodded upwards. "Nice horns, though."

"I accepted nothing."

Shiverrig's senses came back to him as if he was collecting each one from the soupy sludge of a dead swamp. His thoughts were confused, shaken, and drifting aimlessly in different directions. In his mind, he saw distant lands filled with the light of mortal souls. He wanted them. He needed them.

Shiverrig looked upon his followers and the few remaining beast men shamans, who had somehow escaped the mayhem. Each one possessed a similar, flickering light. His eyes fell on Daku once more and he saw the pale demon's soul light was split into two flickering flames, joined at their base. Each flaming tongue sought to overwhelm the other and consume it.

Then, an irresistible urge to kill overcame him. He scanned the grisly remains of the slaughtered tribesmen and he swallowed the saliva gushing in his mouth. This was so much more than Xerthotha had ever granted in him. He squeezed his hand into a fist, marveling at the strength flowing through his arm.

He glanced over the rest of his body. The layers of animal hides and fur he had worn to shield himself from the harsh elements of the chaos wasteland, had been shredded. He cast their remains from his changed and magnificent body. His skin was a thin, charcoal membrane stretched over thick, hard muscles.

He felt enormous and too wide for the space he once held. It was glorious. When he lifted his hands to his head, his palms traveled the lengths of two, spiraling ridged horns that twisted out of the sides of his head.

For once, the cold didn't bother him. The crisp air held a tang of often rubbed limestone and the smell of rotten eggs made him remember his hunger. His eyes stung from the light of the pale sun. It was an irritation now, and he assumed it would worsen when it blazed bright in the sky of Baroqia. Then he saw the twins.

They both looked at him, one with admiration, the other with a feral longing to feast. Shiverrig felt his heart thump excitedly in his chest. One wrong move and Baast would pounce. The thought of grappling with the preternatural *thing,* whether as foes or lovers, excited him.

"Go now. Find the daimus nexus and be worthy of the gifts bestowed upon you," Damiano said.

"If he refuses, I will take him for myself," Baast said, leering at Shiverrig, almost daring him to say no.

"Patience, sister. Give the mortal a moment," Damiano said.

He glanced warily at the twins. "What are you?"

"We are everything and nothing," Damiano said.

"How mysterious," Daku snickered. Still, he stepped back from Baast watchfully.

"Now, my sister would like to know your intentions."

"Daimus nexus," Shiverrig said as an afterthought. He was more interested in watching his monstrous fists open and close. Then, "Never heard of it. How will I know it when I find it?"

"You will hear its call," Damiano said.

"That's it? The world is a big place, bigger than the Three Kingdoms of Hanna. Finding it may take some time. And the angels? What do you think they will do when they discover your hiding place? They aren't fond of anything," he paused, "as unholy, as you."

"We will deal with them in time," Baast said with confidence. "They are flies to be swatted from the sky and crushed underfoot."

"You say that now. But when the firestorms burn this icy place to a boiling river, you may change your tone," Daku said.

"The Lands of Chaos hide us from prying eyes," Damiano said as his hands swept the vast nothingness of the wasteland.

"That's convenient," Daku said. He turned to Shiverrig. "I don't like this. I can smell the charred flesh and melting rock already. I have no desire to test the angels again."

"Be still and stop worrying," Shiverrig said. He then addressed the twins. "Let's say I do help you. We are in the middle of nowhere. The sorcerer led us here, in a rather roundabout way, but he's not much use now."

"You will walk," Baast said.

Shiverrig glanced at the mush that was his horse. "Apparently."

"There are many paths. The sorcerer knew but one," Damiano said.

"Maybe he knew one at the start, but that way disappeared with the arrival of the angels. The rest of the time he was lost," Shiverrig said. "We will need a guide."

"His essence was satisfying but the hunger still lingers." Baast smacked her lips, eyeing the cautious barbarians who remained in the background. She ran her fingers down her bare neck. It was almost seductive. Then she returned her attention to Shiverrig.

"The sorcerer can still be useful."

Baast marched to the dissected body of Dai-Ko-Zior, lifting him off the ground with ease. She threw back his cowl and took a hold of the stringy wisps of hair that hung from the sorcerer's head. Pulling down hard, she exposed Dai-Ko-Zior face to the sky.

The sorcerer's mouth creaked open in a macabre gasp. Then, she pushed her lips down onto his and breathed into him. His entire body seemed to inflate like a brackish-water blowfish. She scratched a simple rune into his forehead, though no blood ran from the surface.

Satisfied, she tossed him to the ground like a broken and discarded thing. Damiano nodded his approval. Daku gave a quick nod over his shoulder. It was clear he wanted to escape while the vampires were distracted. Shiverrig shook his head slightly. "Not yet."

Baast curled a long finger into a hooked position and pulled back as if she had snagged a fish. Dai-Ko-Zior jerked toward her in the snow. She pulled back again, harder this time.

"Return," she said.

Dai-Ko-Zior stirred. His body quivered and then jerked again in an unnatural way until he stood. The sorcerer's eyes were blank, and he swiveled his head from side to side as if seeing the landscape for the first time. Then, he looked at Baast with creamy-colored eyes.

"How may I serve?" Dai-Ko-Zior said in a raspy voice.

"You will guide the warlord out of the lands of chaos. Assist him in finding the daimus nexus," Baast said.

Dai-Ko-Zior bowed his withered head. "As you wish."

"A lich, impressive," Daku said. "Can he dance, too?"

"Your beast talks too much," Baast said and then she was at Daku's side. She tore the golden circlet from his head before his hands could stop her.

"Gerun Shiverrig, you are relieved of the Chaos Devil's influence. He will no longer hold sway over you, or your pets," Baast said, never letting her eyes leave Daku as she curled her long, purplish tongue around the golden circlet's surface and bit down on it with her teeth. The metal of the circlet melted around her mouth and down her chin.

For long moments, the wind was still, and the only sound was the snow falling in a soft whisper.

"That was unfortunate," Shiverrig said.

He gave Daku a watchful stare, then took stock of his remaining troops. They weren't much, but they were loyal to

135

him. It was a start. The loss of the circlet was disconcerting, but no one could escape their inner demons indefinitely. Daku would either conquer Khalkoroth's demon spirit or perish.

Shiverrig inhaled a deep breath, feeling the biting cold fill his lungs, and the raw power of chaos coursing through his veins. He was invincible. This time, the Three Kingdoms would fall.

"I will do as you ask. Just make sure the sorcerer knows the way," he said to the twins. "Daku, gather the rabble. We're going home."

Daku stood in shock, staring at the holes of melted snow where the remains of Xerthotha's circlet had dripped. Hesitantly, he reached a hand toward the biggest hole. The winds howled a hysterical laughter across the plains.

"Daku!" Shiverrig shouted.

"What? I'm coming." Daku's eyes glanced back down into the snow, seemingly embarrassed. "I don't need anyone's help to best Khalkoroth. The demon won't win."

Shiverrig didn't believe him. "I hope so. I would hate to have to kill you in your sleep."

A quick, quivering snarl curled up the side of Daku's purple lip, followed by the heavy breathing of a brute. Daku shook his head like a wet dog, sending bits of snow flying in the air.

"I'll be fine," he said and marched toward the men. "You heard him. We're going home."

True to the promise of Damiano, the lich knew a more direct route out of the barren wastelands. Whether it was knowledge or good fortune, Shiverrig didn't care. Six years of wandering aimlessly was whittled down to a few short months of dull trudging across the wastelands.

Dai-Ko-Zior barely spoke in the past, and the lich version spoke even less, which suited Shiverrig fine. He was never fond of listening to the incoherent ramblings of magic-users.

Eventually, the climate changed into something that would be considered endurable, with a distinct trace of burnt wood drifting through the air. A lucky encounter with a band of brigands brought the arrival of a dozen horses, a surplus of food, and travel provisions.

"We've returned to what was the Kingdom of Trosk," Dai-Ko-Zior said.

"Oh look, His Deadness has finally learned a sense of direction," Daku said.

Shiverrig harrumph. "The sooner we are back in Baroqia, the better. There are scores to settle."

Dai-Ko-Zior led Shiverrig and his small warband of barbarians to the foothills of the Hoarfrost Mountains and into Baroqia. He stopped the procession atop a rolling knoll and pointed to the north.

"The ruins of Qaqal. A fortnight." He then pointed to the south. "Gethem. Longer by three."

"We'll camp here," Shiverrig announced. "We will march to Qaqal in the morning and see what is left of the madness that started it all."

"Sounds thrilling," Daku said. "And a waste of time. You don't think others would have thought the same and looted the place by now?"

"I told you the time would come when the sky would grow so bright as if to be lit by a second sun. My masters will drain this world and I will be delivered to godhood," Dai-Ko-Zior said. "All that has passed, was foretold in my visions,"

"Was being undead part of the bargain, too?" Daku said to the lich as he walked past.

"You cannot hide your fear from me. With each passing day, I hear the demon's howl grow a little louder."

Daku's shoulder twitched in a spasm, and he brought over his opposite hand to smack the erratic muscles, as if to force them to behave. Then, he rolled his shoulder and shook out his arm.

"There is nothing to hear. Khalkoroth is mine to control," Daku said and abruptly moved to a different part of the camp, rubbing his shoulder, and mouthing angry words to himself.

13

DESDEMONIA

Desdemonia's head was groggy from a too much sleep, though she felt as if she had tossed and turned on her bed-box for days. Her body ached from countless muscle strains and ugly bruises. She was on her side when the room finally shifted into focus.

"That was a new kind of horrible," she said, then rolled on her back to see Sekka looming over her like a physician examining her patient.

"Get off me," Desdemonia said, and pushed her away. She raised herself up and rubbed her head. "I have the worst headache."

Sekka squeezed Desdemonia's arms and forearms, then moved her chin from side to side, eventually looking deep into her eyes.

"Enough already!" Desdemonia said. "How about some space? I feel like I've been turned inside out, and I don't need you making things worse."

"Not even the odd snake scale or discoloration of the skin. Hmm... Tell me what happened. Leave nothing out," Sekka said.

"Could you just leave me alone? Don't you have anyone else to haunt?"

Sekka stepped back, scrutinizing Desdemonia. "He did or said, nothing? Besides the light bruises, you look unchanged."

A wry smile crossed Desdemonia's lips. "He did plenty. Then he laughed and said Raguel was a fool. And for the record, Raguel is a fool. I know. I met him."

Sekka's face turned sinister, and her fists clenched. Then she screamed and stormed to the back of the cell. "Impossible! There must have been more. Everything was perfect!"

Desdemonia rolled her eyes. "Oh my, you're so dramatic."

Sekka whipped back around. "What?"

"Nothing, nothing," Desdemonia said and rose gingerly from the bed-box. Everything seemed to be working fine and she was relieved to know she was still in one piece. Then the room spun in a blur and she sat back down.

"What is it?" Sekka said with keen interest.

"Give me a second, would you? You're very demanding apparition," Desdemonia said, holding her head. "It feels like there are rocks smashing against the sides of my skull. What in blazes is a nexus, anyway?"

"Nexus?" Sekka's interest piqued, and her mood brightened. "Did you say, nexus?"

"Maybe it was demon nixes, or nexus hexes. I can't recall."

She came back quickly with an eager expression. "It's time to escape. We will work together and help each other leave this dismal place."

"Why would I ever do that? You can rot here forever, for all I care," Desdemonia said with suspicious eyes and shifted to face the opposite direction.

"You need me," Sekka said flatly.

"Sure, I do. Just like I need another hole in my head. You're not going anywhere."

"Oh, I wouldn't be too sure. Rules that can't be broken can still be bent. The laws of deep chaos magic are filled with loopholes that can be exploited, if one is clever and brave enough to try."

"Or stupid. Listen, you're a dreamer. The *last* thing I would ever do is help *you* escape. It's bad enough you're haunting this cell."

"You may not have a choice," Sekka said, tapping her blue lips with her long, index finger.

"Whatever. I hate you. Leave me alone," Desdemonia said. She lay her head down and was fast asleep.

The following day, Mister Shlub and Hench came for Sekka. This time she went without a fight. Desdemonia knew that was a bad sign—for them. She laid back on her bed-box and stared at the ceiling, mesmerized by the spinning shadows that swirled above her head.

"Another day, another torment," she said, once more thankful it wasn't her receiving Mister Shlub's attention, and glad Xerthotha no longer cared about her. "Once was enough. Besides, he's busy with his war. Go team!"

Then she heard a hiss, followed by a gurgle and a cough. Something wet slapped against the stone floor.

"Serves her right, for all the damage she caused. I hope it hurt," Desdemonia said. The unmistakable fumes of burning magic drifted into her cell.

"That smells like Elemenati magic I use," she whispered, rolling over to her side and closing her eyes. When she awoke, Sekka had been returned to her cell and was a bloody mess.

"Ugh, you got blood all over me. Some friend you are. This will never come out," Desdemonia said.

Sekka slid down the side of her bed-box and sat on the floor. "That had its moments," she said in a weary voice.

"I'd ask if you're ok, but I don't really care," Desdemonia said. She sat upright, looking down at her filthy shift. "Well, it wasn't going to stay clean forever."

"Don't worry. You remain young and beautiful. He'll still want you when we escape and you return to him."

"Who, Kasai? Ya right, but sorry, I don't speak ridiculous. I'm sure he's forgotten me by now."

Escape. The word had no meaning to her now and seemed like it shouldn't even exist. She turned to Sekka.

"I don't ever hear you talking about doors or windows along the short walk to your fun room. I'm not even sure how I was brought to his majesty's throne room for that matter. I don't remember any great halls, hallways or stairs."

"Oh, but the wonders you will see with a set of jailor's keys," Sekka said almost in a sing-song voice. She rested her head on the top surface of the bed-box.

"I'm sure your friends Mister Shlub and Hench would love to hand them over to you, too," Desdemonia said.

"Not my friends, but yours, I think. Lucky for you, I now know who holds the keys while the other has his fun," Sekka said. She lifted her head wearily from the hard surface of the box and looked questioningly at Desdemonia.

"Don't you remember anything I taught you? Wasn't Sess'thra a suitable instructor?"

"The two of you were filled with trickery and deception," Desdemonia said. She came closer to Sekka, surprised that a small part of her wanted to help the archdevil. "Wow, you look terrible. Are you sure you're alright?"

Sekka sighed. "You must learn to use all of the gifts at your disposal, if you wish to leave this place."

"Again, with this notion of escaping. They don't even let me out of this cell."

Sekka closed her eyes, and she rested her head on the edge of the box. "All men have weak parts and can be easily manipulated. When their guard is down you must strike. Steal the keys and escape," Sekka said. "If you are unwilling or unable to do this on your own, I will help you."

"You're dreaming. There is no escape from here."

"Oh, I think there is a way out. Something has changed," Sekka said and inhaled a deep draught of air through her nose. "If you pay attention, you can smell it in the air. It started with the outbreak of war between Azrollorza and Xerthotha and then became more prominent with your arrival. I sensed a weight was lifted and a rule was broken, or possibly just bent enough to temporarily warp it out of place. Gaps will form and they will be enough."

There was a feral spark in her eyes. "Daimus nexus," Sekka said, hissing out the words. "That's what he called you, wasn't it?"

"Yes, I think so. What of it? Geez, lighten up," Desdemonia said.

"Now is the time to act. A thousand years bound to the Abyss as punishment for dying on your cursed world might be sidestepped with a single leap."

"My cursed world? I'm not sure you're clear on where you are, or even *who*, you are," Desdemonia said.

"Yes, yes, with the right host all things are possible." Sekka stood and paced the floor. Her black within black eyes locked on Desdemonia. "If it's true, you would be a perfect blend of angelic purity and demonic passion."

"Wow sounds so exciting," Desdemonia said, sarcastically. "Can you please just stop talking for a minute? You've given me another terrible headache."

But Sekka pressed on. "Let me see your horns. You still have horns, don't you? Never mind, I'm sure my essence flows in your veins. Maybe not as much now that the Chaos Devil has tampered with you, but it will suffice."

"Fuck off. You're like an itchy rash that won't go away," Desdemonia snapped. "Isn't it time for you to disappear so I can get some sleep?"

"If I can reverse the effects of the onyx ring, then just maybe." Sekka mused, then nodded her head, agreeing with herself. "Yes, I'm sure it will work."

Desdemonia held up her hand and wiggled her fingers. "Hello? The ring is gone. Remember?"

Mischievous eyes and a grin to match lit Sekka's face. She stared at Desdemonia for uncomfortable moments.

"I'm going to help you," Sekka said at last.

"Ya, I know you think you are, but that's not going to happen. No thank you. I'm not interested."

"I don't think you understand. That wasn't an offer. It was a fact."

Desdemonia heard the familiar sound of a heavy key being fit into a tight lock, followed by snickering and then the sound of an open hand cuffing sweaty flesh. The jailors had returned.

"It's time," Mister Shlub said as he unlocked the cell door. "How's it gonna go down today, Lovely, easy or hard? I hope, hard, eh?" He elbowed Hench in the side, who was still rubbing the side of his cheek.

Sekka gave him a wolfish grin. "I'm all yours."

Mister Shlub gave her a nervous glance over the shoulder of his hunched back as he turned to leave. "And you will be forever more," he said, just to make sure she knew the rules.

"Our mighty lord has told us you've done some bad things. Many things not to his liking," Hench said as he took her by the wrist out of the cell. "I don't think you will have the luxury of experiencing pleasure ever again."

Sekka was led out of the cell and Hench followed, leaving the door ajar in his haste. Desdemonia sat on her bed-box and slowly counted the seconds to see how long it took before Sekka ripped them to shreds. "One, two, three..."

"Maybe, if you're lucky, I'll be extra gentle today," Mister Shlub said as he walked down the corridor.

Desdemonia heard Sekka yawn and envisioned her stretching her hands above her head.

"Tsk. So obvious," Desdemonia said and rolled her eyes. She knew Sekka's tattered shift rose with her arms.

"What game are you playing, hmm?" Mister Shlub said. "It's not like you to eagerly offer dessert before the main course has been eaten."

What a moron.

Then Sekka was talking. "Tell me, how goes the war?"

"Oh, let me tell you!" Hench said, enthusiastically. "The little goblins are all a chatter, and they tell me everything.

I'm a big deal, you see. Word from the surface says the war goes poorly for our master."

"Shut your toothless trap, ya mongrel. This one doesn't need to hear anything about anything," Mister Shlub said.

Desdemonia could hear his approaching footsteps stomping on the floor as he marched back to his assistant. She heard a second slap of flesh and then Hench yelp in pain. "Twelve, thirteen, fourteen, fifteen…"

"Oh dear. Poor Xerthotha is not winning his little war?" Sekka said.

"It's not little. It's the greatest war in the history of the Abyss. Entire Circles have been lost to the fighting," Hench said, openly defying Mister Shlub.

"I told you to shut it!"

"What a pity. I would have thought the mighty Chaos Devil a better opponent than that."

"You can shut your trap just the same as that imbecile. Lord Xerthotha knows no rival. All of this follows his great plan. I'm sure of it."

"Yes, one must always have a plan," Sekka said. "Now, which one of you wants to be first?"

"I'm not sure I will enjoy it if you are not going to put up a fight," Mister Shlub said. "But there's a first time for everything. Hench, grab her wrists."

Desdemonia heard Sekka's wild laughter and then the crack and pop of breaking bones.

"Ah, now you shouldn't have done that. It will be a hard day for you again," Hench said. "The enforcers will be here soon."

"Not today," Sekka said with confidence. Now, let's see what we can do with you, Hench."

"Just get it over with," Desdemonia said. "I'm exhausted. I just want to sleep."

Desdemonia heard more cracking and then the sound of something ripping like a dry sheet. "Ugh. Twenty-five, twenty-six, twenty-sev—"

The slap of bare feet scurried to the cell door. It flew open and Sekka was silhouetted in the doorway. She held two severed heads by the hair in one hand. In the other was an iron ring, dangling a wide variety of sharp-toothed keys.

"Come on. We're leaving," Sekka said with a wide grin. She tossed the heads to the floor.

"Forget it. I'm not going anywhere with you. My world is no picnic here, but at least I don't have to endure what you do. I know what happens after one of these little stunts of yours and I'm not interested being taken apart, piece by piece by some lecherous demon."

"You're coming with me."

"No, I'm not!" Desdemonia struggled against Sekka's vice like grip. Let me go!"

"I think you may be forgetting a crucial bit of information," Sekka said, grabbing Desdemonia by her thick, black locks, and exposing her neck.

Sekka uttered a series of guttural words in the language of Gathos, and with a quick slash of her sharp fingernails, she opened Desdemonia's throat.

Desdemonia's eyes went wide with surprise as she quickly brought her hands up to stop the bleeding. Sekka brushed them away contemptuously and drank deeply from the gushing blood. When she had taken her fill, she dropped Desdemonia to the floor.

"I'm still the Archdevil of Gathos, silly girl," she said.

"Now, if you *are* a daimus nexus, that little scrape shouldn't be a problem."

Desdemonia woke with a start. She was running. Her feet were bloodied as they slapped on the hard stone floor. Her shift was in shreds and barely clung to her body. She was bleeding in multiple places from scratches and bites. The stingers from a hundred bees jabbed into the palm of her hand every time she squeezed her fist as she ran.

Sekka was gone. She looked down and gasped when saw she was holding a bundle of sharp-edged keys in a bloodied hand. The nightmare was real.

14

KASAI

The morning sun had not yet risen over Nu-Ordu. The first bell, calling the monks to morning meditation, would not ring for another hour, and the monastery was quiet and peaceful. An early bird chirped a melodic song to the shivering stars across a dark sky as it went about foraging for sleeping insects and sluggish worms.

Kasai peered out from the corner of the dormitory hall and watched Cyrus scamper silent as a mouse across the main courtyard. The master monk quietly sped toward the Hall of Artifacts, double checking his sides to make sure no one was awake before slowly pushing open the door. Kasai remained motionless until Cyrus had entered.

"Cyrus, Cyrus, Cyrus," Kasai repeated under his breath, shaking his head in disappointment. "You've become predictable."

Kasai often found his defacto counterpart lurking in the shadows of Ninziz-zida's resting place, mumbling to himself as if conversing with unseen companions.

Sometimes, Kasai caught him standing before the staff, staring, one hand hesitantly reaching forward, but always drawing back.

"It's an honorable thing. Priceless and unique. The Monastery at Symmetu never had such a weapon under its watch," Cyrus had said on countless occasions.

Cyrus' obsession with Ninziz-zida only grew over the months, causing Kasai to worry that his intentions of helping him rebuild the Orders were less than genuine. He was confident Ninziz-zida would never allow a thief to steal her in the night, but he had seen good men take the Path of Ease when their desire for power became too great or life's hardships became unbearable.

Everyone had their breaking point.

Kasai wondered what would happen if Cyrus held the staff. After all, he was a Master Monk of the Four Orders of Light, and Ninziz-zida had an affinity with the higher-ranking monks of Aetenos. But whenever Kasai offered to let Cyrus train with Ninziz-zida, he would politely decline.

"No, I could not. I fear she would find me unworthy."

Kasai wondered at the humility coming from Cyrus. It was completely out of character.

"I understand. I felt the same when she was offered to me," Kasai said.

"Why you?" Cyrus bemoaned. "Why any of the monks at Ordu for that matter? If we had had the venerable Fire Serpent in our vault at Symmetu, and a true master to wield her, well then things may have been different. Perhaps this catastrophe could have been avoided and the world would not have burned."

Kasai was stunned at Cyrus' bluntness regarding his

failures at the hands of Sekka. For six years he had wrestled with the outcome of his actions and the torture of replaying the "what ifs" of different decisions he could have made in his mind.

Who could have done better, Aetenos? Well, he wasn't available, and the burden had fallen to Kasai. He had done his best to right his wrongs, but there were too many other factors that worked against him. Angels, devils, insane warlords, duplicitous demons, and a friend's betrayal. But none of that mattered now.

The world was a mad house, and he was done blaming himself for the actions of others and the misery it caused. He looked Cyrus dead on and held out his hands, palms upward as if showing them to the celestials in the Seven Heavens.

"An archdevil is dead by these hands. I doubt you could have done better, even with the staff. You weren't there. You don't know."

"My apologies, brother. I meant no disrespect," Cyrus said.

"You will address me as Master Kasai," Kasai said, sternly.

"As you wish," Cyrus said and bowed. "I do not wish to upset you and will take my leave. I'm sure there is something of value I can contribute to the monastery elsewhere."

Kasai felt guilty and foolish the moment the words left his mouth. He was supposed to be above this type of petty behavior. His deeds spoke for themselves. He didn't need to prove anything to anyone.

This was not the type of new beginning Kasai had hoped to create with surviving members of the Orders of Light. But he had no patience for naysayers or opinionated, absentee idealists. Where was Cyrus and his mighty fire xindu during the final battle against Sekka?

The open fields of the Last Garrison were littered with the warriors who had fallen in battle. They were the real heroes who gave their lives protecting the Three Kingdoms from Sekka's rampaging demons.

And all that death and destruction came through a Chaos Gate you helped Sekka to create.

"Master Cyrus, wait. I apologize for my rude behavior. I appreciate the fact that you are here and are willing to help and teach. Perhaps there is some common ground we can build on."

Cyrus paused for a moment to acknowledge Kasai but then continued along his way.

Over time Kasai let down his guard and gave Cyrus more leeway. In turn, Cyrus gave Kasai more insight to harnessing his fire xindu as a primary weapon. The message of his teaching ended mostly the same: relinquish the Fire Serpent, for she only serves to hold you back.

"Now show me dragon form. Good. And tiger, then cobra. Excellent. You are well trained in the natural forms. Now, thrust your fire xindu into each of these consecutive while spinning in place," Cyrus said.

Kasai did as he was instructed and a ring of fire formed around his body.

"Let your enemies fight through your inner defenses as well as your outer ones. They will be helpless to reach you without suffering the flames. This is basic Symmetu training.

"You have within you all that you need for a balanced attack and defense. The Fire Serpent has fed you a truth that by joining together you will be a stronger whole. This is a lie.

She has befuddled your mind in such a way that now

you cling to her for security or as the memory of a loved one, long dead. When you release your emotional ties to the past you will be ready to advance," Cyrus said.

Kasai doubted he could or would do either, indefinitely.

But, he had not wielded Ninziz-zida for months, not even to train, and Desdemonia was never coming back. He knew it was not healthy to cling to her memory the way he did, but there was nothing to replace the emptiness he felt from losing her. Better to remain alone and not allow such grief to take hold again.

Kasai felt his self-imposed reclusiveness was a just punishment for his folly outside the monastery walls. If he had just died with his brothers at Ordu, there wouldn't need to be an Ever Hero, the Chaos Gate would never have opened, and the angelic firestorms would not have fallen to clean up the colossal mess caused by Sekka and her legions. More importantly, Desdemonia would still be alive.

But things didn't happen that way. The Ever Hero was alive and Desdemonia was dead. It would have been easier for Kasai to remain in exile, but when did things go the way he wanted? And here was Master Cyrus, ripping him from his melancholy and forcing him to live again.

"Everything changes," he sighed. "And I'm no exception."

The door to the Hall of Artifacts finally opened and Kasai watched Cyrus hurry outside on his way to the Meditation Hall. A moment later the first bell chimed, directing the brothers to morning meditation. Kasai couldn't reveal his position or Cyrus would know he had been followed.

Late for morning meditation again. I guess that part didn't change. Kasai hid out of sight until the third and last bell chimed, then ran across the courtyard to the Meditation

Hall. Thankfully, the door was not shut, but the other monks were absent.

"What's going on here?" Kasai said as he scanned the empty mats lining the floor.

"Come, sit with me," Cyrus said and welcomed Kasai to sit, relax and be calm. A tiny table sat before him with a clay pot of hot tea and two small cups. He deftly poured the steaming tea into each cup, then offered one to Kasai.

"Where are the others?" Kasai said.

"The winds are blowing, and the leaves are falling. There is much to clean. Last night, I instructed our burgeoning brotherhood to small work details outside the monastery walls. I thought it best for us to talk in a peaceful space for a time. Won't you take some tea with me?"

"Was this necessary?" Kasai said and accepted the cup.

"I could think of no better time or place," Cyrus said and smiled flatly. He took up the second cup and sipped gently from the surface. "I have wrestled with the practice of teaching outsiders our ways. This is against every tradition of the Orders of Aetenos. I formally disagree with this practice and I insist you stop."

"You can disagree all you want, Cyrus. This is my monastery, and I grow tired of reminding you that I am the senior master here, not you."

"Yes, you hold the title, but are unworthy of the rank. You lack the years of serious meditation, study, and real-life experiences to warrant mastery over any of the disciplines of the Four Orders."

"Real life experiences? You can't be serious," Kasai said. He put his cup back on the table.

"Yes, I know, destroying the Archdevil of Gathos was a

most astonishing feat. However, whether you unknowingly stole the power of Aetenos or the Great Monk channeled his power through you to slay the beast is still unconfirmed.

"And without the aid of the Fire Serpent, do you believe you would have survived long outside the monastery walls, with a blind, poisoned, and dying master at your side?"

Kasai was about to speak when Cyrus held up his hand.

"Please, don't. We both know the answer. You are a strong student, quick to learn, and have a bold heart. Your skills in combat are impressive. These are commendable traits. But you are not a master of the Ways of Aetenos, or the xindu mysteries he discovered."

"Master Cyrus, it's time you held Ninziz-zida and discovered the truth about me, the staff, and everything else you think you know so well."

Cyrus's eyes widened. "You offer me the staff freely?"

"Ninziz-zida is not mine to give. She will accept you or she won't. She's funny that way."

"No, I could not. Never. The Fire Serpent is not a toy to be played with or fondled like a lover."

"Lover? I just meant for you to pick her up and let her truth speak to you. It's a quick exercise, a test of your purity, if you will."

"Do not play me for a fool. The Fire Serpent will accept only one master at a time. All others will burn at her touch, so the legends say."

"Only those with ill-intent or infernal blood will be consumed in her righteous flame. I've seen it happen, often. But I'm sure you'll be fine," Kasai said. He was enjoying watching Cyrus squirm.

"I will not touch her while you live," Cyrus said, holding

both hands up and shaking his head. Beads of sweat glistened on his forehead.

"Why would you choose to remain in the darkness of ignorance when the light of knowledge surrounds you?" Kasai eyed him suspiciously.

"One might ask you the same question," Cyrus countered.

A silent tension rose between the two monks until Cyrus gave a slight sigh, then leaned back. His eyed roamed the ceiling of the meditation hall searching for an answer to a question he had not asked.

Then he looked Kasai square in the eyes.

"It's time I told you why I'm here. After the cataclysm, I wandered through the Three Kingdoms for many years. Sickness and pestilence ravaged the smaller hamlets and frontier villages once the last of the fires were snuffed out. The harvest was gone, and the water was spoiled. I did my best to ease the pain of the dying, but my efforts proved to be too little and too late to save anyone.

"Then, the first demon sighting came from out of the southern coast. I dismissed this as rumor only, for what foul beast could have survived the fire storms of the Heavenly Host? But then more sightings came, and a formal report stating the same was posted from the demon hunter, Natsue Hime, Clan Mother of the Yoru Ya-iba. The rumors were true. The demons had returned.

"It appeared we were meant to suffer a second invasion from the Abyss. But who was left to stop them? The hopelessness I felt caused a deep exhaustion inside me, one I carried to my core. I doubted if I, or the people of these lands, had the will to fight again.

"Then, I heard a distant voice, calling to me during my restless meditations. At first, I dismissed it as a common distraction from a tired and wandering mind. But then it continued, haunting me for weeks.

"Are you saying you heard the song of Aetenos?" Kasai asked.

Cyrus nodded but padded his hand in the air to say there was more to his story.

"Overtime, the one voice changed in tone to become thunderous in nature, beckoning to me to action, telling me, no commanding me to locate a phenomenal power, which would be used to free the world from suffering."

"That doesn't sound like him to me. Are you sure you heard Aetenos? He's never that specific."

"There's more," Cyrus said. "I received lucid visions of foreign landscapes the likes of which I couldn't comprehend. Awake or asleep, they came to me in maddening repetition. The Great Monk needed my help and was showing me the way."

Kasai was highly skeptical, and it showed.

"And why not me? Do you think *you* are the only one worthy enough to be chosen by the Great Monk for extraordinary deeds?"

"Forgive me, Master Cyrus. Please continue."

"Fine then, for you must hear the entirety of my tale."

Cyrus gathered his thoughts and continued. "At the time, yes, I was convinced Aetenos was leading me to my destiny. I assumed he meant I must locate one or more of his lost artifacts of power, and thus my search began. I knew with any one of these weapons I could create a beacon of hope for others to follow, and if need be, fight back the forces of darkness.

"I searched for Azurn; the legendary wave sword given to Gen Moll during the First Frost War. I travelled throughout the northern reaches of the Sarribe Mountains. Every scroll I read and clue I uncovered, turned out to be a dead end. To this day, the sword's location sadly remains shrouded in mystery.

"Then, it came to me, the Fire Serpent had survived the monastery massacres and had blazed with righteous fire against Sekka's Frost Legions. Finding the staff, and you, of course, if you still lived, became paramount. Though honestly, I thought you were dead. Why else would I have been chosen for this honorable duty and not you?"

"Not dead yet," Kasai said under his breath. The phrase brought back fond memories of a nasty pinch from a feisty wood witch in a cozy cottage in the woods.

"I ventured to the fields of the Last Garrison and found the ruins of Winter's Fury. I set up camp and scoured the battlefield for Ninziz-zida, meticulously marking off the field by sections. For months, I toiled through the ash caked terrain, digging into the dirt whenever I saw evidence of fallen soldiers or demon death.

"I searched what remained of the archdevil's stronghold. The tower was gone, and the upper and lower catacombs proved to be a disappointment. Everything was burnt or melted to slag.

"I implored Aetenos to guide me, but his voice was now silent. It was if he had never spoken to me. I begged for a sign, something to tell me I was still his chosen one. But the Great Monk ignored my pleas and I despaired.

"I thought to retrace your logical steps back to Ordu, carelessly hoping that somehow, you had survived and returned the staff to her home. The entire time, wondering why Aetenos had chosen an initiate to be his next Ever Hero, and not a true master."

"It's not an Artifact of Power," Kasai said sharply, annoyed with Cyrus's constant belittling of his achievements.

"Excuse me?" Cyrus frowned.

"Azurn is an oblivion sword. It was a gift from Artiya'il to Gen Moll during the First Frost War. It's a powerful weapon, but Aetenos didn't craft it. In fact, he had nothing to do with it, other than his friendship with the angel."

"Clearly, you are mistaken. The histories of Symmetu are clear in this matter. Now, if you are finished lecturing me, I will get to the point."

"Please do," Kasai said, sarcastically. He was sure he had something better to do and be anywhere else but here.

"But just as I started towards Ordu, the voice returned. "Come to the north. Find us. Your rewards will be infinite." Finally, the song of Aetenos played in my ears, again, or so I thought."

"You said, "us," not me," Kasai interrupted.

"Yes, I did. I travelled deep into the northern wastelands where a great revelation was made known to me. The memory of that day still haunt me."

Cyrus paused for effect and waited patiently for Kasai to respond.

"What did you discover, Master Cyrus?"

"Aetenos is dead. I saw his broken body under a tree, overlooking a golden city. When I looked again, the tree, and everything under it, was gone. An unbearable sense of loss and sadness overcame me. How would we continue without the Great Monk to guide us?"

"Aetenos isn't dead. He's already in the Seven Heavens with Illyria," Kasai said. "And please, Master Cyrus, do not argue this point with me."

"I'm sure the truth is difficult for you to accept. I held the same disbelief. But the more I reflected on what this could mean, the more it made sense. The Four Orders were shattered, and the monks who survived the war wandered alone and lost through the unknown.

"And now I have found his Ever Hero cannot connect to the higher forms of the xindu mysteries, let alone the divine abundance of the Boundless. Why else would this be if not due to the death of the demigod?"

"You may be speculating a bit there, Master Cyrus."

"There's more. It wasn't the song of Aetenos I heard, but another voice, two to be specific, that were guiding me north. These beings have the power to change the world, but they are trapped by otherworldly forces. They will need men of purity and strength to escape. We are the men they seek."

"I told you, Cyrus, I'm not interested in accepting another holy mission."

"But combined with the power of the staff, we cou—"

"I said, no. Let it rest. If you wish to continue your quest to find Azurn, then go. Ninziz-zida stays with me at Nu-Ordu."

"But Azurn is lost, and I need—" Cyrus shifted in his seat. "Never have I known a monk of any of the Four Orders to be so selfish and self-centered."

"Well, there's a first time for everything, isn't there?" Kasai said and stood to leave.

"You don't understand. I have seen them in the flesh. They will cleanse the world of the taint that rots it from within! The artifacts are but one source of power they seek. There is something else, an enigma that embodies the profound truth of the Great Balance."

"Cleanse? That doesn't sound very enlightening. It sounds more like a sweeping purge by a maniacal tyrant or a self-serving, diabolical devil."

"You must alter your definitions of good and evil. They are both sides of the coin *and* the space in between. They are the same when seen from a particular point-of-view. Your lack of understanding the outside world prevents you from seeing this."

"Master Cyrus, with all due respect, you're confused. Trust me, I've had my fill of extended travel. I know that many things are not what they seem. But following the notion that a great purge of anything unsightly is the answer to salvation is wrong. It sounds more like the ravings of a deranged mind."

Kasai walked to the door. "I think it is time for you to leave Nu-Ordu. I will not participate in a quest that brings dishonor to the Orders, nor allow you to warp the minds of my students."

"You are the Ever Hero, dammit! You have a duty to serve!" Cyrus shouted, then shut his eyes and collected himself. "But of course, this would be your mind. Your training was incomplete when you fled the monastery as your brothers fought and died under the demons' blades. And from that guilt, you allowed the spirit of Aetenos to possess you."

"Cyrus, I'm warning you, let it go. You are about to cross a sensitive boundary."

"One can hardly blame you; any neophyte would

have succumbed to the same fate. Make no mistake, the Three Kingdoms owe the Ever Hero a debt of gratitude for defeating Sekka, but to sequester yourself here for all these years when the lands lay barren and the people suffer, and to refuse the call again when you are needed, well that speaks of cowardice."

"We are finished here," Kasai said, not bothering to turn as he spoke. "Have your things together and be gone before the breakfast bell. Good day, Master Cyrus. I wish you well on your search for missing treasures and forgotten gods."

Cyrus leaped to his feet. "But I can complete the lessons you were denied by teaching you how the Four Orders of Aetenos flow together into a greater whole. Each Order served a purpose, which when combined with the other three, formed a complete set of skills and disciplines. You know this. Unfortunately, you had barely learned one when Aetenos tapped you to be his next Ever Hero.

"And look what has happened since his departure. These last six years have not been kind to you. Without the help of a proper mentor, you will never achieve a higher understanding of the Orders of Aetenos or the enlightenment that comes from combining their teachings."

Kasai stopped walking. His jaw clenched at hearing the truth. Maybe there was still a chance Cyrus could help him.

"Ninziz-zida was my teacher after Master Choejor was murdered, and I have not heard the song of Aetenos in years. The whisperer in the wind is now silent."

"The demigod possessed you," Cyrus said. His voice was calm and gentle. "You heard only what he needed you to hear to do his bidding. The Fire Serpent had a different agenda. She wakes for battle and destroys those that oppose her will, be they friend or foe."

"No, that's not true. She listened to me. We understood each other. I was the wielder, and she was the weapon."

Cyrus gave Kasai a polite, yet condescending smile. "Ninziz-zida is an astral fire elemental, who feeds off xindu energy. She is a parasite."

Kasai sighed, shook his head, and headed back to the door.

"But there is more you should know." The older monk continued. "I traveled through the frontier villages and even smaller towns in southern Baroqia. The people say that the dystopia we now suffer is your fault, for what is the Ever Hero but a mortal extension of the land? You and the land are woven together like a rope, whose bond can be strong and tight or withered and frayed.

"But you are a broken man. If the lands of Hanna are to be healed, then the Ever Hero must be sparked to life. To do this, you must now learn the Way of Symmetu and release the fire xindu locked within your spirit."

Master Cyrus wasn't wrong this time. Kasai was broken. But so much of what the older monk said or believed was not completely true, or just plain wrong. Nonetheless the path to the Boundless remained hidden and he was desperate to find a way back.

Maybe the old man is right and the Boundless is impossible to reach without divine interference. But until I know more of the other Orders, I will always be blind to the truth.

"The fire is there, but it is buried deep under unnecessary layers of control. Why Aetenos chose you as his next Ever

Hero is curious, and it's not for me to know the mind of the demigod.

"He had his reasons, and I must accept them. But his Ever Hero is as sick as the land he is meant to heal and protect. Therefore, my mission has changed.

"Since you have been deemed the avatar of the late Great Monk, then what is painfully obvious to me is that I must start with you if I am to succeed in rebuilding the Four Orders.

"In time, you too will come to understand that finding the lost artifacts and bringing the enigma from my visions to the north is the only way we can save this world."

Kasai stopped at the door. He couldn't turn his back on the world any longer. Cyrus was right, he was the Ever Hero, whether he wanted to be or not. He turned back to Cyrus, wondering if he could trust the man.

"Come, let us sit together in noble silence and meditate on the roles of the different xindu energies, and specifically how your fire xindu will bring you back to the hero you were meant to be."

Kasai reluctantly sat in silence, but he kept his eyes on the Master of Symmetu. He wondered not for the first time if Cyrus was insane or just touched by passion and wanted to make a difference.

And how could Aetenos be dead? That's ridiculous.

15

DESDEMONIA

D esdemonia woke to the blur of stone squares flashing beneath her. She had been thrown over the shoulder of a great beast, running on avian legs, bucking her unceremoniously up and down with each long stride. The creature's black talons clicked, clicked, clicked on the stone floor.

The bouncing motion made her sick to her stomach. There was a lot of blood covering the back of the beast's course, white fur, her blood. It was sticky and grabbed at her skin every time she smacked down into it.

Desdemonia's eyes went wide with anger when she realized who was carrying her.

"Let me down!" Desdemonia shouted.

"Be quiet and stop struggling," Sekka said in a deep, guttural voice.

Desdemonia tried to squirm free but Sekka's grip was too strong. She felt the magic deep within her blood stir. Black vapors rose from the wounded hand that miraculously still clutched the set of iron keys, causing sparks to fly. She looked at her other hand. Cuts and scrapes bled more of the black stuff. When she squeezed her fist tight, she felt a surge of energy shoot down her forearm. Without thinking, she slapped her hand down on Sekka's back.

Sekka arched backward, wincing in pain. She ripped Desdemonia from her back and tossed her across the wide hallway. Desdemonia bounced twice before skidding to a stop. A trail of blood was left in her wake.

Torches were stuck in iron sconces mounted to a row of columns and lit the hallway with flickering light. She saw that the opposite side of the columns offered some concealment, so she scurried into their shadows, fearful of being discovered by one of Xerthotha's jailors, or something worse.

"Where am I? Why am I covered in blood?" Desdemonia said.

She peered around one side of the column, searching for Sekka, but the archdevil had vanished.

"What is going on here?" She wondered and took a breath to calm herself. Desdemonia then turned to her other side and was startled to see Sekka crouched down next to her. The archdevil was back in her human form.

She glanced down at Desdemonia, then edged her way to Desdemonia's side.

"Nice of you to show up," Desdemonia said. "What did you do to them? Don't think for a second, I'm taking the fall for this stunt. This was all your fault."

"Me?" Sekka said, surprised. She peered around the column, stood, and looked farther down the hallway, then nodded with satisfaction. It appeared they had not been discovered. Sekka turned back to Desdemonia. An odd hint of worry in her eyes.

"Get up. You were losing the fight against those two idiots and had lost too much blood. You needed my help, again." Sekka said. She rubbed the backside of her shoulder. "As you can see, the magic I gave you works better here. I suggest you use it next time you're in trouble."

"Fight? What fight?"

"And blood of the Abyss, forget about those little blue missiles you're so fond of casting. I'm talking about the real magic. The dark magic."

Desdemonia glanced at her hands. The black vapors were gone and the wounds on her hands were closing. She rubbed them together and feared she was losing her mind.

"This is just a dream. A very bad dream. I'm still in my cell. I must be."

Sekka's voice dropped to a whisper. "Now be quiet. We're almost free."

"Shut up. You're not even real. How did I get here? When Mister Shlub realizes I'm gone, he'll—wait, you're not actually real, right?" Desdemonia poked Sekka in the side of the arm. Her finger felt a moment's resistance, but then passed through.

"We will be long gone before that happens," Sekka said. "Now stop talking and let me think. We need to reach those doors."

"We? There is no *we*. Ugh, I don't feel well. I'm think I'm gonna throw up."

"It's the chaos magic that saturated this place. Nothing on Xerthotha's world stays the same for long. And you will be the biggest transformation anyone in the Three Worlds has ever seen. Now come on, get up."

Desdemonia was shocked when the spectral Sekka

forcefully took her under the arms and lifted her to her feet. She stumbled for a moment before she caught her balance.

"Gimme a second, will you? You're always in a rush," Desdemonia said. She bent over her knees, staring bewildered at her right hand. Her wounds had completely healed. *What the hell is going on?* After a minute or two, the nausea passed. "Ok, ok. I'm ready."

She stood up straight and Sekka was gone. "Are you kidding me? How about a little consistency?" She sighed. "I pick the worst imaginary friends."

Desdemonia hid herself the best she could behind the stone columns. A quick glance showed her the doors Sekka had mentioned. They were huge, big enough for five giants to walk abreast and still have room to spare.

She glanced around the opposite side of the column, alert for guards or whatever hellish thing wandered through Xerthotha's palace. The hallway was empty. Desdemonia looked back to the door and Sekka was already there, smoothing the surface with her hands, searching for something.

Desdemonia shook her head. "So annoying."

The archdevil looked over her shoulder, perplexed. "Don't just stand there. Hurry up and bring me those keys."

Desdemonia took a few hesitant steps toward the doors, all the while glancing over her shoulder for enemies. "What did you find?"

"Give me those!" Sekka grabbed the sticky keys from Desdemonia's hand. She tried each one in a keyhole that was previously hidden above her head, but none of them fit the lock.

"Blast it!" Sekka tossed the keys across the floor. Her

dark eyes scanned the ceiling and walls. "We have little time. He will know soon."

"By he, you mean the big guy, not Mister Shlub, right?" Desdemonia said, watching Sekka face confirm her answer. "Oh, we're fucked this time for sure. You could've thought this through better."

Desdemonia looked to where the keys lay splayed on the floor. "Shouldn't we save those?"

"They served their purpose."

"Ya well, maybe they could serve their purpose again when we use them to get back into our cell. Xerthotha is not going to be pleased when he learns you killed his guards, again," Desdemonia said.

"You keep saying, me," Sekka said as she continued searching the doors, pushing down here and there over the wide surface. "The war goes poorly for Xerthotha and he is preoccupied with other matters. Raguel has betrayed him and now Azrollorza presses her advantage. It won't be long before she comes here with her full force."

"Oh, and won't that be a treat," Desdemonia said.

Sekka continued to search for a way to open the doors. "We must get outside and find a place to hide before that happens," she said, then eyed Desdemonia knowingly, "Or until you are ready."

"Bahahaha!" Desdemonia couldn't control herself. "You really have a special kind of madness, don't you. You, of all *things,* should know there is no place to hide from the Chaos Devil, especially here."

"Nonetheless, we have to get outside," Sekka said. "It's our best chance to gain precious time."

"You know, if you wait long enough, the inside will

change to the outside, right?" Desdemonia said with a chuckle in her voice.

Sekka stopped short. She looked as if she was calculating outcomes. "Of course. But where to put the body?"

"Wait, what? Whoa, whoa, whoa. Just a minute. I'll just be going back to my cell then, thank you very much." Desdemonia marched over to the discarded keys and snatched them from the floor.

"I grow tired of waiting," Sekka said and quickly moved closer to Desdemonia, watching for any signs of change. "Maybe you need more encouragement. I was sure the gash across the throat would be enough."

Desdemonia brought her hand to her throat. The bleeding had stopped but the wound was still tender. She took three steps back, trying to put the pieces together since she had fallen asleep in her cell.

The dong of bells tolled in the distance, and then again, but louder this time and much closer. The floor trembled under her feet and the walls buckled. Desdemonia stumbled to one of the columns for support and saw that it was now covered in purplish-gray bark. Leafless and withered branches sprouted from its sides. She then noticed that the rest of the columns had also changed to strange, desolate trees.

A long, splintering crack sounded over her head. Desdemonia looked up to see the ceiling splintering into large chunks of plaster, with the smaller pieces raining down on her and Sekka.

"It's happening!" Desdemonia shouted.

Sekka looked up and scowled. "I can see that!" She raised her hands and chanted the words to a spell, but before she finished, the heavy plaster changed into a flock of black birds, scattering through walls that were fading from sight. Desdemonia was sure their squawking would alert unwanted attention and prepared herself for a fight.

Looking back down the hallway now filled with a line of purplish dead trees, she saw the floor had dissolved into an open and barren, rocky landscape. Lines of pebbles grew into larger rocks and then into boulders as they branched out in primitive spiral designs from the last of the purplish trees. The sky above was a flat gray that hung dismally low like a heavy fog.

The deafening sound of giant rock formations grinding together caused Desdemonia to cringe and cover her ears. Another tremor rolled through the earth as a mountain range erupted from the ground in the far distance.

"What fresh new Hell is this, I wonder?" Desdemonia said.

Then, she heard the bellows of angry bulls. Desdemonia turned to her left to see a herd of demonic minotaur milling in a rough circle. They seemed as confused as she was by their current location. They pushed and shoved each other, shouting curses and threats, until one spotted her.

Assuming she was the cause of his displacement, he ran toward her enraged, holding a thick stone club raised above his head. The beast was colossal with broad shoulders and muscular arms, legs, and chest. He ran on cloven hooves faster than should be possible.

"You want to handle this?" Desdemonia said to Sekka, but the archdevil had vanished again.

"Blood of the Abyss is right! That's it, I'm officially disowning you as my prison buddy." Her hands lit with blue witch fire, but the flames grew high into the air and fluttered like thin ribbons.

"Not good. Not good. Come on, Des, get it together."

The demon minotaur put his head down and rammed into her, sending her sprawling. She hit the ground hard and gasped for breath. He rounded quickly and brought his great club up to finish her off. His eyes were bloodshot red, and his breath was foul.

Desdemonia desperately brought her hands up to ward off the blow. She tried to catch her breath enough to mumble a protective spell but failed.

The club came down fast. Desdemonia shut her eyes, waiting for the blow to knock her senseless. She then heard Sekka growl and looked up to see massive, clawed hands holding the club steady over her head. Muscles rippled along Sekka's arms as she leaned into the minotaur's body, while protectively stepping over Desdemonia.

She then ripped the minotaur's club from his grasp and with the other hand she gouged four deep gashes into the demon's face.

"That's it. That's it! Do your stuff!" Desdemonia shouted and scurried out from under the two titans.

The minotaur stumbled backward, howling in pain, then whipped around fast and charged Sekka blind. Before she could react, the minotaur tackled her to the ground.

Desdemonia shot a quick glance to the remaining herd. They had spotted a caravan of sorts, traveling across the newly formed landscape. Desdemonia wasn't sure but she thought she saw a long line of people shackled together trailing carriages pulled by rough beasts. Flying overhead were smaller, fiendish things with long spears, prodding them along.

Desdemonia was relieved to see the herd stampede in their direction, perhaps thinking these newcomers would be easier prey. The fight behind her grew closer and louder. She heard the slapping and slugging of hand on flesh, and bodies hitting the ground.

Sekka and the minotaur wrestled like mad lovers trying to kill one another. Sekka yelled in ecstasy as she ripped at his midsection with her talons, while the minotaur grunted in satisfaction as he pierced and tore into her upper body with his horns.

Then, the minotaur reared his head back and smashed it into hers, knocking Sekka senseless. He freed himself from her grasp and stood up with her in a tight embrace, trapping one of her arms to her side.

Desdemonia's world suddenly went black. She felt her sides being crushed in a suffocating grip. Her scream came out stunned without oxygen in her lungs. Her eyes flashed open, and the barren landscape shifted back into focus.

Sekka was gone and Desdemonia was now held in the minotaur's clutches. He snorted with delight as he squeezed her tighter, laughing in her face as she squirmed in a vain attempt to escape. She couldn't breathe and gasped for precious air.

Have you forgotten everything I taught you, daughter? Use the dark magic.

Time was running out. She couldn't move and weave the magic of the forest through her dance. She could barely suck in a half-breath of air. The flat grey sky began to darken into rolling cloud formations..

USE IT NOW!

Desdemonia sucked in more air and screamed in

desperation. She reached up to the sky with her one free hand as if to grab the dark clouds and pull them toward her. She closed her hand into a fist and held tight.

"Come...to...me," she said through gritted teeth.

The clouds overhead spun together in a wide circle, turning deep blue and bruised purple as they moved. The air became moist and for the first time in what seemed like forever, Desdemonia smelled the glorious and mulchy scent of a pending thunderstorm.

"This is gonna hurt," she said and stared into the minotaur's yellow eyes just as she slapped her hand down on the beast's shoulder.

A thick, jagged fork of white lightning flashed and crackled down from the swirling clouds, striking the minotaur. A moment later a thunderous boom echoed across the rocky plain.

The minotaur's arms went wide as the two were thrown twenty feet apart. Residual electricity sparked and raced over their bodies. Desdemonia stood with ease, miraculously unharmed. She felt alive and super charged with glorious magic.

The minotaur rose from the ground on shaky knees. He shook his broad head from side to side, spewing slobber with each turn. When he saw Desdemonia, he gave a quick snort, spraying more mucus across his muzzle, then wiping it away with his forearm. Angrily, he marched forward, slowly at first, then gathering speed into a charge.

"Oh, this is so on then," Desdemonia said.

The minotaur bellowed, wild with battle lust.

"Strike! Strike!" she yelled, throwing down multiple lightning bolts, pounding the minotaur mercilessly. The dark magic was flowing through her at will. The beast was fried to a crisp long before he slid to a stop on the loose gravel at her feet.

Desdemonia looked for Sekka but the Beast of Gathos was gone, as was any human version of the archdevil. The dark magic still pumped through her veins, yearning for release. She absentmindedly brushed her hair from her eyes and felt two, curling horns protruding from her head. Somehow, they felt right.

Just like old times, I guess.

In the distance, the herd of demon minotaur had finished butchering the lost souls of the caravan. The small, flying caretakers circled overhead, taunting the minotaur with their spears, but remaining out of reach of their swinging clubs.

Desdemonia's lightning strikes had caught their attention and they rustled in her direction, eager for something else to kill. They jostled one another as they approached, pushing and shoving one another to get to the front of the herd.

"I've got plenty more guys. Come and get it." Desdemonia smirked, readying herself by reaching to the sky.

The middle of her back ached and felt itchy at the same time. She tried flexing her arms before her chest to help loosen the sore spots before the next fight. Sharp pain tore through her back as her skin ripped open down her spine.

Black vapor leaked out of her wound and shifting into the semblance of batlike membranes. The herd was almost upon her as another spasm of pain racked her body. She doubled over in agony, then rested her head on the warm ground, panting.

"Oh, Immortal Mother. What is happening to me?"

Grunts and growls echoed around her. The herd had her surrounded. She could smell the musky odor of their sex and felt their hot breath on her skin. Long strands of drool dripped from their nostrils and open mouths. They leered at her as something desirable to play with before the kill.

Through teary eyes, she saw three specs of golden light appear and grow into spinning balls of pure energy that slowly circled her head and horns. The herd paused, sniffing the air, as if sensing a formidable magic.

Their appetite for female flesh turned back to raw aggression. They stamped their hooved feet while lowering their heads or raising their clubs to strike. The balls of energy spun faster around her head until they blurred into a solid circle.

Desdemonia felt a new kind of euphoria. Her magic spread out from her and mixed with the air, the dirt, the purple clouds overhead, and the electricity inside, waiting to be unleashed.

She glared at the herd and shot her arms above her head, grabbing for the clouds.

"To me!" she shouted.

The herd pounced. Brutal clubs fell and sharp horns sought to pierce her flesh. A jagged ribbon of lightning lit up the underside of the clouds, flashing down and into Desdemonia. It filled her entire being before bouncing outward into the herd, sizzling them to nothingness.

When the ashes cleared, Desdemonia was floating just above the ground, hovering from the friction caused by the electric charge coursing through her body and the surface of the ground. She gasped, surprised at the release of so much destructive power.

The environment was changing again. Rock formations crumbled and collapsed. The purplish clouds turned red, orange, and black, like the color of smoldering charcoal. Then, autumn-colored leaves rained down on what was becoming a quagmire of thick mud below her feet.

Desdemonia envisioned using her vaporous wings to fly. The feeling was awkward at first, but nonetheless, the wings responded to her command and opened in a mixture of billowing black smoke, laced with long, finger-tipped ends.

She flexed them once, twice and felt her body rise into the air. A pirate's smile spread across her lips, and she shot into the sky. Soon, the ground below was lost from sight. The dark clouds churned around her and she was happily lost in their formless mystery.

Eventually, the air ceased being warm and grew colder, then it was neither warm nor cool. It just was and Desdemonia drifted alone in the void.

16
XERTHOTHA

A lazy wind drifted across the sandy dunes, spinning thorny bramble bushes into bouncing acrobats over the dry landscape of Dathe. One might think it was a peaceful day in the desert. Xerthotha's ground forces were securely dug in pocket ditches and trenches that stretched in zig-zag patterns for miles in long lines of defense circling a dark citadel.

Fields of spiked caltrops lay before the trenches to stall the advance of larger demons. Smaller, living things, equipped with pinching mandibles tipped with venomous barbs, burrowed just under the top layer of loose sand, waiting for the advancing infantry to stumble over their nests.

The atmosphere shifted abruptly as a new wind churned up sand in grit, turning the air muggy and humid. The enemy was coming. Xerthotha's soldiers moved into better position along the ridge of the trench, the clicking of shifting carapaces rattled down the line.

In the distance, the sky turned an abnormal blueish

gray, the color that preludes a rainstorm, and something completely foreign to the arid Eighty-eighth Circle of Dathe, now under Xerthotha's control.

It was to be expected. *She* would bring a storm before the fight. Intimidation was the first card she loved to play. It was a petty and predictable display of power.

Xerthotha stood with four hands clasped behind his back. He wore a blank, sleeveless robe that slowly bled the colors and design of the swirling clouds from the pending storm on Dathe. Beneath him was a wide basin filled with lime green water, the surface of which sparkled with images of other skirmishes being fought against Azrollorza's massive invasion across the Circle. This was not the only battle but would be the last.

Pasty, white-skinned witches surrounded the basin, gyrating in an erotic dance while a choir of hobgoblin mystics chanted into the water, weaving spells of farseeing onto the surface. The images in the water grew closer until Xerthotha could see through the eyes of his soldiers entrenched across the dunes.

His sand warriors stared into the broadening storm. They were humanoid in shape but resembled stocky dwarves instead of full-grown men. Their heads were covered in a wiry tumbleweed of frizzy hair and coarse hair bristled over the skin of their arms and legs.

Bone armor chest plates covered their torso. One by one, they tightened their grips on swords and spears, while shamans conjured miniature sand devils to be used as material for future spell casting.

Thousands of small dots materialized across the distant sky, reflecting the last of the sunlight being consumed by the darkening clouds. As the dots flew closer, they broke into densely packed clusters, filled with the monstrous slug-shaped bodies of dezemilians.

As the enemy approached, the true size of their enormous bodies became apparent, causing many of his sand warriors to gape in awe and crouch lower in their trenches. Azrollorza had sent her strongest assets to take the Eighty-eighth Circle, and this made Xerthotha chuckle.

"Oh my, she brought the whole gang," he said with amusement.

The storm clouds rolled over the trenches like a thunderous wave, dumping stinging, acid rain over his soldiers. Tempest level winds swirled and sprayed the raindrops like a swarm of haywire bees, injecting sharp barbs into anything they touched.

Fiery explosions covered the battlefield, shooting shrapnel bullets of buried rock and vaporized sand that seared skin from flesh and tore holes into those unlucky enough to be in the line of fire.

Percussion bombs of pressurized water sealed in magical casings dropped overhead. Upon impact, the water detonated and blasted sand warriors apart or threw them into the weapons of their comrades.

Waves of Takuur's floated overhead and lowered writhing tentacles into the trenches, searching for anyone who survived the initial barrage. They wrapped their slimy appendages around warriors and raised them to mouths filled with grinding teeth. Piercing screams were added to the din of battle as orange blood sprayed from mangled bodies.

The sand warriors fought back honorably for their lord,

thrusting their blades and spear tips into the tentacles, but it was not enough. D'xyston sky riders encased in vermillion armor and wielding long, black spears, fell from the Takuun's backs and targeted the shamans before they could mount a proper ranged attack at the flying demons.

Xerthotha's battle view shifted as each soldier he inhabited died. The experience of being slain countless times was an interesting sensation for the Supreme Devil. The body he now possessed looked back to the massive citadel built into a towering rock formation. It would not be long now.

Forces had been reserved to protect the stronghold, but defeat was inevitable. Based on what he had observed in the farseeing basin of similar battles raging across the Circle, when the citadel fell, he would lose Dathe. Azrollorza would control the Eighty-eighth Circle and Xerthotha would make her bleed for it.

The Supreme Devil brought one hand to his face and twisted the end of a long moustache he had grown for the occasion. Azrollorza's leviathans and the legions of D'xyston sky riders who fell from their backs had overwhelmed the insufficient legions he had left there to stall her advance.

His rival thought she was being clever by controlling the sky against his sand troops. He was sure she thought she had outwitted him.

"Sire, the desert operation will fail."

Xerthotha watched Azrollorza's massive troop movement across the dune surface. His minion wasn't wrong.

"It's an acceptable loss," Xerthotha said. "Send the command for all remaining troops to proceed to their predetermined underground rendezvous points. The surface of Dathe will fall today, and I will reclaim it tomorrow. Launch the subterranean campaign."

Xerthotha wrinkled his nose as the stale air in the chamber turned sweet.

Rose pedals, Xerthotha thought and scowled. "Continue monitoring. Let me know when the citadel falls. I'll be in my private chambers."

The summons came repeatedly. Xerthotha dismissed each attempt to establish an astral connection to his mind with bothersome contempt. He decided to stroll through his palace instead, admiring the changing edifices of a newly constructed hall, and the exotic creatures born into existence, some of which he had never seen before.

Xerthotha arrived at his private chambers and found a favorite reclining chair composed of still "living" soul-slaves. He smiled appreciatively and eased himself back in comfort. A hundred bodies had been contorted, twisted, and bent to construct a divan of agony. Oh, how he loved this chair.

Another attempt was made, this time more insistent and furious at being ignored. Xerthotha manifested a chalice of wine and reached down to snap off some delectable body parts from his chair. He sighed dramatically and reluctantly established the mind connection to Lord Raguel.

+This had better be the clarion call of salvation. Where are the white doves to ease my woe? I have lost another world to that bloated sea hag.+

+I have assembled a warband of shock troops to assist you. They will provide the support you need to tip the scales in your favor. However, before I send them, you must return the wood witch, Desdemonia Mishi, to me. This is nonnegotiable. She belongs in the Seven Heavens.+ Raguel's thought came to Xerthotha's mind.

Xerthotha's booming laughter shook the walls of his chamber. Windows shattered. The falling pieces of glass turned to a swarm of bright blue murder hornets, which darted after something small and furry, scampering out of sight.

+A warband did you say? Ho, that's rich. What can a meager flock of pretty birds do to stall the advance, or tip the scales as you say, against Azrollorza? She brought a legion of dezemilians to Dathe just to insure victory.+

+The Heavenly Host is preoccupied with internal matters.+

+Yes, I heard. Mother took away your toys and sent you to bed without a kiss good night,+ Xerthotha taunted. +If you hadn't guessed by now, you've never been her favorite son.+

+Mistakes were made but soon I will have ultimate control,+ Raguel countered. +That is all you need to know.+

+And the Heavenly Host, when will they fly? And I mean all of them. I will not be satisfied until every barrack and stable is cleared and conscripted to my cause.+

+When I have the wood witch. No sooner.+

+And the Barrier? How do you intend to pass through it with such a force? What prevents me and mine from invading the other two worlds will stop you too. The Immortal Mother's laws cannot be broken.+

+I am the first and finest of Mother's creations. There are powers I possess you cannot fathom. Now, fetch me the witch.+

Xerthotha rolled his eyes, yawned, and smacked his lips.

+Yes, well, I've grown rather fond of Desdemonia Mishi. We've become...close. I'm keeping her.+

+That is not your decision to make. If you refuse me, the angels will not fly for you. Keep in mind, it matters little to me who rules the Abyss, though I will enjoy congratulating Azrollorza on her conquest over you.+

+Oh, you wound me so, big brother. But it seems we are at a bit of an impasse. Send your birds or not. Either way I am committed to ending Azrollorza. Know this, if the birds do not fly, I will find a way to visit your peaceful land of puffy clouds and pluck out every single colorful feather on your back.+

+Show her to me,+ Raguel commanded.

Xerthotha stalled. +No. I think I'll keep her until you prove yourself trustworthy. As of now, your credibility is lacking. When I see your birds dropping their fiery shit on Azrollorza's forces, then we will talk of trades and pacts of good will.+

Xerthotha wiped away the connection. "I hate the smell of rose pedals."

Bells tolled in the distance, and the walls of his private chamber turned emerald, then melted into a dark, soupy marsh as Xerthotha walked in pensive contemplation. A moment later, thousands of wet ravens burst from the spreading ooze and flew into the air, cawing and flapping for height.

Gooey, black bits fell from their feathers and sprayed like pebbles, raining into the greenish morass. The Supreme Devil paid the spectacle no mind as he squelched across ankle-deep muck. His mind was occupied on how best to leverage the opportunity Raguel had mistakenly given him.

"He's desperate. The daimus nexus must be stronger than I initially imagined, perhaps even strong enough to dismantle the Amaranthine Barrier. That's Raguel's play. All those souls for the taking, unless I get there first.

"With a daimus nexus at my side, the worlds under my control could flow into the Mortal Realm. And then the true war would begin."

Xerthotha glanced speculatively into the open sky. "Or I could hand over the anomaly to Raguel and watch in glee as the Heavenly Host annihilated Azrollorza and then Morrdilliax, and then...me. Oh no, that won't do."

He walked on, stepping on heads bubbling to the surface. Coiling appendages wrapped around his ankles and wound up his shins, attempting to prevent him from leaving. Only a greater dimensional demon would be so bold. But everything had to eat.

Presumably, the beast lurking in the shallow flow of muck also existed in a parallel pocket of space and time, thus hoping to catch Xerthotha unaware and make him its next meal.

Xerthotha felt the pinprick of thousands of thorns digging into his flesh. He appreciated the moxie of the beast. The demons and devils throughout the Abyss were either busy killing or busy dying. There wasn't any peaceful in between, not even for him in his own palace.

He yanked his legs free from the fleshy tentacles and with a casual flick of his two first fingers the muck hiding the dimensional demon boiled and then burned. He walked on without much consideration to see if the thing was dead.

"The arrival of the Ancients remains the unpredictable variable. I imagine they have hidden themselves from

Raguel's prying eyes, and are weak, but they are there, somewhere. I know it, Raguel knows it, and I'm sure that unsavory hag and the hundred-headed worm knows it, too."

A new sun warmed a field of golden reeds which had sprouted from the now hardened muck. The ravens circled above in a tight ring. They flew together in a dense, black cloud until their forms merged into a multi-faceted, onyx crystal and dropped to the ground, shattering into a thousand pieces.

Millions of tiny beetles erupted from each crystal piece and scurried into the reeds. Xerthotha heard the chewing of countless mouths and watched the reed stalks fall like felled timber, one after another.

"Small steps, not great leaps, wins the pinnacle of the mountain," he said. "Until I know the strength of the Ancients, I will keep my assets close and play them accordingly."

Xerthotha brought his hands together until magical energy shot between his palms. He widened the space between his hands and stretched a fine layer of film before him. Foggy images took shape, eventually coming into focus as giant mushroom formations towering across a damp, misty marshland.

He zoomed into the damp landscape and saw spidery webs crisscrossing floating balls of florescent moss, which lit fungus, oozing with slime. Salamanders scurried under moist, rotting logs, slugs moved through the muddy ground, and worms wriggled away from noxious gas bubbles, that had boiled to the dank surface.

Flittering bugs dived on unsuspecting centipedes only to be snatched mid-air by waiting tree snakes or snagged by clever web traps. The swamp gas smelled of rotten eggs and wet shit. He smelled it as clearly as if he waded waist deep into a thick marsh.

"Morrdilliax!" Xerthotha said into the astral plane. "We will come to terms concerning the fate of the Abyss."

"Yessssss," a voice slithered through the purple membrane. "One of the Great Three must fall. Are you willing to accept your defeat? Morrdilliax will kill you quickly and painlessly. Glory and prizes we will claim with your death."

"No!" another voice quickly asserted itself. "We kill the Chaos Devil slowly. Let him watch as we carve him up and feed him to the minions. He deserves no less for his trickery."

"There must always be three, not two or one. There are no terms. The Great Balance must remain less we all perish under Her displeasure," a new voice said.

Xerthotha sighed. Conversing with Morrdilliax was an exercise in patience. "No doubt, you have heard of the arrival of the Ancients."

"They cannot breach the Amaranthine Barrier. They are helpless, trapped in the great void," another new voice said.

"Their avatars walk the Mortal Realm. We are doomed. Nothing will survive their thirst," a fifth voice said.

The Supreme Devil, Morrdilliax, possessed one hundred heads, some male, some female, which sprouted across its bulbous, caterpillar shaped-body like an infinite field of spotted mushrooms. The land was filled with an echoing din of arguing voices for each of Morrdilliax's heads constantly competed for attention to be heard and to decide what the juggernaut would do next. No decision was undebated which left the Supreme Devil in a state of eternal neutrality.

His body was plump and tubular, stretching across the

marshlands like a mountain range. Attached to its great bulk were thousands of stiff hairs, which preformed the function of legs and feet when Morrdilliax moved, which was seldom.

"We have something they need, or rather I have something they need," Xerthotha said. "Without it, they will never manifest into their true forms. The Chaos Gate is gone. The tear has closed to a fraction of its former size."

"We are saved!" a new voice said triumphantly.

"Xerthotha will use us. His deceit knows no limit."

"He schemes and betrays."

"Trust the Chaos Devil."

"Never!"

Xerthotha inwardly sighed. "Might I suggest a spokesperson?"

"Xerthotha does not command the great Morrdilliax!" a thundering voice spoke out.

"Forgive me. I meant no disrespect. Would the great Morrdilliax be open to a proposed agreement?" Xerthotha said.

"Speak," the thunderous voice said.

"Raguel takes me for an obedient dog. But it's you and I, Morrdilliax, who will come out as the ultimate victors. A final battle approaches, one that will end all wars. The Seven Heavens will fall, and the Abyss will reign over the Mortal Realm. Think of the bounty of souls we will claim!"

"Azrollorza will prevent every attempt Xerthotha makes to gain the Mortal Realm," a voice chimed in from one of Morrdilliax's heads.

"The Chaos Devil lies. There will be nothing but scraps for Morrdilliax," a distant voice echoed across the astral connection.

"We will not allow it. The Great Balance must remain," a new voice said. "Morrdilliax keeps his neutrality when the younger devils fight."

Then the mighty voice bellowed over them all. "We will help Xerthotha and claim half instead of a third but will do nothing in the conflict to come."

"Ah, perfect! The "do nothing" approach wins the day. Brilliant! The simplicity is genius. The Heavenly Host will destroy Azrollorza, and we will both be stronger from the spoils. In time we will invade the Mortal Realm and seize it for our own."

"But what stops us now, will stop us then. There is no way past the Amaranthine Barrier."

"Xerthotha must know how to break through. He is cunning and resourceful."

"We must wait and be patient."

"Yes, we will need more than a thin sliver to breach the barrier, but luckily, I have just the blade to slice it wide open," Xerthotha said confidently.

"If you fail us in anyway be assured, Azrollorza will receive our aid and cast you into oblivion."

"Understood." Xerthotha severed the connection. The arguing beast that was Morrdilliax would spend the next century debating itself over the merits and weaknesses of the Great Balance. But an agreement had been struck and was binding by the laws of the Abyss.

"Now, to unwrap my little present and find out what's inside."

Xerthotha morphed into the figure of a dapper, young rogue, outfitted in wide brim hat, billowy shirt, and puffy pantaloons. He strapped a rapier at his side for good measure. Then, he snapped his fingers and was transported outside the door to Desdemonia's cell.

Blood and gore were sprayed across the walls and floor.

"Well, this is unfortunate," Xerthotha said, mildly irritated that his black leather boots were ruined. He looked down the corridor and saw two, headless and mangled bodies slumped awkwardly against the wall.

"At least she's enjoying herself," he said and turned to the door. When he grabbed for the outside latch, the door pushed opened easily.

"Knock, knock, little one."

He peered inside wearing his most rakish smile. The cell was empty but for the heads of his jailors, staring at him from the solitary bed crate in the room. Xerthotha frowned.

"This is most unfortunate, indeed."

17
DESDEMONIA

Desdemonia flew through the formless void. If she was meant to be somewhere, she would be lost. But there was nowhere to go, and nowhere to be. There was only more of the same nothingness no matter which direction she chose. Time was irrelevant to her and distance had no meaning.

She wasn't sure if she had real wings or not, since what was behind her back was more of a backwash of inky smoke that reformed into the resemblance of leathery wings whenever she cared to look, but then shifted back to vapors as she looked away.

Memories of her past tumbled through her mind. She saw the exotic flowers and vibrant-feathered birds found in the jungles of Sunne. A young girl with long black hair, streaming behind her as she raced along an earthy path of soft, dead leaves, agilely skipping over roots, and dodging low-hanging vines. She saw the adoring faces of loving parents, taken too soon by wicked and vengeful men.

Next, the wilderness of Baroqia opened before her

eyes. The jungle trees and foliage turned to a dense forest filled with deep green pines, red maple, white birch, and ancient oak trees. It was autumn and the leaves had already turned, creating a spectacle of colorful flurry whenever the northern winds blew down from the snow-capped Sarribe Mountains.

A cozy cottage appeared, nestled in a clearing in the woods. A thin line of smoke rose from a small stone chimney. Honeybee hives and fruit trees lined the edges where the clearing met the wall of the forest. A chicken ate rocks instead of seed. Dumb bird.

Inside the cottage a young monk sat inside, nervously eating soup. He wore the robes of the Order of Ordu and knew nothing of the real world outside his monastery walls. Only a few days earlier, the boy was forced to become the man who would be the Ever Hero.

She smiled at that memory. Kasai was the hero everyone needed, but he just couldn't get out of his own way. Good thing she was around to help keep him out of trouble.

She heard the deep laughter of Khalkoroth and felt despair and loss when the shadow demon murdered Kasai's mentor, Master Choejor. The imaginary world inside her head turned as snow-white as the pale demon's fur coat. Her skin turned to gooseflesh and her body shivered as she watched herself trudge through knee deep snow on windswept plains of ice. A lone tower rose in the distance, waiting.

A red devil with the wings of an angel, flew like a comet across the sky. She gasped as a black ring pricked her skin as it slid down her finger. Then she was someone else, a doppelganger imposter, a traitor, a lure to bring the one she loved to his knees. The images cascaded together in a jumbled mixture of truth and lies.

When the haze lifted, she was on a battlefield. The clamor of swords against shields rang in her head as grossly outnumbered mortal warriors fought against a limitless demon horde raised from the Abyss. A lone monk stepped apart from the melee and confronted a wicked archdevil. It was a brave, if not hopeless challenge.

Somehow, in the splinter of a moment, the chaos of battle ceased, as onlookers watched in fascination as the monk's hands glowed brighter than starlight and were thrust into the devil's chest. A feeling of relief followed and then nothing. That was the last memory she had of the Mortal World.

They were her stories, but seen this way they became distant tales, as if spun by a traveling merchant, retelling a fantastic story of a long-forgotten war, fought by faceless people in a faraway land.

She helped save the world, and what reward did she get for her troubles? Death, and then the shame of being cast out of the Seven Heavens, only to be abused and tortured in the Abyss. She found doom no matter where she went and wondered why she had tried so hard to do the right thing.

"The Great Balance must remain. Ha! What a joke. There was no balance. The powerful took from the weak and the weak were broken." Desdemonia said into the nothingness. There was no response, nor did she expect one.

The saying was meaningless to her in the same way that the words fate and destiny were nonsense, better to be used by poets and minstrels than anyone trying to live a good life. And that was the problem. No one took the words seriously because complete balance was impossible to achieve, let alone maintain.

For what was "good" but a point of view, conveniently named for the opposite of evil? Two words set at opposing ends of a great scale and depending on where one stood, a case could be made for the "rightness" or "wrongness" of either. The hypocrisy of the archangel, Raguel, came to mind.

"There is no good without evil, and no evil without good. One defines the other although they are part of the same," she decided. The fact that she flew using devil magic but saw her way with the light of an angel's halo were testament to the harmony of opposites.

A balance through opposites? she thought.

"You're quite the philosopher," Desdemonia chuckled to herself and flew on, beating her vaporous wings and drifting onward.

As she traveled along, she realized the bland nothingness was becoming brighter beyond the glow of her halo's luminance. Soon, she found herself squinting as the light became excessive. The haze thinned and she soon saw a pulsating, golden barrier stretching beyond sight.

"Have I reached the sun?" she wondered. But she felt no heat and beat her wings faster toward the barrier. When she eventually arrived at the surface, her curiosity overrode her better judgment, and she tentatively reached out and touched the golden wall. Yellow and white sparks tingled across her fingertips but were harmless.

This is the Amaranthine Barrier. Sekka's voice whispered in her head.

"Sure, why not? That makes as much sense as any of

this does," Desdemonia said, replying to her horrible but convenient, imaginary friend. Her eyes roamed the surface, searching for the end of the golden wall, but it extended beyond sight.

You are free.

"Hahaha. I told you I wasn't staying," She laughed aloud, then her mood became somber. "Clearly, I've gone mad, or worse, I'm lost in the void and trapped by the Amaranthine Barrier. That s just great."

She pumped her vaporous wings once, then glided parallel to the golden surface. Up or down, it didn't seem to matter which way she went, the barrier did not end.

"This got dull real fast," she grumbled.

Find the tear and you can pass through. Again, Sekka's voice, not her own. *You are close to the breach.*

True enough, the barrier's rigid surface now felt gooey, and its golden sheen turned brownish-green. She easily pushed her hand through the soupy surface.

"So, this is how you did it," Desdemonia said as if the archdevil floated next to her.

The barrier will never fully heal from the afterbirth of the Chaos Gate.

"Whatever that means," Desdemonia said, but nonetheless, she pushed her arm through to the shoulder. The sensation felt strange, like pinpricks traveling through her arm and out the other side. She pulled her arm out and saw that it was covered in moisture.

You, see? There's just enough room for one such as you to fit through.

"A freak like me, you mean?"

You are the most unique creature in the Three Worlds.

"Whatever," Desdemonia said as she eyed the gooey surface quizzically. "Might as well take the plunge and get this over with. Besides, it's not like I have anything better to do."

She flexed her wings to push her body through. The appearance of the other side was the same as the one she just left except the atmosphere was wet. Desdemonia pushed away from the barrier and coasted through a foggy mist.

She soon caught the scent of burnt wood in the atmosphere. Eventually, dark shadows came into focus through the mist, which became more distinct as she flew closer.

"Well, would you look at that," she said.

A white capped mountain range extended in a long line from north to south curling down a left side horizon. Below her and to her right was an open plain, to her left, a vast forest carpeted the land for miles. A second, cold and desolate mountain range was to the far right, just visible in the distance.

If the mountains to the right of me are the Hoarfrost, and the open plains are where I... Could it be true? Have I found my way back? she thought.

Desdemonia tucked her body and willed herself into a dive. The taste of burnt wood and charred things filled her throat and made her cough up phlegm. She spotted an area of blackness that appeared to be more of a target from her vantage point than a natural transition between climates. The snow seemed to avoid falling here as if it was forbidden. Then, the ruins of a mountain stronghold came into view.

"And if I've reached the Hoarfrost Mountains, then that must be Rachlach Fortress, or what remains of it,"

Desdemonia said, though she thought she would have more of a visceral reaction to seeing Maugris's lair. Then again, what did she care now?

Desdemonia touched down gently on the soot-covered ground, causing a small cloud of ash to swirl around her legs. Her body had weight. "Strange, I don't feel dead."

She spun around the desolate ruins. The boulders looked like globs of melted wax, while anything that may have once been cut stone for building material was pockmarked with holes and as sharp as sea coral. The area had been sterilized by fire and was now void of life.

"This place has seen better days," she said.

The temperature was mild, and a cool breeze blew through the ruins. She reckoned it was either late Spring or early Autumn. A clump of damp hair fell across her face. When she used her hand to smooth it back in place over her head, she found her horns were still protruding from her forehead.

"Some sight I must be," Desdemonia sighed as she walked around the edge of the hardened surface of the Chaos Gate.

"What do you call a freak that is half angel and half devil?" She raised her hand. "That would be me." Then chuckled despite herself.

"Oh, hi, I'm Desdemonia Mishi. Nice to meet you. Ya, I know, horns, right? And explaining the smokey wings is no picnic either."

She stopped to stare at the lifeless portal. "At least that foul thing is gone."

You did this. You were the reason he succeeded, Sekka's voice whispered in her head, taking her out of her playful antics.

"Oh no, no, no. You're not gonna haunt me here, too,

are you? Ugh. Don't you have somewhere better to be, like on Xerthotha's rack?" Desdemonia said.

We still have much to do together, child.

"Listen, it was fine when I needed a prison buddy to get me through that rough patch. But I'm home now and you need to be somewhere else."

The thought of Sekka, and the misery the archdevil had caused to the Three Kingdoms, made Desdemonia realize her appearance was going to be a problem.

"I'm way too fancy now."

It wasn't hard to make the horns recede back into her head. She had lots of practice in a previous life. The smokey vapor and halo orbs were a bit trickier to control. She couldn't figure out where they were supposed to go.

"And this outfit has seen its last day. I'm such a hot mess."

She took one more look around, though she didn't expect to see anything different.

"Nothing helpful here," she said and turned to leave the ruins.

"Oh, I wouldn't say, nothing," Sess'thra's voice spoke but her body remained hidden.

"Show yourself!" Desdemonia shouted.

"You're looking well, sister."

"I said, show yourself!"

Sess'thra materialized above the solid depression of the Chaos Gate with dark wings unfurled and stretched wide. "Ta-dah!" she exclaimed and laughed.

"How are you even still alive?" Desdemonia said, pointing an accusatory finger at the succubus. "I was told all of your kind were destroyed by the angels."

"My kind?" Sess'thra said while trying to hold back

more laughter. "Aren't you just adorable? Your horns aren't showing, but I can still see them."

"I should vaporize you right now," Desdemonia said.

"Oh stop. And I love the smokey wings? The dark and mysterious look fits you. Who did you have to sleep with to get them? I have a hunch, but tell me everything, anyways!"

"Ugh, and the nightmare continues," Desdemonia said and turned again to leave. "I should blast you into smithereens.'

"Wait! I'm coming with you. All the fascinating people are gone, and I've been terribly lonely. Well, not entirely," Sess'thra said and gave Desdemonia an exaggerated wink. "Plus, so much has changed. I'm sure you will need a guide to go wherever you are going."

"Leave me alone. I just want to go home."

"No, wait! You owe me," Sess'thra said. "If not for me, he'd be just as dead as you...were." She teleported to Desdemonia's side and sniffed around her neck and the side of her face. "You smell different."

"Time in the Abyss will do that to a girl," Desdemonia said and used her hand to swat away Sess'thra's probing nose like a bothersome gnat.

Sess'thra's eyes lit up. "I know where he is," she said, gleefully. "I can take you to him."

"Who?"

"Your Prince Charming, who else?" Sess'thra said teasingly. "Come on, that cute monk, you were so fond of before, you know, *kkkkch.*" Sess'thra drew her thumb across her throat and stuck her tongue out to one side.

"Guess what? He's all grown up now. Sadly, he spends his days sulking in his broken monastery. Such a shame. I could show you the way if you promise to play nice with me."

"Absolutely not."

"Why not?" Sess'thra stopped short and put her hands of her hips. "Well fine then, suit yourself. Next time you and your boyfriend are fighting for your life, don't expect me to butt in, no matter how interesting the outcome might be."

Desdemonia knew the succubus couldn't be trusted, and letting her live was a mistake, but she did feel a certain kinship with the demon, as horrible as that sounded. *At this point, what's the worst that can happen?* she thought.

Finding Kasai did seem like a good start to a new life. *But where to begin. Ordu? Like I have any clue where to find a hidden monastery in the mountains.*

"Ok. Only until we find Kasai. Then, I'll consider the debt paid and most likely, try to kill you."

"Wonderful!" Sess'thra said, clapping her hands excitedly.

Desdemonia wondered why she didn't feel more enthusiastic about the idea of finding Kasai. *I'm just too tired. Tired of mind and tired of heart. Or it's because I know he is going to hate what I've become.*

She took a few steps, then pivoted, thinking the way to Storm Wind Pass was in the opposite direction.

"You're not thinking of *walking* there, are you?" Sess'thra said from behind.

"Well, I'm not going to fly. That's the last thing anyone needs to see."

"Sigh, if I only had more time with you," Sess'thra said, and crossed one of her arms over her chest, while raising the other, her finger pointing in the air. "We could, oh, I don't know, teleport there."

"Ya well, I can't. Tell me where it is, and I'll meet you there. If you tire of waiting, you can leave."

Sess'thra rolled her eyes. "Seriously, sister? Sometimes, you can be so crabby. How about we try something fun? Remember when we used to do fun things together?"

"If you try to kiss me again, I will punch you right in the face. Got it?"

"Ok, ok, that can wait," Sess'thra said. "Repeat these words after me and let's see what happens. Now, concentrate on those three glassy rocks."

"There are glassy rocks everywhere," Desdemonia said in a huff.

"Just do it."

Sess'thra chanted out words, which Desdemonia repeated as instructed, albeit with little enthusiasm. Nothing happened.

"See? I told you," Desdemonia said, turning to leave. "I'm walking."

"You're either trying too hard, or not hard enough. Envision yourself at the destination and let your magic curl around the words of the spell. Now, try again," Sess'thra said. She repeated the words, slower this time.

"Fine," Desdemonia said and did as she was told. She closed her eyes and felt her magic rise as she spoke each word properly.

When she opened her eyes, she was standing by the three rocks. The smell of charred wood and stagnant air was replaced by sulfur and cinnamon.

"See! You can do it! There's hope for you yet."

"How about that, I guess I can," Desdemonia said. "Okay, let's go to Ordu."

"Slow down, hot shot. You'll need more practice before you can navigate such a far distance without seeing it first. Let's start with some shorter jumps."

"Ok, take me home," Desdemonia said.

Sess'thra gave Desdemonia a wolfish grin. "I thought you'd never ask."

18

KASAI

Kasai spent the next two weeks contemplating the connection between the Ever Hero and the lands he was meant to serve. Could it be true? Was his vitality tied to the wellbeing of the land? What if he died? Then the land perished as well? That made no sense.

Woven together like a rope, Kasai thought. He then sucked the air between his teeth, disappointed at the symbolism he conjured. *A frayed and brittle rope at best. How much time have I wasted, wallowing in self-pity? I should've been stronger. Cyrus was right. I shouldn't have turned my back on the world. But there is still time to change, to be better.*

"I need to know," Kasai said. "Cyrus is not going to be happy about this one, but when is the man happy about anything. What's one more thing going to matter?"

Kasai turned from the wall walk and made his way to the courtyard. The second of three bells were chiming. Morning practice would begin soon. He looked down to see the other monks and his friends coming out of the Zazen Hall.

Run-Run looked like a hermit from the wilderness. He

had let the stubble on his face grow into a thick beard. He couldn't speak, but the man spoke more truth than most with his clever eyes and expressive gestures.

Pallo walked slowly to the courtyard's center toward the sparring circles. He had been thrown particularly hard yesterday and was doing his best to loosen up sore spots.

"A little stiff today, old man?" Kasai chuckled.

Gift came next, followed by a trail of monks, eagerly listening to stories of Sunne and the Frona jungle tribe. She was a creative storyteller and often spoke long into the night of the histories of her people. Needless to say, Cyrus was absent during these gatherings.

Today, Kasai was going to put the teachings of Master Cyrus to the test. If he was to increase his martial skills and master his fire xindu in the ways of the Order of Symmetu, then Kasai would learn as much as he could from the crotchety master.

Cyrus often spoke of attaining enlightenment through purging one's emotions, casting them into the heart of one's fire xindu. He compared it to stoking smoldering coals to whirling flames by adding dry kindle. A monk blazing with an inferno of fire xindu could not be stopped, ever, and that was the goal.

But no matter how much fire xindu Kasai expelled, he could not settle into stable fighting style. Heightened fire xindu sparked more aggression, but it was reckless. The earth and water xindu used for balancing attack and temperament were sacrificed to the flames and left him craving more violence.

According to Cyrus, the alternative was to remain blinded, frustrated, and defeated. Kasai's strikes became faster and harder, but he was not merging his spirit xindu with the four energies of his being. The harmony and balance of fusing his xindu energies together changed to anger and frustration. A battle of wills ensued, and he was losing to himself.

It's only because I'm doing it wrong, he thought. *I just need more practice.*

Master Cyrus was last to join the group in the sparring circles. Kasai assumed he was fawning over Ninziz-zida as he was prone to do at this time of day.

"Forgive my tardiness, I was examining some old scrolls I found in misplaced crates in the catacombs, detailing the arrival of the Fire Serpent during the First Frost War," Master Cyrus said aloud, then softer for Kasai to hear. "Fascinating reading."

Kasai gave Cyrus a displeased look, then addressed the initiates. "Today we will be sparring using our fire xindu for protection rather than attack. Brother Frick, this is your first and only warning, no hurricane strikes laced with xindu energy. For that matter, any brother, who uses their fire xindu to strike instead of to defend, will face me in the circle. Understood?"

The brother monks bowed to Kasai and let them know they understood.

"Fine. To start, I ask Master Cyrus to join me in the center ring."

This startled the older monk out of his musings of scrolls and fire serpents, but Cyrus bowed his acceptance and stepped into the circle.

"Master Cyrus, please choose a position, offense or defense," Kasai said.

"Offense, of course. A Master of Symmetu always moves forward in battle."

"Fine. Now pay attention to the various blocking techniques you will see. When done correctly, each will place you in an opportunistic position for an effective counter strike, if that is your intention," Kasai said.

The two masters faced one another and bowed. Cyrus leaped forward with a knee kick that Kasai blocked with both hands. He let his fire xindu rise and felt the warm sensation fill his muscles. He stepped back and readied himself for the next strike.

"While a strong defense is admirable, a stronger attack is preferable," Cyrus said as he circled Kasai. "This has always been a shortcoming of the teachings of Ordu. At Symmetu, we learned to strike first as hard and fast as possible. Watch for your opponent's weakness, then exploit it."

The temperature within the center circle felt like the vents to an underground furnace had opened, and now billowed hot air into the cool courtyard. It was obvious to Kasai, and most likely the watchful brothers, that Cyrus was loading up his next strike with fire xindu.

Kasai braced himself. He consciously held his water xindu down to allow his fire xindu to spike. Cyrus came at him in a flash. Fire xindu lit his steps and the man moved faster than humanly possible. The blow that hit Kasai came from the opposite side of where he expected it to land.

Kasai responded quickly and spun in a pirouette to let the momentum of Cyrus's strike build speed into his own attack. If Cyrus was going to ignore his rules of engagement, then so would he. Kasai planted his foot and shot back toward Cyrus.

He launched a fist that burned with fire xindu energy past Cyrus's face. Then, in the same moment Cyrus turned away from it, Kasai kicked out and struck the back of Cyrus's leg.

Cyrus absorbed the blow by arching his body into the kick, leaving him momentarily off balance. Kasai planted his foot and caught Cyrus in the jaw with the elbow of his extended arm. The movement was fluid, exact, and painful.

Cyrus hit the ground. He scrambled crablike to regain his footing, but Kasai was there and sent the heel of his open palm into Cyrus's face. Blood exploded from the older monk's nose, and he hit the ground again. Kasai wasn't sorry.

Master Cyrus looked up at Kasai in dazed amazement as he wiped the blood from his face. Then he nodded knowingly, perhaps acknowledging that he had been defeated or that Kasai had mastered a new level of xindu control.

"Thank you for your participation, Master Cyrus. I think they understand the lesson now."

Kasai reached his hand out to help Cyrus up. He brushed some debris off Cyrus's shoulder and bowed, then stepped out of the circle. Cyrus followed.

"I see not everything I say to you is worthless," Cyrus said, straightening out his robes.

Kasai directed Brother Sondru and Brother Mando into the circle and signaled them to begin.

"I was simply doing as your masters instructed you," Kasai said, then decided to breach the subject of a walkabout. "It's time to revisit the Three Kingdoms. There is much we can do to help the frontier villages, even if it's just one family at a time."

"Monks of the Orders of Light carry a heavy responsibility. They're not ready for the burden they will encounter or the blame of fault they will receive," Cyrus said, mustering up an air of superiority to calm his wounded pride. "It's a wonder any of them managed to survive for this long."

"I wasn't ready the first time I left the monastery either."

Cyrus raised a bushy eyebrow at that remark.

"But help is needed, and we will do what we can. The Three Kingdoms will benefit knowing the Monks of Aetenos are still here and ready to serve."

"Let us discuss this matter later, in private, shall we?" Cyrus said. He then gesticulated wildly with his arms. "No, no, no, not like that Sondru. How many times must I repeat myself? It's forearm block, step, step, then kick."

Kasai slowly shook his head as the older monk walked into the sparring circle to show Brother Sondru the correct movement to block and counter a high kick using fire xindu.

"I don't much care what you think, Cyrus. We're going," Kasai said to himself.

"What's the matter with him?" Pallo said, coming over to congratulate Kasai on his decisive sparring match.

"He's a little ornery, just like my old masters. But he's helping me learn a new way. I'm thankful for his guidance," Kasai said.

"Ever Hero, you've walked through Heaven and Hell. What guidance can he give one as you?"

"You were there with me, and we have learned a great deal of the workings of the Three Worlds. But no matter our personal experiences, there is always something to be gained by listening to and understanding the perspective of others."

"But—"

"Pallo, old friend, we must never stop learning, otherwise we will never move on from the thoughts that hinder our growth."

He had wrestled with this thought himself for many years. Living a content life had seemed dishonorable to Desdemonia's memory, when she had paid the ultimate price, and he had lived.

Perhaps Cyrus was right when he said the Ever Hero and the people he was meant to serve were connected. As he wallowed in self-pity and reclusion, the people of the Three Kingdoms suffered. That was wrong and selfish. But it wasn't too late to change. He would honor her sacrifice by living life to its fullest.

Kasai spotted Gift spinning in a whirling kick across the courtyard that knocked Run-Run out of their sparring circle. Then, quick as a shadow cat, she shifted her weight and planted her kicking foot, took a step back with the other and threw a sharp punch at Brother Tran. The younger monk never saw it coming and dropped at her feet.

"She has a balanced attack, using all of her xindu energies," Kasai said proudly, pointing her out to Pallo. He had taught Gift the move just yesterday. She was a quick study.

Gift looked in Kasai's direction and gave him a broad smile. Her body glistened with sweat and the residue sheen of water xindu energy.

"Does Master Cyrus know you are teaching her something different?"

"She's marvelous," Kasai said. The muscular curves of her body were strong and subtle. He had always thought of her as a fierce warrior-mage who wielding magic as easily as any weapon. But now...

"Ever Hero, you look genuinely happy," Pallo said. "I believe this is a first for you."

"It's good to be surrounded by friends again."

"I think a little more than that, eh. Don't worry, your secret is safe with me and Run-Run."

Kasai's gaze drifted back to Gift. She was sparring again. This time, three brothers rushed her from different angles. "She is a well-balanced fighter."

"And?"

"What do you mean? That's it. Gift is a blessing to all of us."

Pallo patted him on the shoulder and walked to the sparring circles to see his brother. Run-Run was sitting on the ground, tuckered out.

"You've always been a poor liar, Ever Hero," he said over his shoulder. Then, "Run-Run, I saw that kick coming from a mile away. You're getting slow, old man."

Run-Run scowled at his brother and got up. He moved to a different sparring circle, pointed at Pallo, and signaled him to follow. Kasai's eyes shifted back to Gift.

"Stunning," he said, feeling a queer jolt of excitement shoot through his body.

The night air was unseasonably warm as the Southern Winds blew a last breath through the Sarribe Mountains. The full moon bathed the courtyard in blue light as dead leaves rustled and tumbled across the open ground.

"Just once I'd like to sleep throughout the night," Kasai mumbled to himself as he moseyed through the square on his way to the wall walk. Warm nights always brought him outdoors. Sometimes he would just stand in the moonlight, staring up at the night sky and sparkling stars, thinking of her.

"I should've done more sooner," he said. "Something. Anything."

"Master Kasai, am I disturbing you?" Gift whispered from behind him.

He had heard her coming and didn't choose to turn around. "Why are you awake?"

"I never sleep well away from the jungle. I sense there is something troubling you. Not just now, but always."

Kasai sighed. Nights were worse for bringing out bad memories. "It's been six years and it still feels as if it was yesterday."

"Only because you cling to your guilt as if it would save you from drowning," Gift said as she walked beside him. "Yet, it is the same weight which holds you under the water of your sorrows."

"You're probably right. Still, waking up each morning in a cold sweat from seeing the face of death framed in snow-white hair staring at you, can darken any man's day. If I had died here with my brothers, then..."

"Then the world would be without the Ever Hero and that is a disheartening thought. I remember the day you decided to leave the stupid monk behind and become Master Kasai. What happened to that man?"

"I think he died with Des, just in a different way."

"You mustn't let you best memories bring you sadness. Enjoy them and hold them safe in your heart until the time of reawakening."

"Hold it safe," Kasai said. "She once said that to me."

"Hold what safe?" Gift asked.

"It was a special secret we shared," Kasai said, looking back into the night sky.

"You can find love again. It exists in abundance all around you. You need only ask for it to join you."

She was close to him now, close enough to smell the exotic fragrance of jungle wildflowers on her skin, in her sweat. The moonlight gave a blue sheen to her dark skin. She was tall, slender, and muscular, yet still held the curves of a woman.

"And your nights need not be lonely," she said softly.

Kasai looked deeply into her dark eyes and his throat tightened. His heart thumped against the walls of his chest. She edged closer, eyeing him like a hungry predatory. He wanted her and she was there to be taken, the sway of her body told him as much.

"You should probably go back to bed before I do something stupid," Kasai said, though half-heartedly.

"And what stupid thing would that be, Master Kasai?"

He kissed her, hard, like Desdemonia had done in the jungle years before.

She kissed him back, harder. A warm breeze blew past. He was hot. Sweating. Her clothes needed to come off. She didn't object.

"Maybe we should take this inside."

"No, Nayche's sister will witness our joining," Gift said, raising her eyes to the full moon.

Kasai kissed her again. He didn't care about sister moon, or brother sun or whatever any of her mumblings meant. All he wanted was more of her. His mouth kissed down her neck and his hands moved over her swelling breasts.

Her hands reached down under his robes. She grabbed him and squeezed. Kasai stopped worrying and started enjoying life's abundance.

Just like a strand of rope, Kasai thought while laying entwined with Gift's body after they had finished. His breathing had calmed, and a cool sweat coated his body. He could feel his blood pulsing through his chest with each heartbeat.

"Now, will you tell me what troubles your nights?" Gift said as she curled into him.

"I've lost something and I'm not sure if I will ever find it again."

"You must let her sleep, Master Kasai," Gift said. "She will awaken when it is her time."

"I'm talking about the Boundless. It only came to me in moments of dire need, and even then, I'm not sure how or why. Master Cyrus is convinced it is because I was possessed by Aetenos, and it was his power I wielded and not my own. Either way, now it's gone. Have I been judged an unworthy coward, who hides behind walls when the land suffers?"

"You are not a coward," Gift said, "You are a warrior. You *are* the Ever Hero."

"That may still be true. Maybe not. I don't know. I no longer hear the song of Aetenos," Kasai replied. "And who races into the jaws of death as a way of life?"

"It's fear. But I think you are misunderstanding the value of fear. One must always understand the times of life and the times of death. You have known too much death and perhaps are fearful you will never know the equal proportion of life, and the love that comes with it, and that is why you hide."

"It's getting cold. Time to go inside and sleep."

Kasai kissed Gift again and disentangled himself from her arms and legs.

"I'll stay and commune with Nayche," Gift said.

Kasai dressed and returned to his room. He fell asleep quickly but suffered through a nightmare of Desdemonia blocking the metaphysical entrance to the Boundless.

"Don't leave me," she said. "You can't abandon me. Not again."

He woke suddenly and with a touch of the shakes.

"It's my fault you're dead," Kasai said. "And my guilt is blocking me from entering the Boundless. I must let you go, Des. I'm sorry."

Unconsciously, a single tear rolled down either side of his face. Then he remembered Gift's words. "Too much death and not enough life."

"She's right. It's time for more life."

The next night, Kasai waited patiently at the center of the courtyard where he had been standing alone for almost an hour, trying to calm his mind. A travel pack rested on the ground at his feet. His sleep was restless, and his thoughts darted from one uncomfortable memory to the next. There was a chill in the air as the northerly winds pushed into the southern regions of the Sarribe Mountains.

Master Cyrus approached from the master's dormitory.

"Winter will be here soon," Kasai said, as a cloud of breath escaped his mouth. The morning sun had not risen, and the older monk had a heavy frock pulled over his head, cloaking him in darkness.

"Master Kasai, a word before we speak with the young ones."

"Yes, Master Cyrus?"

"During my evening stroll through the complex, I ventured by the Hall of Artifacts. I noticed the Fire Serpent had been removed."

"She's tucked away. No more distractions."

"I see. Maybe you should tell me where she is kept. The staff must not be lost if anything should happen to you on this expedition."

Kasai eyed him suspiciously. "I'll be fine."

Gift was next to appear. She moved gracefully across the yard, smooth and purposeful. The cold did not agree with her, but she didn't complain. Pallo, Run-Run and the ten monks of Nu-Ordu came last. One by one they filed into two lines before Kasai and Cyrus, each equipped with a pack filled with traveling supplies.

Kasai waited for everyone to settle down before he began.

"There is more to following the Ways of Aetenos than endless training, chores, and meditation," Kasai said, eliciting some hopeful looks from the older monks in the front row.

"You must also be of service to the people of the Three Kingdoms. We are leaving the monastery and traveling to the frontier villages of Baroqia. Our mission is to help with the last harvest, mend roofs, cut wood, and tend to the sick."

"Are we to become Traveling Masters, then, Master Kasai?" Sondru said, hopefully.

This elicited a scowl from Master Cyrus. "Brother Sondru, you of all people shouldn't be asking such a ridiculous question." He shook his head from side to side. "Ordu has been known to elevate rank too quickly. I assure you those days are gone."

The old, cranky master stepped in front of Kasai to pace parallel to the monks. "Now, as you have witnessed during the six years before coming to the monastery, the aftermath of the war left scars not only on the people who fought, but also across the land where the battles raged."

When he reached the end of the first line, he turned his head quickly to the right, looking past Brother Che's shoulder to stare at Brother Tran, who had made the mistake of yawning at that exact moment.

"Brother Tran, perhaps you would like to remain behind as caretaker of the monastery, since this is of such little interest to you."

"I'm sorry, Master Cyrus. Forgive me."

Cyrus sighed angrily. "How do you expect to master the xindu mysteries if you cannot master your basic bodily functions?"

"Yes, Master Cyrus," Tran said, straightening his back and looking straight ahead.

Cyrus turned back and paced to the other end of the first line, clearing his throat.

"The world beyond these walls has always been a dangerous place, perhaps more so now than ever before. Demon sighting has become commonplace, and the people are sick, starving, and desperate.

"Although your training is far from complete, you will use what you have learned to serve and protect the kingdoms. You are conceivably the last monks of the Orders of Light and are forbidden to bring shame to the monastery. Your actions will reflect on all of us."

"Thank you, Master Cyrus," Kasai said. "All right, let's get a move on then. There's plenty of work to do."

The small expedition traveled down the Sarribe Mountains along the foothills into the Kingdom of Baroqia. With the help of Run-Run and Pallo, Kasai had laid out a route that connected one village to the next, like the links in a chain. The monks would offer their time and service, then move on.

The group would journey through four seasons before returning to Nu-Ordu the following Autumn. Kasai estimated they would visit roughly ten frontier villages and two smaller towns in that time, traveling in a northern pattern parallel to the mountains. He was optimistic the settlements still existed, though Cyrus was quick to put a damper on that hope.

Kasai wondered how the village he was born in had faired through the years. The home he grew up in and the woods surrounding it seemed a distant memory, belonging to someone else. He wondered how much of that little boy still existed within him.

"So much has changed," he said softly. His eyes drifted to Gift. Although he didn't feel the same awkward and intense emotions that he had felt for Desdemonia, Kasai knew he cared for the graceful warrior. She was an apt student and a good friend.

For her part, Gift was teaching him how to live not only as a monk, sheltered behind monastery walls, or as the Ever Hero, savior of the Three Kingdoms, but also as a man. She was a sleek and strong panther while sparring, and an adventurous lover when they shared their nights together.

He watched her move over boulders with ease. She was as one with nature as she was with fighting with a bo staff or wielding Elemenati magic. Gift was perfect.

Kasai adjusted the pack on his back. He was still sore from their love-making the night before. His legs ached with each step over the uneven and rocky terrain. A fond memory of her back up against the outer monastery wall, her legs wrapped around his waist as her body rose and fell with his.

The trek to the first village was uneventful. Although there was no direct route, or marked path, Run-Run was a competent guide and kept the group surefooted and safe. Within ten days, they arrived at the first village nestled within the foothills of the Sarribe Mountains—and found it deserted.

"As I have said, much has changed," Cyrus said. "The fires destroyed everything it touched. The fall harvest was lost, and the few frontier villagers that survived fled back to the safety of the bigger towns and cities, or what was left of them."

Kasai scanned the village, though he was not sure of what or for whom he was searching. Then, the cool, crisp air of Autumn turned humid and the gentle breeze that had accompanied them for much of their trek, picked up to a warm, gusting wind.

"Smells like a heavy rain pour is nearby," Kasai said.

"I can't recall experiencing thunderstorms this late in the season," Pallo said with a concerned expression. "By this late month the scent of the first snow should be in the air."

Run-Run's eyes scanned the sky, and the dark skin across Gift's knuckles turned white as her grip on the spear shaft tightened.

"That's not the smell of snow," Gift said, taking a defensive position.

"Oh no," Kasai said.

Three balls of electricity crackled to life, surrounding the small party within the three points of a perfect triangle. Kasai instinctively put his arm up to shield his eyes. The younger monks weren't so quick and stared wide-eyed into the blinding light.

Then, three successive booms pounded the ground around them, followed by accompanying shock-waves that slammed into the blackened timber of the surrounding, derelict buildings. The outer porch of one collapsed in a heap. When the light and heat from the charges dissipated, three angels stood surrounding the small party. While their divine faces were beautiful and flawless to behold, their eyes held the small party in terrible judgment.

Kasai immediately recognized Lord Raguel's equerry, Sonnalle. The angel's long, blonde hair flowed down to his armored shoulders. He was clad in golden battle gear etched with various markings and equipped for war. The two Protectorates accompanying him held spear and shield ready.

"Did you think you could evade us so easily by leaving the mountain hideaway? Your trail was easy enough to follow from the jungles. Now, where is she? You cannot hide her forever."

"To the Abyss with you and your demands!" Gift said menacingly. "The Frona Tribe protects their own."

She stepped forward. Her magic flared to life and her body sparkled with a thin blue sheen. "She is protected by Nayche and is beyond your reach."

"So convinced are you in your primitive beliefs and superstitions," Sonnalle said. "She was sent to the Abyss, where she belonged. Is that where your false goddess dwells as well?"

"The Abyss? That's impossible!" Kasai's heart missed a beat and his throat tightened. "You had no right! We did what was demanded to prove our innocence."

"And she died. Yet, the wood witch's soul has an uncommon strength and perseverance."

"What? Des is alive?"

Sonnalle smirked. "My lord Raguel believes she has somehow managed to slip through Xerthotha's fingers and has escaped the Abyss, though I think this is highly unlikely."

He stepped closer to Kasai. "Nonetheless, I am here to follow my lord's orders and bring her back to him. I will not ask again. Where is she? We will have her back."

"No, you won't!" Kasai said, stepping back. "Leave her be."

Kasai felt his fire xindu ignite into a ball of fire in his heart. His hands burned like hot coals. Sonnalle glanced down at the amber and orange radiating from Kasai's hands and gave him a patronizing smile.

"Desdemonia Mishi has changed. She is no longer the human you once knew."

"If your divine eyes can track a Sunnese warrior so easily, why would the one you search for be so elusive? What else hides from your ever seeing eyes I wonder," Cyrus said, matching the angel's haughty attitude. Kasai was surprised at his boldness.

"If you do not comply with my wishes, you will be destroyed," Sonnalle said with finality. The two Protectorates lowered their spears into an attack position.

Then a flash of lightning followed by a thunderous

boom presented another angel to the group. He rushed to Sonnalle's side.

"My lord. We've found her. She's close."

Sonnalle glanced at Kasai and held up his hand to stop the angel from revealing more.

"Are you sure."

"Yes, my lord."

"Show me."

Sonnalle muttered undecipherable words of power and four bolts of lightning hit where each angel stood. When the dust cleared, small fires burned on the ground. Sonnalle and the Protectorate were gone.

"What's going on here?" Pallo exclaimed, coming to Kasai's side.

"Get everyone together. We're leaving," Kasai said. He removed his pack from his shoulders and placed it on the ground. After a quick rummage, he pulled out a package wrapped in blue cloth.

"What is that?" Cyrus said in disbelief.

"It's time," Kasai said, and headed across the town square.

"The Fire Serpent is here?" Cyrus said aghast while trailing behind Kasai. "Where do you think you are going?"

"If they want a fight, I'll give them a fight."

"Fight? Are you insane? We cannot get involved in the business of angels. *You,* especially, should not get involved," Cyrus said, trying to hold Kasai back. "They are likely to steal the Fire Serpent, or worse, destroy her."

"Desdemonia is alive. Release me. I'm going."

"If you must be so careless with your own life, so be it. But you will do so without the staff. It is an artifact of the Orders and must be protected at all costs," Cyrus said, releasing Kasai's robe and folding his arms across his chest. "The Fire Serpent shall remain with me."

"Don't be ridiculous. She loathes cowards and would burn you to a crisp if you touched her."

Cyrus's face went pale, unsure if what Kasai said was true. "You would give up everything you have learned to the Fire Serpent's greed. This is a crucial time in your training," he pleaded. "You will never rise to the rank of a true Master of Ordu, while you rely on the staff as a crutch."

"Des needs me. The angels want her dead. I know it. Now is not the time to test your theories."

"It's the exact time to do what must be done. You will do more damage to yourself, and those you profess to love, if you fail to heed my warning.

"Think about your reckless intention for a moment. You intend to wield the honorable Fire Serpent against the lawful angels! That is heresy!"

Kasai stopped walking. *He might be right. But to go against angels unarmed was insanity.*

Kasai gripped Ninziz-zida tightly. "Are we still stronger together?"

Always, the staff pulsed back.

He looked to the edge of town and gathered his determination. Kasai had a hunch that if Des was close, that probably meant home.

"Pallo, get the others and follow me. I'm not losing her again," Kasai said, and marched off to find the cozy cottage in the woods.

19

DESDEMONIA

Desdemonia's first teleportation brought her
and Sess'thra to the fields outside the ruins of
Winter's Fury. They arrived holding hands, which
Desdemonia quickly dropped. Sekka's tower was gone,
melted like every other diabolical thing that had tarnished
the land.

Good riddance, Desdemonia thought.

Any of the dead that had not been consumed by the
flames and turned to ash had been cleared away long ago.
Late blooming wildflowers surfed on a sea of flowing long
grass. There was a scattered mix of violet toadflax, lavender
devil's bit scabious, and bright yellow, nettle-leaved
bellflowers as far as the eyes could see.

Desdemonia waded through the long, flowing blades as
if she was traversing a shallow pond. Her fingers pricked
against the seed heads as they brushed passed. The land was
slowly healing itself. Balance was being restored.

She made her way to the ruins with Sess'thra following
close behind. Piles of glassy rubble and mounds of molten

slag replaced the buildings of the city. A raised path of stone lining the perimeter was no more than a thigh-high reminder of the great wall which had once surrounded the interior.

A short time later, she was at the edge of the pit that had surrounded Sekka's tower like a bottomless moat. Her legs felt weak as she peered into the deep chasm. She had no fear of heights, but the blackness of the pit left her feeling nauseous.

"We need to leave. I think I'm going to be sick," Desdemonia said. Her insides squirmed like a thousand earthworms rushing out of the ground after a rainstorm.

She glanced over at Sess'thra, who stared at her with curious wonder and then turned her head to the central column in the pit. Desdemonia figured the sneaky succubus was up to one of her tricks.

"This wasn't the home I envisioned in my mind," Desdemonia said, doing her best to steady herself. "We're not staying. This place is haunted."

"Yet, your magic brought us here, mistress," Sess'thra said, subtlety, as if she were probing for a particular response.

"What did you call me?" Desdemonia demanded.

"Mistress. You're the new mistress of the tower, aren't you?" Sess'thra said, as if that was obvious. "Blood of her blood, no? Someone must carry on the line."

"Mistress of the tower? You're crazy. That's not going to be me. Come on. Another jump will take us to the foothills of the Sarribe. I want to check on an old friend."

"Perhaps a slight rest first," Sess'thra said, watching her carefully. "Teleportation requires a steady mind, and one misstep can lead to disastrous results."

Desdemonia felt as if the days and nights without rest had suddenly come due. Her body felt heavy and sluggish, and she couldn't keep her eyes open. All she wanted to do was sleep.

"Maybe you're right. I do feel a bit off. No funny business, now. I'll rest for an hour and then we'll go."

"Funny business? Me?" Sess'thra said with a shocked expression. "I would never think of such a thing, *mistress*."

"Whatever. Just wake me in an hour. I want to jump again before nightfall."

Desdemonia's body and mind faded into a deep slumber. Soon after, the nightmarish scene of a magnificent, infernal tower rose from a pit of darkness in her mind. She saw Sekka standing between the crenels of a high wall. Her white hair unfurled in the wind.

An army of demons marched across snow-covered grasslands. Villages and small towns fell to their cruel madness. Sekka's gleeful laugher echoed in the distance. It rolled toward her like the tumbling clouds of a thunderstorm, amplifying as it gathered momentum.

Sekka's laugher swept her up in a rush, pulling its way through her until it was gone, leaving her feeling empty and alone. Desdemonia woke with a start. She looked around and realized the afternoon hour had turned to early morning.

"Why did you let me sleep all night?" Desdemonia said, annoyed and still feeling drained. She eyed Sess'thra suspiciously. "What did you do to me?"

"Why do you always assume I'm the villain?"

"Because you are one."

"But in the best possible way, right?"

"Ugh. You're impossible. Let's just go."

The next landing spot was a meadow walled by three cliff sides and the opening to a forest, which had burned in the fiery aftermath caused by the angels' wrath. Now, silent, black statues stood as ghostly reminders of the ancient trees' former glory.

But the forest's roots were strong, and after years of hibernation, the trees had reawakened to a new life. The rich smell of saplings and new growth of ground brush along the foothills of the Sarribe Mountains filled the air. More wildflowers had pushed through the blackened earth and bloomed with the Autumn rains.

Desdemonia was sure she was in the right spot. This was where she and Gauldumor had rescued Kasai and Master Choejor from the pack of vargru. That memory of that meeting seemed like a lifetime ago. Oh, the stories she would tell Gauldi when she was finally home.

Desdemonia immediately headed for her cottage, knowing in her heart that it had somehow survived the fires. Gauldumor's magic was strong. He would keep it safe.

Life and death, she thought. *Another balance of opposites. There is not one without the other.*

"I must say, you're a quick study. We've crossed a third of the Three Kingdoms in only two jumps. You've learned a thing or two while you were away," Sess'thra said as she hurried to Desdemonia's side. "You've been with Xerthotha, haven't you? I can tell. He's just the worst, isn't he? What did he do to you? Something fabulous, I'm sure."

"Don't you ever stop talking? Come on, we're almost there."

"Oh, don't be such a grouch." Sess'thra said as she

looked right and left, taking in their new surroundings. "This certainly looks like you, but a bit too colorful for me."

Then Sess'thra stopped short and looked behind her as if they were being followed, then turned back to Desdemonia. She took in a deep draught of air and held it. Her eyes shifted back and forth as she deciphered the smell.

"What is it?" Desdemonia said.

Sess'thra raised her eyebrow and then wrinkled her nose. "Well, that's unpleasant."

"What, the wildflowers?"

"No, it's something else," Sess'thra said, "Probably nothing, but I'm gonna pass on this sentimental homecoming. I have something better to do."

The succubus's eyes raised upward and her expression turned worrisome. "Plus, it looks like rain."

"Suit yourself. But remember your promise. I will meet you back here in two days. Then we will continue to Ordu," Desdemonia said. "Got it?"

"Don't worry, I'll be back. I can't wait to see the look on that cute monk's face when he sees you again."

"You'd better. I'm only letting you live so I can find Kasai."

"Mmmhmm. Well then, ta-ta, time to fly." Sess'thra blew Desdemonia a kiss and vanished with a pop.

"Stupid succubus."

Desdemonia turned towards the woods and hopefully her cottage. The rainclouds gathered quickly and soon the pitter patter of falling drops echoed around her.

"Well, she got the rain part right."

The cool water collected in her hair, then dripped down her face. Soon her skin was wet and covered in gooseflesh. It was wonderful. It felt like home.

The rainwater was cleansing and gave her hope that things might be different from now on. Maybe she would find Kasai, maybe she wouldn't. If she did, and he didn't approve of her transformation, well then that was going to be his problem.

For now, she would stay in her little cozy cottage and forget about the world for a while. The rest would do her good. She was tired of fighting. Let the world solve its own problems. She had done enough.

The cottage was not far, and she soon saw familiar trees that had miraculously survived the cataclysm. Their bark had been scorched, and many boughs had been reduced to unsightly stumps, but the ancient trees had persevered through the fires.

Desdemonia stopped to watch the gentle giants swaying in the wind, bending to one side, then curling back the other way. The tranquil movement was in perfect harmony.

Everything returns to a balanced center, she thought.

Soon, she recognized the clearing where her modest home still stood.

"Gauldi, I knew you'd keep our home safe," she said with a smile and wiped water from her face. "Come out and see me, old mud pie!"

Then, the isolated and lonely feelings she held for the cottage returned. She had left the jungle to start a new life after the death of her parents. But the world outside of Sunne was ignorant, and those who lived in the towns and cities of Baroqia were driven by fear, hatred, or lust for power.

She had been an outcast and needed to stay hidden

from those that would persecute her for her magic. They did stupid things, hurtful things, to anything they didn't or refused to understand.

She could hear their cruel voices in her mind. "Watch out! It's the Wicked Witch of the Forest! Catch her! Burn her! Don't let her touch you. She'll turn you into something nasty."

Is it even worth it?

Desdemonia called to Gauldumor again. This time, the earth rumbled softly under two old logs, leaning against a pile of rocks. A whirlwind of dead leaves, spun together with mud, twigs, and mulch, then compressed together into massive, humanoid figure.

Two gleaming eyes opened and narrowed upon seeing Desdemonia.

"The forest mourned your death. Yet here you are among the trees and flowers of the vale. You're reawakening should not be so soon."

"Sheesh. Everyone's a critic. How about I'm happy to see you, too, Des?" Desdemonia said with her hands on her hips.

Gauldumor stomped closer. "Your scent is different."

"I get that a lot these days."

"And the boy monk?"

"You were right about him, and I helped him as best I could. But so much has changed now. I feel like I've lived a hundred lifetimes since we parted."

"Was your sacrifice worth it?"

"You mean to save the realm? Yes, of course. Well, I think it was." Desdemonia sighed. "I don't know. Sekka was a horror, but the other side of the coin wasn't much better, at least not for me."

"And now you've becomes a being of light and a creature of darkness," Gualdumor said as he lumbered along beside her.

"I could never hide anything from you, old friend." Desdemonia released the black vapor that formed her wings and let her horns sprout from her forehead. The halo orbs appeared and continued to spin around her head.

"It's a cruel joke, I know. I'm still me, but I feel... uncontained, like I've been stretched beyond sight but I'm still physically here."

The earth golem grunted and frowned. "Your essence extends into the Outer Realms. You have been touched by the divine and filled with deep chaos magic."

"Lovely. As if the horns weren't enough. Come on, I'll tell you all about it the after I've had a rest. I'm exhausted." She shifted back to her normal appearance. For now, it seemed like the right thing to do.

"By the way, what's a daimus nexus?"

Gauldumor stopped and craned his neck, twisting his enormous head upward, searching for a scent in the air. A low rumble from the earth golem turned to a deep growl.

"A storm comes."

"What gave it away, the rain?" Desdemonia said.

The air became charged with static, lifting her hair off her skin. Something was burning. Then, a bolt of lightning lit up the forest, pulverizing the tree that dared to stand in its way. The environment shimmered out of focus just before another intense light blinded her. The following BOOM tossed Desdemonia several feet into the air.

When she could see clearly again, Sonnalle and a squad of armored Protectorates were arranged in a semi-circle around her. Each held a long spear and shield, with a sword sheathed at their side. Their golden armor glimmered with residual sparks.

"Wood witch. You are ordered to return to the Seven Heavens," Sonnalle said in commanding tone.

"I'm not going anywhere with you," Desdemonia said, picking herself off the ground.

"This was a command by Lord Raguel, and not a request. You're coming with me. Take her."

The angels leaped at her and Gauldumor attacked. He snatched the nearest angel as it shot past him. The air burned with the smell of chaos magic as his earthen hands flared with Elementati energy. The angel grunted then screamed as he was crushed in Gauldumor's powerful grip. A second angel agilely swerved away from the earth golem and grabbed Desdemonia.

She shouted in anger then let her magic erupt from deep within her soul. What had once been the yellows and greens of the forest now bloomed as deep purples and blues, surrounding her in a protective aura, repelling the angel. A symphony of howls and screams from unseen allies surrounded her and kept the angels at bay.

"The trickster wields the forbidden magic of the enemy!" the angel cried out.

Gauldumor tossed the angel he had killed into the trees. The mangled warrior landed awkwardly among the branches, looking like a broken scarecrow. Desdemonia yelled out a warning when she saw three angels rush behind Gauldumor with their spears leveled at his back.

Gauldumor howled in agony as electricity ripped through his body. Large chunks of his midsection exploded in bits and pieces of wood and stone. The golem twisted fast and took the angels off guard, forcing them to lose their grip on the spear shafts.

Four more angels flew at Gauldumor. Two attacked from above, while the other two spun off in a wide arc to either side of the earth golem. The three who had lost their spears drew their swords. Gauldumor charged blindly, but the airborne angels spun away like diving raptors. They were too fast for his blind rage. Each of their connecting blows, blocks, or stab wounds carved off more of the mighty earth golem.

Desdemonia gathered her magic as she had done in the Abyss. She felt the storm clouds heed her call, rolling and rumbling together.

"You want a fight? I'll give you a fight."

Her hand shot above her head and ripped down a bolt of lightning that bounced off the ground, splintering into separate chains before striking the angels coming at her. The electric bolts did little to stop them. They reached her at the same time, grabbing her arms and holding her tight.

"Get off me!" Desdemonia said, struggling to free herself. She glanced over at Gauldumor. The earth golem was on his knees and surrounded by angels pummeling him from all sides. Crackling strands of lightning bounced across his back. One arm had been severed from his shoulder and was quickly decomposing on the ground.

"Gauldumor! Escape! Return to the earth!" Desdemonia shouted.

Gauldumor's eyes found hers and he let out a mournful bellow and tried to rise one last time. Desdemonia caught the bright light of a sword being drawn. Sonnalle walk casually towards her friend and protector, drawing his sword from its sheath. The blade glowed as if lit from within.

Desdemonia had heard of oblivion swords, the holy blades of divine champions. The weapons were made to banish the creatures of chaos to the realm of non-existence. Sonnalle held one now. The True-born angel gave her a look of disappointment, saying without words that this could have been avoided. With an elegant swipe, Gauldumor's head came away from his body.

The rocks, roots, branches, and dirt that composed his body separated and fell in a burning heap of discarded mulch. The magic which had knitted his constructed form together escaped in a hiss.

"Gauldi!" Desdemonia shouted.

Sonnalle's smile was smug and cruel. "Now, you will…"

Desdemonia screamed the high-pitched wail of a banshee devil. The angels holding her fast were thrown violently to the ground. Blood leaked between gauntleted fingers from their ruptured eardrums. Their cries of pain were drowned out by Desdemonia's agonizing howl.

The angels surrounding Gauldumor's remains fell to their knees, covering their ears. Sonnalle took two steps back, then wiped the bright red snot from his nose.

"One way or another, Abomination, you're coming with me," Sonnalle said.

The angels closest to him rose on shaky legs but soon regained their composure. Their armor shimmered as sparkling light danced over its surface. The painful grimaces were gone, replaced by a look of serenity. They found their swords and stalked toward her. Desdemonia saw other angels crawling on the ground, searching for their lost weapons.

"Your primitive beast should not have gotten involved," Sonnalle said. "Though, I think this world will not mourn the loss of another demon."

"He wasn't a demon! He was my friend. Gauldi didn't have to die. He was only protecting me. Why can't you just leave me alone?"

"Your fate is not mine to decide. Perhaps, you were simply made to suffer."

She gritted her teeth as tears ran down her cheeks. "I hate you."

The squad of Protectorates slowly edged closer, surrounding her. She could fight, and die, again or run for her life. Leaping into the sky came to mind, and she absentmindedly looked upward.

"Your feelings are irrelevant," Sonnalle said. His eyes followed hers and he sadly shook his head. "There is nowhere for you to fly to that we cannot go."

Then, a sly smile came to her face. "Well, see, there you're wrong. See you boys around."

In a flash, Desdemonia teleported away.

20

SHIVERRIG

The morning's moist autumn air was warming in the breakfast sun. If the clouds held off, it would be a mild afternoon. The air was filled with the mulchy scent of tilled earth, freshly picked vegetables, and slowly dying leaves.

The farmstead was absent of idle conversation or the gruff sounds of hard work. Sensing perhaps the arrival of unnatural creatures, blue jays and robins had flown elsewhere looking for uncovered worms and grubs for their morning breakfast. Only the cawing crows remained, circling overhead, waiting.

Shiverrig's troops had descended on the farm just before first light. The family overseeing the harvest had died quickly to blades in the dark. Foolishly, they had tried to run. The laborers who rose at first cockcrow were already in the fields and were easily rounded up.

"If your lord had pledged his banner to me, this madness could have been avoided," Shiverrig said to the scrawny man he held aloft with one massive hand wrapped around his throat.

"But the greed of House Conrad slithered into his veins, and like a parasite, it sucked away any small amount of loyalty and honor he might have possessed."

"I don't know who or what you are," the terrified man said, unwisely trading words for precious air. "I'm just a farmer. We work under Duke Nathor's protection. His manor is a day's ride from here."

"Nathor? There is no duke or noble house by that name."

The farm hand shook his head in the affirmative, eyes wide with fear. Shiverrig watched as the other frightened farmhands nodded the same. Each one flinched away when he looked in their direction. Presumably, it had been years since they had seen a monster.

Lord Nathor, and whatever guards or men-at-arms he bankrolled, had not bothered to confront Shiverrig and his men as they trespassed the boundaries of his estate. Likely, the man was hiding, assuming another band of bandits had come to steal some supplies and possibly one or two women and leave.

Nothing had changed. The noble class was weak and held power through the lure of shiny coins, not will of force. There were no champions to protect the vulnerable, no battle lords or war dukes to repel invading marauders. These were feeble men acting as merchants, dealing in human need from suffering.

The kingdom was mine by blood right. But those who were honor bound to follow me, kept their coffers full of gold by betraying me. And so, I have become the monster they feared.

Shiverrig's eyes narrowed. He would deal with the self-proclaimed noble in time, just as he had the others.

"Who am I?" Shiverrig growled in the face of a farmhand. "I am your Aj-Kahun."

"What's an Aj-Kahun?"

Shiverrig gave a sideways glance to Dai-Ko-Zior. "Should we impale the lot to appease your dark gods as we did the with the jungle-dwellers of Sunne?"

Daku bounded to Shiverrig's side. "Stop it! We can use them."

"For what, food? These people can barely work, let alone fight."

"Would you stop and think for a moment? Do you think we will march across the Three Kingdoms without drawing attention? Armies will rally against us when they know you have returned.

"What armies? All I see are the deserters and weaklings who choose not to fight."

"We will need more men. I don't know, they can forage, they can cook, carry supplies. It's a start."

Shiverrig brought the man's face closer to his own and looked deeply into his eyes. He had no idea who the man was, nor did he care. The acidic smell of human piss reached his nose. Shiverrig knew he had found a coward. And he hated cowards.

A cruel smile curled at the sides of his mouth as he tightened his grip on the man's throat. The farmer's eyes bulged, and his face turned purple. Impulsively, Shiverrig grabbed the man's hair and held him aloft by his scalp, eyeing his throat with wolfish hunger.

"Your Aj-Kahun is Death and I have come to collect my due."

Shiverrig's mouth opened constrictor wide. Rows

of shark-shaped teeth glistened with thin lines of saliva, extending from the top of his mouth to his lower jaw.

"Don't," Daku said.

Shiverrig ignored him and bit deeply into the farmer's throat. Warm gore slid down his chin as the man shook violently in the air. The raw, mercurial taste filling his mouth was invigorating. Blood drooled over his lips and his eyes shifted to the other farmhands.

He tossed the dead man to the ground and watched in mild fascination as the body spasmed and twitched with uncontrollable convulsions. Eventually, the man lay still and Shiverrig's attention turned towards the nearest farmhand, a teenager whose facial hair was still thin and sparse. Then, he heard a guttural moan rising from the ground and nodded in satisfaction as a ghoul rose to serve.

"That's a better start," he said, turning to Daku. "Round up the rest."

"Barbarian Devil," whispered a young voice.

Shiverrig turned fast and saw a boy shoved behind a woman's back.

"You, there! Step forward. What did you call me?"

Hesitantly, the boy peaked out from behind the woman's hip. His eyes were full of fright behind a dirty face and tangled hair. Nonetheless, he came forward, timidly at first, but then he stood fast, puffing out his small chest.

"You carry the devil's hex, so I called you a barbarian devil."

Shiverrig glared at the boy. A lust for more blood overcame him. The boy would be a tender morsal, but Shiverrig held his desire in check. Chuckling, he put his meaty hands on his hips.

"Barbarian Devil," Shiverrig pondered the title for a moment, then a broad smile lit his face. "Finally, I have found the lost courage of Baroqia. I see now it skipped a generation and lives in our youth. What's your name boy?"

"Thomas." the boy replied in a shaky voice.

"I need brave men at my side, Thomas, who possess the strength to do what is right. Will you help me defeat those who would prevent the glorious revival of Baroqia?"

The boy looked back to the woman, who was shaking her head no. Tears streamed down her face. She held out both hands for him to return to her.

But Thomas didn't go back. Instead, he turned back to face Shiverrig, defiant.

"My father was taken under King Conrad's banner to fight in the war. He didn't come back. Ma died when Gethem burned. Auntie took me and we fled to the capital, thinking it would be safer in Qaqal, but there are evil things there, too. Now she's gone."

A broad smile bloomed across Shiverrig's bestial, blood smeared face. "You are a man of Gethem, then!"

"Yes, my lord," Thomas said.

"Why, I am your lost duke!" Shiverrig perused the crowd of prisoners. "Who else here once called Gethem their home? Come now, step forward. Don't be shy. Your liege lord is here to protect you."

Of the thirty adult field hands, five hesitantly stepped forward.

"Excellent! Daku, take them aside. The rest I want over there."

When the laborers had been divided, Shiverrig approached the larger group. "Your service is required to save Baroqia. Consider yourself conscripted to the war effort."

He fell upon them, ripping at their throats and drinking their blood. Some stood stone still in fear, others tried to run, though none escaped. As each one fell in death, a ghoul rose in life.

"I guess that's it for the knives and forks," Daku said, shaking his head as he shepherded the living away from the undead.

The countryside of Baroqia had been altered in the aftermath of the war. Thriving towns had been incinerated. The buildings' foundations remained a spotted pox of charred wood and blackened stone on either side of the cobblestone streets. The people were gone, scattered to whatever haven they could find.

Vast farmlands lay barren. Hectares of ancient forest burned and now were overrun by sickly scrub brush. The hardy plants somehow managed to breach the deep layers of ash and stole the light from the sapling children of the great trees.

"Surprising, isn't it?" Daku said as Shiverrig's troops departed from another deserted farmstead.

"What's that?" Shiverrig replied, while picking something fleshy out from between his teeth.

"One would think the ash from an angel's fire would be life-giving, instead of this," Daku said.

"Everything dies," Shiverrig said.

"Do they know that?" Daku said, pointing with his thumb over his shoulder at the ghouls shuffling aimlessly behind them.

"Harrumph. Be happy it's not you." Shiverrig kicked his horse forward to the front of the line.

Shiverrig's handful of warriors had grown to the size of a battalion as whispers flourished through black market channels of the Barbarian Devil from the north, who marched through the eastern provinces, culling the false nobles, and claiming their land and title under the law of combat.

Bands of cutthroats, thieves, and ruffians sought him out, possibly thinking to commandeer his men until they saw the monster in the flesh. Just one look at him, and the throng of hideous, half-humans that followed like a pack of gruesome canines, was enough to change the mind of any opportunistic brigand.

The decision was simple. Join him and reshape the land under one ruler, or shamble along in the ranks of the undead. No one chose the latter.

Shiverrig was pleased to see that his first brood had transformed into something more fiendish. Their backs had hunched over, and their arms grew long. The clothing of their past life was shed as a necessity for it was ineffective and constricting to their metamorphosis.

Their heads swelled to a size larger than should be possible and lagged like heavy weights below their shoulders. Saucer-shaped eyes filled with a creamy, opal substance, shined in the moonlight. They were lanky things with rugged hands made tough from honest work, but now sported claws better suited for rending flesh.

During daylight hours, long, purple tongues lolled out of wide mouths like dogs panting from the heat. The creatures were more effective killers at night when they roused out of their lethargic bumbling and stalked with hungry purpose.

Shiverrig noticed the stronger ghouls transfused his tainted blood into those they killed, effectively multiplying the mob of ghouls under his command. He had to admit, he was appreciative of the gifts given to him by the otherworldly twins in the north.

Resistance to his horde was minimal. The newly proclaimed lords of Baroqia were craven and chose to avoid confrontation by fleeing on swift steeds, rather than facing him in battle or joining his cause. The food supplies left behind were appreciated, and any hideaways they hauled out of panic rooms were added to his growing ghoul army.

"You may want to leave a few of them among the living. Someone needs to be left to rebuild these towns, and your followers don't look much like the industrial type," Daku said.

Occasionally, a bold lord would choose to fight, rather than surrender his title and rights to Shiverrig. The noble would barricade himself and his family behind the high walls of his stately manor, lining the parapets with men-at-arms, or whatever number of conscripted fighters he could muster. Unfortunately, the people he taxed in meager coin, food, or flesh in return for protection, were left outside to fend for themselves.

At nightfall, Shiverrig unleashed the ghouls, commanding them to scurry over the walls like rats. The sub-humans climbed over one another, obsessed to be first to reach the top and the promise of fresh meat. Their shrill cries tore at the courage of most men and the opposing soldiers fell like wheat stalks to the ghouls' scythe-like claws and biting teeth.

When the battle was over, Shiverrig was pleased to see more soldiers returning than had original left his camp.

Whether the humans he encountered held their ground or ran, the eventual outcome would be the same. Living, or undead, they would be his to rule again.

Three day's travel brought Shiverrig and his growing army to the outskirts of Qaqal. He was disappointed with what remained of the once grand city but expected no less. Miles of cityscape had been reduced to something resembling petrified pudding. The angelic fire melted rock as easily as it burned through dry wood and the City of Spires had been eradicated.

The city's orderly and precisely laid out streets were now a maze of pathways, winding around heaping mounds of slag and rubble. Nothing of the grandeur of Qaqal remained. Shiverrig couldn't care less.

The debauchery of Conrad's greed has come full circle, he thought with a certain satisfaction.

"Daku, keep the troops alert. We may need a hasty retreat out of this mess if we find anything holy in there."

"Holy?" Daku said anxiously, scanning the sky. "You mean like angels? This is becoming more and more of a bad idea. We should rethink this."

Shiverrig eyed Dai-Ko-Zior. "Well, lich?"

Dai-Ko-Zior waved a cursory hand across the ruined walls and broken gates of Qaqal. He then lowered his hand. "The angels are elsewhere today."

Shiverrig raised an eyebrow. "As in the cosmic elsewhere or elsewhere in the Three Kingdoms?"

Dai-Ko-Zior cursed and kicked his steed forward. Then, his cold, dead eyes rolled back into his head, and he moved his hand across the melted city. Sooty symbols rose over his shoulders and arranged themselves in chaotic patterns behind his back as he muttered a divination spell.

"They are not your concern today," Dai-Ko-Zior said in a raspy voice when he was finished. A thin, malicious smile crossed his deathly face.

"Fine, then. Daku, lead the way," Shiverrig said.

"We should be laying low while building our strength. There's nothing here but regret."

"I will not hide like a den of thieves. Let's go."

The pale demon grumbled under his breath then loped ahead of the main group, finding a usable path for the men and ghouls to follow. Soon a long, single file line wound its way into the heart of dead Qaqal.

Shiverrig remembered the fateful day six years past, when the angels had arrived and destroyed everything. He envisioned the winged warriors of the Heavenly Host swarming above the city before unleashing their wrath in the form of massive fire column over the madness he had wrought with his violence. The city, and any person or thing still living there, was surely liquified in an instant.

He assumed the palace was first to be razed. It stood before him as a massive, relief sculpture of melted stone and iron, looking more like dead coral rather than something glorious built by man. The precious metals that lined its outer surfaces were now paper-thin films of color, flaking away in the dirty air.

Every illustrious spire that once reached for the heavens had been brought low and mixed with the melted remains of mercantile buildings, shops, and street level, lower cast homes. Now, everything was a continuous pool of hardened slag.

"There's nothing here," Shiverrig said after an hour of exploration.

"Surprise, surprise," Daku said. "Can we leave now?"

Then Daku's white snout raised into the air in alarm. "Wait, I know that scent." His bear-shaped head twisted back around, pointing in the direction of a large pile of gooey-shaped rubble.

"Come out!" Daku growled.

"Only if you say, pretty please," Sess'thra said as she emerged from the shadows between fallen slabs of reshaped stone. She walked with sensual grace as her lithe body swayed on narrow hips.

"Hello Daku from Ordu," she said while studying Shiverrig suspiciously. "You remind me of someone. It's in the eyes."

Then recognition hit and she leaped through the air and into his arms. She kissed him savagely with open mouth and flickering tongue. "It is you!"

Eventually, she pushed herself off his broad chest and appraised him thoroughly.

"Well, well, well, you've changed. Horns appears to be quite the fashion these days. You look like a true prince of the Land of Eternal Strife."

She reached down and grabbed his crotch. "Did the new you come with any additional bonuses I might like, big boy?"

Shiverrig pried her hands away. He was in no mood for her antics, not yet.

"Where have you been? I wandered aimlessly for six years in the winter shadowlands of Trosk! You could have saved me that time."

"But then you would not have done what was needed of you to do. nor would you have gathered so many new recruits." She eyed the barbarians with a keen interest. "They look healthy."

She eyed the throng of ghouls, mindlessly swaying in the sunlight and mewling like sick cats. "And them? Can they fight or do they just look pretty?"

"With the half-breeds gone. I was forced to make do with whatever stock was available," Shiverrig said.

"They're not much to look at, but are good in a scrap," Daku said.

"I bet," Sess'thra said, but kept her eyes glued to Shiverrig. "And how is your dear father figure?"

"Xerthotha? He can rot in the Abyss for all I care. His favors proved useless to me. I've terminated our agreement. He's gone."

"Gone?" Sess'thra frowned. "You forsook the gifts of the most powerful Supreme Devil in the Abyss, and for what? Pride?" She sighed with disappointment. "That was careless and thoughtless, especially after all I did for you. I have no use for dimwitted mortals. You have ruined more than you can imagine."

"I have made other arrangements."

"Yes, I see that." Sess'thra's look of suspicion returned, but then she quickly turned playful and excited.

"Tell me who!" She eagerly clapped her hands together. "Azrollorza? Please say it's Azrollorza. Oh, that would just be splendid! Can you imagine the look on the Xerthotha's face when you command her troops through his lands?"

"I'm not commanding anyone's troops through even one of the countless Circles of the Abyss. Enough with the questions. Where have you been?"

"Excuse me? I'll have you know it was no small feat escaping the wrath of the Heavenly Host. They are like hounds on a fox once they get your scent. Luckily, this girl has a few tricks up her sleeve, and I still know a few reliable hiding places."

"What of Dax? Where's the assassin? Lurking where I least expect him, no doubt."

"Oh, I'm sure he is around here somewhere. Maybe he's doubling as one of your little experiments."

"I'd sniff him out if he got too close," Daku said putting his snout in the air.

Sess'thra's expression became thoughtful. "Though, I suspect he's had enough of devilish frost storms and angelic infernos. And who can blame him? Just look at this place. What a mess." She sashayed closer to him.

"But less about him and more about me! You left your poor, little Sess'thra, all alone in the big bad world with no one to protect her."

"They ruined everything," Shiverrig said. He raised his face to the sky. "A thousand curses on the Seven Heavens!"

"Oh, don't be such as poor sport. You lost a round or two in the forever war. There will be other, better opportunities to claim your glory."

Her eyes shifted and narrowed ever so slightly as they wandered to the lich. Shiverrig watched her tail twitch like a cat contemplating a potential target.

"You've looked better, wizard, though not much."

"The gifts of my masters cannot be measured in life or death for they are eternal."

Sess'thra did her best to stifle her laughter. She failed. The succubus then turned her attention to Daku. "And how is my second favorite monk? Still fighting the good fight?"

"I have complete control."

"Do you now?" She clapped her hands in a slow, mocking

gesture as her eyes searched for Xerthotha's golden circlet. "Congratulations."

Shiverrig caught the skeptical look and was sure she suspected the same as he did. Daku wasn't strong enough to hold back the spirit of Khalkoroth without the talisman.

Perhaps best to end the beast now, Shiverrig mused.

Sess'thra moved closer to the ghouls. She poked one, then another, and then smelled the tip of her finger. "Eww."

"Why are you here? Did anything else survive?" Shiverrig said.

"I'm glad you asked," Sess'thra said.

She gave Shiverrig a quick wink and then whistled. Rocks tumbled and slabs of stone grated together, sounding like the removal of a sarcophagus's lid. Three full companies of half-breeds came out of the rubble. These were the wingless variation and still wore the dented and dirty armor of Shiverrig's last campaign against the Ever Hero and his savage army from Sunne.

Rather than receiving a warm welcome, Shiverrig was greeted by snarls and growls. Crude maces were raised above reptilian-shaped heads and pointed tips of chipped swords angled at him.

"As you can see, the more intuitive of our offspring found hiding places of their own. Some things have a way of surviving through the darkest of days. Though, I don't think they can see you the way I do. Then again, maybe they do."

Shiverrig understood the rules of the Abyss, they were not much different from the world of men; you don't get power, you take it. This group of half-breeds no longer knew him as their sire or the dominant threat without Xerthotha's taint coiled around his soul.

The half-breeds pressed in on him, effectively separating himself from his long line of troops, not that it would matter. This was his fight. He focused on the circling demons and fixed his eyes on the one he would kill as an example for the rest.

"What's the plan here, boss?" Daku said. "There's a lot of them."

"This won't take long," Shiverrig said. Then they rushed him and tackled him to the ground. His arms were pinned by the weight of their overwhelming numbers. Steel glinted in the oppressive sunlight as his half-breeds, his children, jabbed cold steel into his flesh. A red haze collected at the edge of his sight as sharp, painful bites dug into him.

Shiverrig kicked out and smashed the knee of a demon with a raised sword. The entangled half-breeds that grabbled with him on the ground were so close he could bite them, so he did, tearing out the throat of the nearest one.

"Daku!" Shiverrig shouted after spitting out a mouthful of flesh and feeling another blade slide between his ribs. The half-breeds were finding unprotected organs and inflicting mortal damage. He felt the pain, but it did not slow him down.

"Prove yourself a worthy champion of my masters," Dai-Ko-Zior said as if his eerie voice whispered directly in Shiverrig's ear. "The pale demon cannot interfere."

As Shiverrig struggled to free himself, he drank in the blood flowing from the demon's open throat. The warm fluid filled him with vigor. He heaved upwards, scattering the demons holding him down.

Scrambling to his knees, Shiverrig grabbed a half-breed by the ankle, and pulling him closer. He jumped on its back and dug his nails deeply into its course hide, ripping through its back down to the bones. Blood gushed into his face and over his chest. He bit down into the back of its neck, savoring the muscular meat.

Shiverrig howled with a predator's delight after a kill. The unholy baptism was a rebirth into a new world. He raised himself up and stomped on the neck of the squirming demon beneath him, snapping the vertebrae like dried kindle. To the side, he saw the throatless demon rise from the ground.

"To me!" Shiverrig commanded and the demon-ghoul responded, as did the one beneath his legs.

"Oh, Gerun Shiverrig!" Sess'thra said with glee. "You never cease to amaze me."

Hearing his birth name only added to his bloodlust and preternatural hunger. The failures of Gerun Shiverrig, the War Duke of Gethem and the Aj-Kahun of desolate Baroqia, would not be attached to the conquest of the Barbarian Devil. He would slaughter them all and enjoy the bloody feast that followed.

The half-breeds who had foolishly attacked him now kept their distance. The demon with the broken back, somehow managed to right itself. Bones cracked back into random positions, giving the demon a permanently deformed posture. It took heavy steps to join Shiverrig's side.

Shiverrig smiled wickedly as he licked the blood from his mouth. He was panting with bloodlust and craved more carnage. The world had gone blood red.

"The taste of Xerthotha is so much sweeter this way. Who's next?"

Sess'thra was talking but he could barely hear her words. She stood there before him, tiny, frail, and so vulnerable. He felt messy drool dripping over his chin. She would be a tasty treat.

"That's enough," Sess'thra said and stepped forward. "I think you've proven your point. Are you listening to me?"

Shiverrig glared down at her. She didn't flinch. The red mist cleared from his eyes.

"What?" Shiverrig said, still panting but regaining control.

"I said, you have won the day, Now, what will you do with them, oh fearless leader? Or would you like to stay here and chit chat over some tea and cookies?"

"I intend to rebuild," Shiverrig said after a moment, and wiped the slobber from his mouth. "Gethem. They will go to Gethem. Perhaps others are already there, waiting for my return."

"You will honor your promise. My masters will have the daimus nexus before you squander their gifts," Dai-Ko-Zior said ominously.

"That's right," Daku said as he pushed away an idle spear still held against him. "Those things won't wait forever."

"Well now, that's a very rare treasure you seek. Today is certainly your lucky day, lover. I know where to find one!" Sess'thra squealed with delight. "Oh, this is rich! What a fabulous turn of events. You must do exactly as I say or no daimus nexus for you."

"We're wasting our time. She has no idea what we're looking for. Everything is one big game to her," Daku said.

"I do! I do! You can trust me!" Sess'thra pleaded.

"If the succubus knows of its location, you must go there first," Dai-Ko-Zior said.

"The succubus will fetch it and bring it to me. We are going to Gethem."

Sess'thra gave him a sly smile. "See, that's the thing. It or I should say *she*, is not close. Nor will she come with me, even if I ask nicely."

"Shadow walk with Daku, then and take her together. I'll wait."

"Nope. I won't do it. I've been so lonely, and this is just the type of adventure I've been longing for. If you want my help you have to work for it."

Shiverrig pointed to one of the half-breeds. "You, or whoever leads you, march to Gethem and secure what is left of the city. And try not to attract attention until you get there."

The half-breed glared at Shiverrig, then his eyes shifted to Sess'thra, who nodded her approval. The demon squawked loudly and led the rest of what remained of his conquering legions to the city of his birth.

"Daku, round them up. We follow the succubus," Shiverrig said, then turned to Sess'thra. "Lead the way."

The trip across open country was uneventful. The succubus came and went as she pleased, 'gathering information,' as she said. Shiverrig often found himself eavesdropping on Daku for lack of anything more interesting to do while she was away. The ongoing struggle against Khalkoroth was taking a toll on Daku's moods and more than once, he lashed out at the soldiers.

The last one to fall was a ghoul, who lost his head and undead life with one swift swipe. The rest of the ghoul troop wasted little time consuming the remains. Nothing went to waste.

Today was a dull day. The road stretched ahead for miles and the sun was an annoyance. His eyes wept red tears if he didn't guard them in some way from the daylight.

"Your threats don't scare me, demon. I control you," Daku whispered angrily to himself as he stomped in pace with Shiverrig's horse. "Even without the circlet, I am still more than a match for you."

"Everything alright, Daku?" Shiverrig asked.

"Fine. Why?"

"I'm wondering if I need to kill you or not."

Sess'thra trotted nearby on the horse she appropriated from a peasant turned undead soldier. The succubus was in a playful mood and wore a wry smile.

"Inner demons got you down?" She had the laugh of an angel but under the surface was the wickedness of an ancient demon. Her purple eyes scanned his face and body, searching for something.

"Khalkoroth is mine now," Daku said defiantly, pointing his pointy thumb into his chest. The human gesture was comical on the pale demon. "It was me. I won. I bested your champion."

"And I thought it couldn't be done. Just imagine, a boy monk straight out of a monastery overpowers a three-thousand-year-old shadow demon in a battle of wills," Sess'thra said as she directed her horse around Daku's hulking body. She appraised him while her fingernails drew lines through the white fur of his shoulders.

"Just to think of it is mind boggling. I'm *very* impressed."

"Don't mock me. I haven't forgotten or forgiven the

duplicitous trick you played on me. Too bad for you it backfired."

"A truer champion I have never known," she said. But her eyes told a different story.

She's waiting for him to snap, thought Shiverrig.

21

KASAI

Kasai jumped over a fallen tree as he ran through the forest, heedless of which direction he turned. He would find what was lost and this time, keep it safe. For the first time in many years, he dared to hold hope in his heart.

Desdemonia lives!

But finding her was proving more difficult than he expected. The forests had changed since he fled the massacre at Ordu with his wounded master. Trails were overgrown and tree patterns were jumbled with new growth. Kasai scolded himself for not paying more attention to the terrain but kept running.

"Ever Hero," Pallo said through huffing breaths as he ran next to Kasai. "If you could describe the landmarks surrounding Desdemonia's cottage, maybe Run-Run could find it faster,"

"It's close, I know it!" Kasai replied. "Can't you smell the smoke? She's in danger."

"That's not angel fire," Pallo said and grabbed Kasai's

robe to slow him down to a stop. Then, he bent over with his hands resting on his knees. "It's the villagers. They're burning wood in the hearths of their homes. Only wood, Ever Hero, only wood."

"Let go of me. We must keep going," Kasai said anxiously, looking back in the direction they were heading.

"Not until we know where we are going. We're running blind."

Run-Run trotted over to his brother and nodded solemnly. He pointed to a rock formation jutting from the ground, then took his finger and pulled the skin down under one eye and pointed again.

"Run-Run says…"

"I know what he's saying!" Kasai said, turning in a circle, trying to get his bearings. "It's here, somewhere. These paths are familiar to me." He lied.

Run-Run gestured again, this time just to Pallo.

"Run-Run says there's a village less than three miles south of here. We can get more information there and restock our supplies," Pallo said. "That was our initial plan, remember?"

Kasai searched the weary faces of the ten brothers under his care. None of them were in peak condition and couldn't continue at this pace. Only Gift had the endurance for more forced runs.

His gaze drifted to the proud warrior-mage. She stood tall and her breath was calm. He imagined a sheen of sweat coating her muscular body under her travel skins and felt a pang of guilt for the way he desired her, even now. Her eyes gave away nothing of her emotions, and that made Kasai feel even worse.

But if Des had returned, and was being hunted by the angels, then he had to save her, regardless of who he hurt in the process. He was honor bound to try.

"Master Cyrus, your thoughts?" Kasai said.

"One must know where he is going if one is to lead," Cyrus said.

Kasai reluctantly conceded. "Alright, Run-Run, Pallo, lead the way.'

It took less than an hour to reach the next frontier village. Kasai, Pallo, and Run-Run entered first but came to a quick halt when they reached the village square. The rest of the group spread out to either side of them. Sondru put his hand to his mouth in shock. Some of the younger monks turned their heads away.

The village had not been deserted like the previous one—this one had suffered a worse fate. Soot explosions peppered the exterior face of the meager buildings. Debris from small shops and outdoor market stands littered the square. There had been a brutal fight and the dead lay strewn upon the ground.

Kasai was callous to the loss of life before him. He didn't know these people and right now, he didn't care. The snap and crackle of fires and trails of smoke drifting across the village told him whatever happened here was recent.

He searched the ground for Desdemonia's familiar black hair, hoping not to find her among the dead. Then his eyes connected the dots of six black spots arranged in a wide circle. He walked to the nearest one and crouched down. It was still smoldering, and hot to the touch. Angel markings.

"I told you," Kasai said through clenched teeth, containing his anger.

"These people thought salvation had finally come. They didn't know what hit them," Pallo said. "Ever Hero…how is this possible?"

"The villagers got in the angels' way," Kasai said as he stood and rubbed the blackened dirt off his fingers.

"Horrible," Pallo said, shaking his head in disbelief.

Kasai nodded and looked around the square in disbelief. "Pallo, recon the village. And take your brother with you. Maybe someone survived and can tell us what happened and why. The rest of you, stay close. See if any of them are still alive and need help."

The two brothers nodded and jogged into the village.

Gift examined a nearby corpse, then moved on to another, and another, perplexed with each body she turned over. "I cannot find a wound, bruise, or broken bone. Their lives were taken from them by other means."

"Why would angels do that?" Kasai said. "They were just people."

Gift shrugged her shoulders.

"This is quite interesting," Cyrus said from nearby. He looked more curious than appalled. "Reach out to the vibrations in this area and tell me what you feel."

Kasai closed his eyes and concentrated on opening his xindu energies. His fire xindu came to life and blazed fiercely like a flash flame over dry kindle, stealing the energy from the others. It made him feel overly aggressive and off-balance.

He calmed himself and focused his attention on a patch of broken ground and then the air above it. The air was alive with activity. Tiny dots of energy collided together and hummed with an easy resonance. But the dirt was dead, and

Kasai suspected anything once living in the soil was gone as well.

He quelled his fire xindu and focused on using only his earth xindu to communicate with the ground, seeking understanding. Try as he might, he couldn't establish a connection between himself and the soil. *This can't be right,* Kasai thought.

"I cannot feel the essence of the soil. It's as dead as the villagers laying on its surface," he said at last.

"Exactly. Something or someone has stripped away the living vibrations," Cyrus said. He too had placed his hand on the ground. "I suspect the same fate fell on the villagers."

"Angels wield the same death magic as demon sorcerers? That seems unlikely," Kasai said.

Cyrus held his tongue. The master knew something, Kasai just didn't know what.

"Ever Hero, we've found someone!" Pallo said from afar.

Kasai then saw Pallo and Run-Run walking from the alley between two smoking buildings with a scared and dirty child between them.

"Can he talk?" Kasai said impulsively. "What did he see? Was Desdemonia here?"

Pallo looked at Kasai with concern, then prodded the child to answer. "It's ok. You're safe now. Just tell us what happened here."

"I saw...angels in bright armor," the boy stammered with wide, saucer-shaped eyes. "And a devil."

"Devil? What sort of devil? Was she a woman? White hair? Describe her, now!"

The boy took steps back with each question. "Yes...a woman."

"Sekka," Kasai hissed. "But how? It's too soon."

Pallo looked anxiously at Run-Run, who had drawn both of his blessed short swords.

"Did they fight? Did she use magic? Kasai pressed. "Come on boy, speak. Did she kill the people of your village?"

The boy nodded quickly. "There was magic."

"She's back," Kasai said. He felt the weight of the dead for the first time. He turned and paced a few steps away from the group "How could it be so soon?" He scanned the village. "There's no snow. Something should have remained, patches of ice, maybe."

His mind fell into war time thoughts of enemy dispositions, raising armies, and battle strategies against another horde of demons from the Abyss. He shook his head, searching for an answer where there was none. "We don't have enough men."

"Black hair," the boy whispered.

"What's that?" Kasai said, whipping back around to face the group. His eyes burrowed into the boy.

"The devil had black hair."

"Ever Hero, you mustn't get your hopes up," Gift said. There was caring and a touch of sadness in her eyes. "He said devil, not Desdemonia."

Kasai looked in the opposite direction from where they entered the village. He pushed through his companions and started to walk south.

"Where are you going?" Pallo shouted. "What about the child?"

"Can't you see there is a pattern? There's a sister village nearby," Kasai replied and began to run. "Brother Mando will stay behind to see if there are others and tend to the wounded. I'm getting her back."

The next village was a long day's hard run away. It was well into the night when Pallo called a halt for the day.

"Ever Hero, we must rest. If there is to be a fight, we will need our strength. You have pushed us close to exhaustion."

Kasai knew his friend was right. He was half awake and more than once tripped over an obvious root or caught a low hanging branch across his face. The salty sweat, dripping from his dirty forehead made the cuts and welts crisscrossing his face sting.

He followed the path they had run along with his eyes as it vanished into the night. A crescent moon lit a wide band of stars in the night sky. They were a wonder to behold, but Kasai realized if angels were flying overhead, they would have the same direct sight to them on the ground.

"We'll stop for the night, but off the trail. And no fires. I don't want anyone to see us coming," Kasai said.

His companions agreed. Run-Run quickly located a large fern patch off the trail, which was surrounded by leaning pine trees. Kasai was satisfied. The overhanging tree branches and curling fern fronds would hide their numbers from watchful eyes.

He doubted the angels worried about a surprise attack, but if Desdemonia had escaped their last confrontation, there would be scouts searching for her. Best they didn't know he was searching for her as well.

"Pallo, set a perimeter. Give the duties to the younger monks. If it comes to a fight, I don't want them in the middle of it. If they see or hear anything, they are to alert the rest of us using the old signals."

"Perhaps we should send the youngsters back to regroup with Brother Mando. This is no longer a mission of service to the frontier villages," Cyrus said.

"You're probably right. I'll dismiss them at first light."

Kasai watched Gift walk to find a place to rest, one that was far away from him. He felt a sad sense of rejection, but what did he expect?

I can't save everyone, Kasai thought, though he wasn't sure if he meant Gift or himself.

He approached Master Cyrus, thinking it best to devise a strategy to free Desdemonia if the angels had already captured her. But the older monk had already found a suitable spot for himself and sat with his back against a tree in deep meditation. He was a darker shadow within the shadow of the tree.

Eventually, the small group was bedded down and Kasai found his own spot to meditate. He closed his eyes gave himself a moment of reflection.

Could it really be her? he wondered. *But the boy said the devil had black hair. Was there a new threat to the Three Kingdoms or was this just another cruel joke by Raguel?*

He dared not hope, but the thought of Desdemonia somehow being alive filled him with unrulable passion. It drove him mad with hopeful bliss. He knew he could be complete if he just had her by his side again.

Kasai drifted in and out of restless sleep throughout the night. Somehow, the quick silence of the monotonous drone of crickets' humming in the night startled him awake. Then he felt the sharp prick of a knife at his throat just as the call to alarm sounded.

Kasai instinctively slid to the side. He saw the glint of a

steel dagger flashing past his head and into the dirt. His eyes focused on the shadow looming over him as Master Cyrus raised his dagger for a second strike.

"You have no hope against the angels. They will destroy you," Cyrus whispered menacingly. "Which would do the world some good, I think, except they would claim the Fire Serpent, which I cannot allow."

"Cyrus, no." Kasai said, seeing the bundle Cyrus held in his other hand.

"The Fire Serpent must be kept safe until I reunite with the twins in the north. The power of fire elemental will aid them in their holy quest to cleanse the lands."

Kasai heard two quick dashes through swishing fronds. Then Pallo and Run-Run crashed into Cyrus in blur of motion, knocking him to the side. The dagger somersaulted through the air and was lost in the fern patch.

Cyrus tumbled and rolled with Pallo and Run-Run in a tangle of arms and legs until the momentum of the assault died. Cyrus caught Pallo under the chin with his elbow. Run-Run hung on tight to the master's waist, only to receive a sharp blow to his spine from the butt end of the bundle. He released his hold with a yelp.

Cyrus twisted his body and rose fast, cursing. The moment of surprise was lost. Kasai sprang to his feet and reached instinctively for Ninziz-zida. Cyrus gave him a wicked smile and tucked the bundle into the sash at his waist.

"Ninziz-zida will never accept you," Kasai said, stalling for time. The rest of the camp scrambled to attention and were closing in. "She will burn you until there is nothing left but ash."

"Ordu was always considered the weakest of the Four Orders, and now I know why. I came to the monastery to find the legendary Ever Hero but found you instead. The Fire Serpent deserves a true master and not a crippled soul, who will only burden her in battle."

Cyrus's hand flashed into the sleeve of his robes and revealed a small glass ball. He threw it against a rock. When it shattered, a billowing cloud of choking gas filled the area. Kasai heard glass shattering three more times and soon the area was engulfed in a thick fog.

"Remember your training! It will save you!" Kasai shouted as he activated his air xindu to push away the gas cloud and create a path to where Cyrus stood. He was there in an instant, but the monk, and the staff were gone.

Through watering eyes, he saw the color of Cyrus's deep maroon robes darting between trees in the distance. Kasai gave chase, dodging brush and leaping over stumps. Trees flashed by in a blur of blinding speed.

Cyrus stopped fast and shot a column of fire at Kasai, hitting him square in the chest. The mark of Oh-hur on his forearm absorbed much of the heat, as it was designed to do, but Master Cyrus's fire xindu was strong. Kasai rolled to the ground and burned along with the dry leaves and needles on the forest floor.

"No time to burn," Kasai said, gritting his teeth and activating his water xindu. He pushed himself off the ground, searching for Cyrus, but the thieving master was gone.

In the distance, Kasai heard the younger monks coughing. He knew he had to go back. They were not equipped to deal with the poisonous vapors as would a senior level monk. He followed the hacking sounds and found them crawling on their knees or curled up in a fetal position on the ground.

It took some time, but Kasai managed to purge the gas from their lungs using his own air xindu. Pallo and Run-Run were battered and bruised, but otherwise unharmed. Sometime later, he sat with Pallo, Run-Run, and Gift, trying to understand the motivation behind the betrayal.

"That was his plan all along. Cyrus meant to steal Ninziz-zida, but the question is, why? She will refuse him," Kasai said.

"The story of the wicked is never straightforward or logical," Gift said. "If he cannot use the Fire Serpent himself, it must be for some other reason. The Tribes of Sunne sacrifice artifacts of evil to Nayche to receive her blessing before battle. Perhaps this is his intention."

"You said he spoke of twins in the north. Who do you think he meant?" Pallo asked.

Run-Run gestured with a sad face to his brother.

"I don't know what makes a master monk go bad either, Run-Run," Pallo said.

"Life. Too much life and the experiences that come with it," Kasai said bitterly.

"He must be on his way back to Symmetu. He's got a half-day's lead on us but Run-Run will find him fast enough. He has the nose of a hound," Pallo said.

"Possibly," Kasai said. Then looked to the south. "I can't leave without Des. Not now. Not when I am so close."

"Desdemonia is dead. You were there. You saw it. You buried her yourself in the jungle," Gift said. "Retrieve the Fire Serpent and let her rest. "

"Ever Hero, she's right," Pallo said in a reasoning tone.

"What hope do you have without the staff? Wielding xindu power the way you do is amazing, but you won't be fighting base-level demons. These are True-born Protectorates."

"I cannot have a crutch. I will find the Boundless again, or I will die trying. Either way, I will not abandon her to the angels. I defeated Sekka without the staff. I will do the same against the angels."

"The stories say it was the witch who disarmed the devil with her magic. Help is always needed, no matter the hero or the fight."

"And the staff?" Pallo asked. "Do we just let the rat bastard keep it?"

"I ask one last favor of you, old friend. Take Run-Run and find Cyrus's trail. If he heads to Symmetu, follow him there and learn the way.

"But do not engage him. He is a Master Monk and is dangerous. Your blessed weapons do not carry power over him as they did against demon kind. Then, return to Nu-Ordu. I will meet you there."

"What do you say, Run-Run?"

Run-Run agreed enthusiastically, then pulled out his short swords and sliced the blades against each other.

"Run-Run says the blades are sharp and will cut his flesh just the same," Pallo said.

Run-Run nodded and grabbed Pallo's shirt to leave.

"Find her, save her if she lives," Pallo said and dashed away after his brother. "Until we meet again, Ever Hero."

Kasai turned to Gift. "You should return to Nu-Ordu with the others or go home to the jungle. This is not your fight."

"The spear you thrust is not meant for me, but the

enemies of your heart. Desdemonia is an honored member of the Frona Tribe. I will go where I choose."

Kasai nodded. He wasn't sure what he was going to do when he found the angels, but if he couldn't find them in time, it wouldn't matter anyways. He would need a competent tracker, though how one tracked aerial beings who could vanish from one location and appear at another was beyond him.

"What about us, Master Kasai?" Sondru said.

"Go back to the last village and help Brother Mando. Then, return to Nu-Ordu. If the boy is alone, bring him with you. I never should have brought you this far. Somehow, I thought everything would work out differently. I was wrong."

"I won't fail you, Ever Hero," Sondru said.

"When you get to Nu-Ordu, you must ready the monastery for war. I leave the preparations in your capable hands," Kasai said. "This time, we will not be taken in our sleep."

22

SHIVERRIG

Shiverrig rode stoically at the front of his war column. The horse under him snorted and struggled under his enormous bulk as it trotted along the wide, but now seldom used road to the ruins of Winter's Fury. The clip-clop of hooves was like a metronome ticking in his ears and causing his mind to wander.

A lifetime ago, the road brought young nobles to the Last Garrison to be trained in military tactics and how to lead men to war. For many it was a right-of-passage to manhood, to young Gerun Shiverrig, it was already a way of life. When he entered the academy, he was already a seasoned fighter, accompanying his father on more than one campaign to repel the barbarian warbands from the north. How times had changed.

Sess'thra sat upright and lively on her roan to his left side. His nights with the succubus were filled with carnal delight and lustful, savage play. She was never one to disappoint and her curiosity for his new physique was insatiable. But what did he expect from a sex demon?

He only wished the days with her were more tolerable. She divvied out information about the whereabouts of the daimus nexus in bits and pieces, but never enough for him to solve the riddle on his own. His impatience with her fun was wearing thin.

"What good is being part of the living if you cannot enjoy the adventure?" she chided him as they broke camp earlier that morning.

Am I? Shiverrig wondered. His connection to the living things around him seemed to revolve more around the notion of food, rather than assets or servants. He absentmindedly licked his lips remembering the bold, young Thomas from Gethem. The lad was a tasty morsel.

Daku sulked to his right, mumbling angrily to himself. If Khalkoroth won the fight for Daku's soul, then so be it. He no longer cared. Either way, the shadow demon was useful muscle in a fight.

Dai-Ko-Zior sat motionless on a plow horse he has transformed into something more suited to serving the undead lich. Over the miles, it slowly decomposed into a stinking, rotting corpse. Bones and fibrous muscles were visible to anyone who cared to look, though the barbarians who followed Shiverrig tended to avoid the gruesome abomination and his steed.

"Why are we headed North?" Daku said, seeming to come alert to his surroundings for the first time since the morning march. "You said you came from the frontier villages, which are to the west."

"You never were much of a clever boy," Sess'thra sighed.

"Isn't it obvious? This is the road to Winter's Fury. She's bringing us back to the land of ruin and shattered dreams,"

Shiverrig said hunched in his saddle, trying to shield his eyes. The sun was mocking him in its warmth and brightness.

"Who knew we had a poet in our midst," Sess'thra said, giggling.

She then turned back to the line of trailing troops and ghastly things. "But you won't accomplish much with that motley crew. I'm betting Winter's Fury will hold a secret or two for you to use."

"Doubtful. The angels destroyed it all," Daku said with a snarl. "Nothing can stand against their wrath."

"And how would you know? Those who *did* survive, saw you beaten and broken by the Ever Hero. I'm surprised he didn't finish the job. That soft heart of his will get him killed one day."

Daku growled low and menacingly. "Take away his staff and he's nothing."

"But he has the staff, and you do not. Which makes you…?"

"Sess'thra, enough," Shiverrig said with a raised voice. "This had better be worth my time. I'm in no mood for your games."

"Oh hush, both of you. Do you want your nexus or not?" Sess'thra said.

Shiverrig squinted into the horizon and frowned. The daylight irritated his eyes and soured his already miserable mood. The thought of traveling at night was becoming more and more appealing.

Winter's Fury, what a colossal failure, he thought. *So much military potential squandered due to the hubris of a greedy devil. If I just had more time, I could have easily taken the Three Kingdoms and the lands beyond its shores with such a force.*

He scanned the way ahead. Long grass had grown high between the burnt remains of ancient trees dotting the landscape on either side of the road. Birds darted from charred branches, chirping out warning calls to others as the column pushed on.

"Daku, scout ahead," he said. "Find horses, men, food, or equipment—anything useful we can appropriate."

"My dear Gerun, have some faith in your little succubus. If nothing else, you will need a location to establish a new base of operations, and what better place than where Sekka met her ruin? I would think you would enjoy some satisfaction knowing you built your new empire on her grave."

"Stop calling me that name. The Shiverrig legacy is just as dead as the black bark of this ghost forest."

"When did you get so temperamental?" Sess'thra said.

"Since I met you," he said and kicked his horse forward.

Eventually, the trees thinned and disappeared altogether. It was unclear whether the fires took the trees to the ground, or it was simply the end of the forest. Ahead of him was an ocean of grass swaying under a big, blue expanse. Puffy white clouds dotted the sky.

Hours later, Daku returned and jogged up to the side of Shiverrig's mount, causing the horse to shy away until it was brought to heel.

"What is it?" Shiverrig said.

"We're being followed. Riders. A mile or so back," Daku said.

"Numbers?"

"More than ours."

Shiverrig turned in his saddle. The rest of his men were

oblivious to the enemy trailing them. They trudge forward with heads down, watching where each foot fell rather than their surroundings.

The ghouls were worse. They had a propensity for wandering off and needed to be herded wayward sheep. Shiverrig commanded Dai-Ko-Zior to gather them into something resembling a pack and keep them moving with the group.

"The riders will make their intentions known soon enough. Until that time, we continue to the ruins."

"A brilliant idea!" Sess'thra cheered. "See? Everything is falling into place perfectly."

For two days, the riders kept their distance. Shiverrig could see the sparkles of light reflected off distant armor, obscuring his ability to get a decent count of their numbers.

"No nearer, no farther. They're content to keep pace with us," Shiverrig said.

"Of course. They are afraid to engage in battle and are just waiting for us to leave their territory," Daku said. "Why not send the ghouls at night to pick them off?"

"Maybe," Shiverrig said. He scanned the open prairie. All flat. "Maybe not. I'd never get them back."

The following morning, the enemy riders had split into two groups and trotted parallel to Shiverrig's men. The barbarians hooted and hollered at the small bands of horsemen, challenging them to fight.

"They barely have half our numbers, Daku. You need to learn to count better," Shiverrig said. "They are tempting us to attack and draw our lines thin. An impatient man would oblige them and be caught in their trap. For now, we will let them be."

Shiverrig knew he was being goaded into making a mistake. Ranged weapons would do nicely to keep mounted soldiers at bay. His men had none. If he had caltrops, he would scatter them in the night before the attack. But he lacked the hardware for such an endeavor, as well as a secured position to defend.

Those with spears would have some advantage against the men fighting from horseback. He had three spearmen. These barbarians were brutes that craved the intimate fighting of hand-to-hand combat with bludgeoning maces and sharp-edged swords.

Then there were the ghouls. *They're miniature versions of the monster I've become,* Shiverrig thought dismally. Not quite the fighting force he envisioned, but effective at the necessary messy work required to conquer a land. *But against charging horses?* It didn't take a genius to see that a straight fight was a losing proposition for his bourgeoning army.

Then a thought touched his mind, something his father had said to him on their first campaign together. Gerun had been fifteen at the time, but the lesson had always remained true.

"Professional soldiers are predictable, it's the amateurs and the politicians that are dangerous."

He glanced to either side. The enemy riders kept pace with his war column. Then he scanned the open horizon. *What are they thinking? Nowhere to hide in ambush, unless...*

Shiverrig's eyes dropped to the ground. The memory of his father's murder hit him like a hammer striking an anvil. How could he have missed such an obvious stunt? It had all happened before in this same spot with disastrous results. He could not escape the Shiverrig curse.

"To me! To me!" he shouted, but it was already too late.

Trap doors sprung open on either side of the dirt road and a multitude of soldiers in dusty padded leathers erupted from hidden burrows just under the long grass. The doldrums of a long march quickly gave way to pandemonium. Limbs were severed and skulls were smashed under metal helmets from those caught unaware. Soon, heads rolled, and bodies fell.

The ghouls scattered. Sess'thra's membranous wings unfurled, and she leaped into the air. Her girlish body now resembling a hunting falcon rather than an alluring demon. Daku snarled like a feral wolf and launched into three men that had singled him out to destroy. Another trapdoor opened and he was hauled beneath the surface.

Unarmed barbarians grappled with their hands and fists until fingers found eye sockets and throats. His troops not felled in the ambush rallied into smaller groups, only to be trampled under heavy hooves as the enemy riders charged, crisscrossing his ranks at murderous velocity.

The hardened faces of his men transformed to fear and panic as the enemy soldiers on horseback sliced and smashed with sword and cudgel. His men were outnumbered and suffering heavy loses. If he didn't change the momentum of battle, their defeat was inevitable.

Shiverrig drove his horse into a cluster of enemy soldiers. His sword cleaved heads from bodies and sprayed his face with blood. More of the enemy stormed from hidden tunnels. Their numbers seemed endless.

The legs of his horse were smashed, and it collapsed beneath him. The impact of its body hitting the ground headfirst tossed him from the saddle. His sword flew from his hand. He rolled with the momentum of the fall and rose in a fluid motion, snarling like an animal. His preternatural growl gave pause to the enemies surrounding him.

Then the nightmarish whisper of Dai-Ko-Zior's death magic hovered over the din of battle. A slithering green mist wove through the wild melee. Friend and enemy soldiers alike suffered the same grisly fate. The clashing of steel was replaced by screams, then the agonizing gurgle of melting throats and bodily flesh carried the field. There was no glory here, only death.

The aftermath of battle was perversely serene. The few remaining ghouls, which had mindlessly scattered far enough away into the fields to survive, raced back as the green fog dissipated, and set about feasting on the viscous soup dripping of the dead.

Some distance away, Daku emerged from a different tunnel opening. His white fur was covered in clumps of dirt and blood oozed from numerous wounds. His breath was ragged though his feral eyes searched for something else to kill as he lumbered closer to Shiverrig.

He felt the eerie presence of the lich hovering at his side.

"All of them?" Shiverrig said, angrily, snatching his sword from a tuft of grass. He cleaned the blood from the blade and replaced it in its scabbard. "Was that necessary?"

"I do not think my masters intend for you to die before you have accomplished your task. I am owed much and will not be denied my ascension," Dai-Ko-Zior said. "I did what was needed to preserve you."

Shiverrig harrumphed. He turned to Daku. "Did you root out the remaining rats?"

"It's impossible to know. The tunnels are endless," Daku

replied, clearing his throat and spitting out something thick and white.

Sess'thra floated down to the ground, pouting. "I missed all the fun. The lich didn't leave any alive."

"Take a ghoul if you're so desperate," Daku said. His head twitched to the side, ever so slightly.

Shiverrig took stock of what remained of his army and saw a handful of worthless fiends playing in the human slime. The horses didn't survive and their sloppy remains spoiled the meager supplies they had left. He was fortunate to have sent the half-breeds to Gethem.

"It's still another three days to Winter's Fury. Now that our forces are less formidable, I suggest we find an alternate route," Shiverrig said. "Sess'thra, come here."

"Yes, my darling and delicious man?"

"You will teleport me to the ruins. Daku, drop back underground and shadow walk to the pit. Focus on the southern bridge. I doubt it still spans the expanse, but it's a good enough meeting point."

Shiverrig turned to the lich, who gave him a rotten smile filled with black teeth.

"I will arrive in time and by my own means," Dai-Ko-Zior rasped.

"Understood," Shiverrig said. "Let's move."

"As you wish my fascinating man," Sess'thra said.

In a blink of an eye, Shiverrig and Sess'thra materialized at the edge of the pit where Sekka's tower once rose. As expected, the bridge that had once connected the two sides was gone. Everywhere Shiverrig looked, he saw failure and ruin.

"This is a dead place," he said.

A whisp of smoke rose from somewhere deep within the pit.

"Look! Something survives. Let's go see what it is," Sess'thra said gleefully.

"This is all just a big game to you, isn't it?" Shiverrig said.

"Of course, it is, silly," Sess'thra said, then burst out in childlike laughter. "How else do you think I've endured the boredom of endless time? Life would be so dull and dreary otherwise."

Shiverrig scanned the looming mountain range to the right, remembering where he had knelt on glass rock as a captive of the archangel, Raguel, and his Protectorate Guard. One does not easily forget the spot of a death sentence.

If not for the sorcerer, he would have died with the rest of his legions at the hands of the angels. Shiverrig turned completely around. There was no sight of the lich.

"Where is that cursed spellcaster? I don't intend to stay here any longer than necessary."

"Shall we have a picnic and wait?" Sess'thra said.

"It shouldn't be this cold. Winter's first snow hasn't fallen," Shiverrig said. He looked suspiciously at Sess'thra. Something wasn't right. She looked too eager.

Then Daku materialized a league away and bounded to their position. When he arrived, his breathing was heavy, and his head lolled beneath his shoulders. A queer smile curled around his mouth as he wiped the strands of drool and spittle from his snout.

Shiverrig walked to the edge of the pit, then gazed across the chasm. The middle column remained, though the tower had been vaporized, reduced to blackened lines of ruined foundation and scattered rubble. The smoke continued to drift upwards.

"Bandits and thieves have made a home in the tunnels to avoid attention. This was a colossal waste of time," he said.

"Oh, don't be so negative. Let's have a look. You never know what you might find in the dark."

"She's right. Maybe Sekka hid something of value down there," Daku said in a tired voice. He hacked as if he had something caught in his throat.

Shiverrig squatted down and grabbed a handful of grayish dirt. It was filled with crystalized shavings. Most likely the ashen and molten remains of his troops. He rattled it in his oversized hand, then raised himself up and tossed the earth into the pit.

"We're leaving and heading back to Gethem. I'll start there with the half-breeds."

"Where's the dead wizard?" Daku said, clearing his throat. He hacked again.

"What's the matter with you?"

Daku spit out a wad of pinkish phlegm. "Nothing. I'm fine."

Shiverrig narrowed his eyes, unconvinced. He then looked to the open plains. "We're returning south to raise a new army," Shiverrig said.

"Do you think anyone will side with you? Clearly, by our warm reception across the grasslands, they haven't forgotten Qaçal."

"Damn that lich. He is just as careless with his sorcery in death as he was in life. Nothing has changed since the jungles of Sunne. If I am to retake the Three Kingdoms, I will need more troops. The Lesser Houses pretending to have noble blood will be the first to join my ranks."

Shiverrig watched a ghoul scamper after a rat until it raced into a hole. "One way or another."

Daku rubbed his eyes until his sockets were raw. When he took his hand away, his eyes were bloodshot red and leaking tears.

"And the daimus nexus? What's your plan? Those two things in the north don't strike me as the patient type."

"Bah. I gave them no promise of time. If they're so mighty they wouldn't be trapped in the wastelands. They can wait."

"Xerthotha was just a voice in your head. Those bloodsuckers are here, now, and are more powerful than you think," Daku said. He took an unsteady step, then stopped walking. A fit of coughing took him and he spit out more pink phlegm. "Send the succubus."

Shiverrig watched the pale demon carefully. He didn't have time for this. Maybe it was time to end the charade. Daku had tried his best but without the golden circlet he was no match for the true shadow demon lurking inside.

"If you are going to puke, get it over with."

"You don't even know what they want," Daku said after the coughing had stopped. "What if this nexus thing is another Sekka, or worse? We both know that didn't end well."

Shiverrig walked past Daku, scanning the ruins for Dai-Ko-Zior. "Where the fuck is that sorcerer?"

"This feels like we're back in the dirty water circling the drain," Daku said, then doubled over in another coughing fit.

"Are you finished? We have work to do," Shiverrig said. "Go see where the lich has lost himself. I'll have a word with the succubus."

He turned in the opposite direction to see Sess'thra spinning in a carefree pirouette. Then, the unmistakable sound of a sword being drawn from its sheath caught his attention. Before he could turn the sharp tip of a blade bit into his flesh.

"Time to die, mortal."

Shiverrig spun fast to see the pale demon standing before him. Menacing, pink eyes glaring beneath a furrowed brow.

"Daku?"

"Ho, ho, ho. Not today, hero," Khalkoroth said as he thrust the fell blade, Eishorror, through Shiverrig's gut in a smooth, easy motion.

Oddly, Shiverrig felt little pain. He instinctively grabbed the sword and watched in fascinating horror as both hands froze solid.

"I have lived for thousands of years and have thousands more to come. Did you really think that boy would prevent my return? I told you my time would come, and I would hurt you when it did."

"What kept you?" Shiverrig said. He heard clapping coming from somewhere and a mature woman's voice floating through the air. Where was Sess'thra?

"Well done, my loyal shadow demon."

"I knew it was you, mistress!" Sess'thra squealed in excitement somewhere to the right.

Khalkoroth looked over his shoulder. "Your servant has returned to you and slain this enemy in your honor."

Shiverrig looked passed Khalkoroth through watering eyes and saw the specter of a grown woman approaching. Long, white hair billowed from a gust of wind before it settled around a face, framing black on black eyes.

"I am pleased," Sekka said, then looked smugly at Shiverrig. "Very pleased, indeed."

"Curse you to the bowels of Hell," Shiverrig managed to mumble through chattering teeth.

Khalkoroth stepped back and ripped the frost blade from Shiverrig's gut, shattering his hands though no blood ran from his wounds. Shiverrig dropped to his knees and was mildly aware of Sess'thra sauntering toward him.

"Does it hurt?" she said. The look of admiration and lust she'd normally held for him was replaced by contempt. She traced her finger along the curled surface of one of his horns.

"Hel-p...me," Shiverrig pleaded.

Sess'thra leaned in close, brushing her lips to his left ear. "You, silly man-child. Who do you think convinced Xerthotha to make you his champion? We could have ruled the Three Kingdoms and beyond, uncontested and together. But you had to resist and do things your way."

She straightened her back. "Tsk, tsk, now look at you, gutted like a pig and whimpering like a babe. You're a far cry from the Golden Son I had envisioned."

"You used me," Shiverrig mumbled through numb lips.

Sess'thra melodic laugher grated on his thinning senses. She stood before him with the body of a seductress, the face of innocence, and the cunning mind of a jackal.

"Have you learned nothing? Yes, I used you and given the opportunity I would do so again. But you were fun for a time, brief as it was. I would say, see you soon, but considering where you are going, I doubt that will be for some time."

"Sess'thra," Sekka called. The archdevil was already

returning to the pit. Khalkoroth slaughtered the remaining simple-minded ghouls before loping to her side.

"And the game continues." She gave him a playful wink. "Coming, mistress."

The succubus walked away and didn't look back. His face hit the ground, though he didn't feel it. Then there was nothing.

23

DESDEMONIA

"Sess'thra knew they were coming, oh, that little bitch! She'll be sorry when I get my hands on her," Desdemonia said through gritted teeth and clenched fists.

She had teleported to the first place that came to mind. It was the central square of a small village on the outskirts of what she would consider her trading territory. Plus, it was in the direction of the Sarribe Mountains, which hopefully meant Kasai.

She would occasionally come here to resupply when she took long treks away from her cottage, or to hear the latest gossip filtering through the kingdom. Though, she knew by the time the news arrived here, the facts had become rather skewed. The outside world rarely made sense anyway, at least it didn't to her.

Nonetheless, it was something to do and laugh at with the few friends she had made here. Desdemonia was saddened to see the village had not survived the finality of the war. It had been destroyed long ago, ravaged by the angelic fires. The villagers were gone or dead within the collapsed structures.

"Oh no. What did these poor people do to deserve this? Devils and demons on one side, True-born angels, and their righteous soldiers on the other, and these poor souls were caught in the middle. Where was their justice?"

Desdemonia took a few more steps toward a shop she traded in. *Would you have helped them if you could? Do you still care enough? Are you even still one of them?*

She let out a sigh. "I don't know. I just don't know. But someone needs to protect the weak and innocent."

Desdemonia turned in a full circle. There was nothing here and eventually, she would need supplies if she was going to find Kasai. *Did she, though? She hadn't even thought of food since...being mortal.*

She spoke the words of the teleportation spell and blinked out of existence. Then with a pop, she arrived in the bustling village square of Warren.

"I think I'm getting the hang of this," she said, blinking as her eyes became accustomed to the new environment.

She came here once a season to trade herbal potions for spices and seeds, that for some reason, could only be found here. It was a thriving village than could never quite become a town. The people here accepted her for who she was and didn't bother with horrible labels or superstitions. To them, she was just Desdemonia, the girl who sold the most delicious honey.

She searched for familiar faces in the crowd of people scattering out of her way with all kinds of startled, confused, and fearful expressions.

"Note to self, next time, concentrate on a spot outside of

town," she said and waved to a villager staring at her with her mouth wide open. "Hi there. Sorry, sorry, I know. A bit of a scare."

She walked quickly toward the Old Crow, a merchant's shop where she knew the owner. He was a bear of a man and always treated her nicely. She called him Little Joey V and he didn't seem to mind.

Those monks must have traded for supplies, right? Maybe I can enchant a useful item like my dad used to do and get some information, she thought, hopefully.

Electricity crackled in the air as a squad of Protectorate angels popped into existence throughout the town square, effectively surrounding her and ready for battle.

"Dammit," she said and searched for a way out. The power radiating from the heavenly warriors was palpable. She could feel it on her skin. It was cleansing and deadly at once.

The villagers in the square either scattered like mice or dropped to their knees, frozen in place, mumbling prayers to the Immortal Mother.

"There's nowhere to run to now, witch," Sonnalle's melodious voice echoed over the shouts of the frenzied villagers. "There's no need for this hovel to be destroyed because of your stubborn resistance. You will come with me."

"What are you, part hound?" Desdemonia said. Then she tried to teleport away, but only managed to shift a few paces.

"Your clever trick is useless now," Sonnalle said. "Come peacefully and I will see that you are treated fairly, or at least as well as can be expected for one such as you."

Desdemonia heard the memory of Sekka's voice whispering inside her head. *Use the dark magic, daughter. It will set you free.*

For once, Desdemonia did as she was told.

Her wings materialized in a billowing, inky-black, vaporous cloud. She leaped into the air, leaving a spinning spiral of smoke in her wake. The angels rose with her.

All the better, she thought, thinking of the lives of the innocent villagers. *I guess I do still care.*

Instinctively, her hands flashed outward, shooting slimy, black tendrils of organic matter that slashed like whips across the celestials' armor. The protective steel fizzled and their eyes were blinded by stinging, charcoal-colored smoke. The residual slime splashed over the angels' exposed faces, causing them to scream in pain as the mucus burned their flesh to the bone.

She heard Sonnalle's voice echo around her and watched in disappointment as the slime covering the angels dissolved from their armor and flesh. More angelic words were spoken, and tiny sparkles cascaded over the angels' damaged skin. The sight of the divine magic reminded Desdemonia of fireflies in the forest. But that was where the pleasant memory ended as she saw the flesh of her foes reknit and heal as if new.

You must go deeper into the forbidden.

"I'm trying and you're not helping! Where are you when I need you?" Desdemonia shouted as she climbed higher into the air. Her smokey wings beat hard and soon she had put some distance between herself and the angels.

Desdemonia headed into low hanging cloud cover and for a moment she dared to hope that she had lost them.

I am only a sliver of a memory of what could have been.

"This is Raguel's fault. It should have been him that destroyed you. Killing demons and archdevils is not the work of mortals. If he had just done what angels are supposed to do, then Gauldi would still be alive, and I'd still be normal."

Bahahaha you were never normal.

"Well, I wouldn't be this thing! Geez, can you get on my side for once?"

Desdemonia watched in wonder as her raven locks rose in stiff sticks above her head.

"Oh no. This isn't good."

The searing sizzle of multiple bolts of lightning shocked her body. She was paralyzed in midair as the static energy ripped through her. She screamed in pain as the world exploded with bright white light. When the attack ceased, Desdemonia fell from the sky.

She was vaguely aware of a sea of treetops and then a clearing of rooftops rushing to meet her. Somehow, she gathered enough wits to will herself to stop, and the inky vapors responded. They swirled around her in a gaseous cocoon, which cushioned her impact on the ground.

She bounced twice but managed to tuck and roll, then come up fast. The angels were already there. More lightning hit her and tossed her through the front window of the Old Crow.

"Ugh. That really hurts."

She raised herself slowly from the floor. Shards of glass dug into her face, arms, and hands. Fires quickly kindled and choking smoke filled the small store. Little Joey V was sprawled over the counter. Fire still burned his body where the lightning had ripped through him.

"No, not him. He did nothing wrong!"

Somehow, a few villagers inside the Old Crow managed to survive the lightning strike and ran blindly outside, screaming in fear. They flew back inside, riding the next wave of angelic lightning, dancing into the merchant's store. The smell of their roasted bodies hit her like a slap across the face.

"I'm so sick of this shit." Desdemonia's magic boiled in her veins. She clenched her hands to fists and marched outside.

"Ah, I see you finally understand the hopelessness of your flight," Sonnalle said. He pushed away an old woman, who mistakenly thought he was there to save her. She was dead before she hit the ground.

"You can go ahead and wipe that pompous smile off your face," Desdemonia said, planting her feet firmly in the dirt of the square. "I'm not going anywhere."

"Take her," Sonnalle said.

His smug expression was infuriating. Desdemonia willed fire to appear and a swirling column of blue flames wrapped around her body. The cylindrical wall of flames expanded away from her body and slammed into the advancing angels. She saw the dark silhouettes of the angels through the flames.

"Let's see you get through that."

One by one the angels walked through the wall of fire. Small tongues of flames smoldered briefly on their armor, then were snuffed out. Their flesh suffered no harm. The angels glared at her and stalked forward.

"Whoa. That's not good," Desdemonia said.

"You cannot hope to best divine might with your feeble magic," Sonnalle said.

An angel rushed forward. His sword held back, ready to strike. Another approached from the opposite side. Desdemonia could feel her magic swelling inside of her. It was now so much greater than anything she had experienced while under Sekka's influence.

Use the forbidden magic. Send them to oblivion! Sekka's voice hammered into her mind.

"Perhaps something with a little more kick, then," Desdemonia said and conjured a small ball of pure darkness, big enough to hold in her hand. "And add a little spark to light the way. I learned this from my foster mom."

Chain lightning traveled over the surface but the space inside remained pitch black. She threw it at the nearest angel.

"Catch!"

The angel instinctively swatted the ball away like a gnat, but it stuck fast to the back of his hand and no manner of shaking could remove it. Then his expression changed from annoyance to horror as the shadow ball grew and engulfed him in a bubble of darkness.

The electricity swirled rapidly over the bubble's surface. A moment later, the shadow ball popped, leaving nothing of the angelic warrior.

The remaining angels rushed her, heedless of the danger. Desdemonia conjured more black balls, this time sending them to their targets with her mind. Each one gave a muffled shriek before being snuffed out of existence.

Sonnalle stood dumbfounded. Then desperately summoned a surging bolt of lightning and shot it at Desdemonia. It pushed her backward. The pain was intense, but she took it, and remained standing. The black vapor seemed to feed off its energy and swirled like a hurricane around her.

He sent another lightning strike at her, but the protective vapor somehow slowed the bolt enough for her to grab it and let it circle around her hand like a giant lantern. The strength of her magic was incredible.

"Isn't this a pretty thing."

"Impossible," Sonnalle stuttered. "You are only mortal."

"Am I?" Desdemonia smirked. She let her horns curl out of her forehead. A moment later the halo orbs spun in a lazy circle above her head.

"You know, I've always wondered why the Great Balance was soooo important. But now, I think I get it. When things shift too far one way or the other, everything in the middle goes to shit," she said and laughed. "It doesn't even matter which side you're on, either."

Sonnalle backed away as Desdemonia stalked forward.

"It's best when everything remains equal, right down the middle. So, if you take from me, I have no choice but to take from you. This way, everything stays balanced."

Then she glared at the True-born angel. "And you took Gauldi from me. It was a cruel act committed by the cruel dog of a cruel master. Well, I can be cruel too."

Desdemonia hurled Sonnalle's lightning bolt black at him. He uttered a defensive incantation, but nonetheless, the lightning exploded into his chest.

"Oh, I added a little something extra to that, sorry. It seems Xerthotha gave me his blessing, too."

She advanced on the injured True-born, waving her hand over him and speaking the word "fail" before blowing him a kiss.

Sonnalle's incredulous expression told her that her hex had worked.

"What's the matter, healing powers not working? I bet you can't blink away, either."

"What are you?" Sonnalle said through labored breathing.

Desdemonia watched with satisfaction as blood dripped from his chest plate. He tried to rise but she stomped him back down.

"I haven't a clue," she said. "But now is not the time for introspection or self-discovery. It's time for judgment. You killed my friend, and he will be avenged. After all, the Great Balance must remain."

She molded another black ball into her hand, letting the spinning lightning grow fierce on its surface. The look of fear on Sonnalle's face was priceless.

"I'd be lying if I said I wasn't going to enjoy this," Desdemonia said as she raised her arms. "I only wish it was Raguel under my foot instead of you."

Just then, another Protectorate materialized in the square. He was stunned to see Desdemonia standing over Sonnalle and quickly drew his sword. The angel ran at Desdemonia with deadly purpose.

"Escape! She is beyond you! Warn Lord Raguel," Sonnalle commanded.

The angel stutter-stepped to a stop. Then the sound of galloping horses filled the square. A makeshift militia under the banner of an unfamiliar Lesser House fluttered in the air. Nine soldiers and their captain pulled the horses to a stop.

"You, there! Halt!" a soldier at the head of the group

shouted, though it was clear he was unsure of what he was seeing.

"Sorry, Sonnalle. The cavalry won't save you," Desdemonia said.

"This is not over," Sonnalle said through bloodied teeth. "Lord Raguel will see you destroyed."

"It is for you."

She opened her hand and dropped the black ball. Sonnalle's scream was cut short and then it was over. He was gone. She then brought her gaze to the sole Protectorate. He was torn between attacking her or fleeing with the news of what he saw.

"Don't worry. I have more," Desdemonia said and formed another black ball between her hands.

The Protectorate shouted as Desdemonia threw the ball of darkness at him. He blinked out of existence just as the ball flew past his position and hit the front porch of the rice wine vendor across the street. The small building crumbled in on itself and was gone.

Desdemonia sucked the air between her teeth. "Just missed." She then watched with detached interest as the horsemen pulled their mounts back. She didn't bother hiding her new features from their view with a glamour. They stared at her with spooked eyes and gestured signs of protection across their chest.

"Listen, I'm not looking for a fight. The angel and I had unfinished business and now, everything is mostly settled."

The captain of the group stared in wonder then managed to speak. "We have been charged by our lord to purge his lands of demonkind."

"Demon hunters, are you? How nice. I thought you were

supposed to be women from the Archipelago of Mith. Well, I'm not a demon so you can be on your way."

"Witch then, or whatever foul thing you are, you cannot be allowed to live."

Desdemonia sighed and lit her hands with blue flame. "And I woke up in such a good mood."

24
KASAI

Kasai and Gift navigated through a wheat field. The grassy stalks had dried to a golden yellow color and the crop was ready for harvest. Gift had taken the lead and pushed through another row, searching for a faster way through the lines in the field. Kasai watched her move like a determined jungle cat trailing prey. The tension between them was only getting worse.

"I'm sorry, Gift. I never meant to hurt you," Kasai said as he pushed wheat leaves away from his face. His apology sounded hollow to him, and he could only imagine how it sounded to her.

Gift continued walking in silence, then she struck at an unfortunate stalk that was in her way, taking it down with quick swat of her bo staff. A murder of crows took flight to the left, squawking and cawing as the flew away.

"It is understood. We all thought she rested during the long sleep. But if somehow, she lives then I will not abandon her to those who would bring her harm. The honor of the Frona Tribe demands that we do not forsake our own.

"How this has come to be is a mystery only Nayche can solve. Desdemonia died on the battlefield many years ago. If she is alive, I fear she will not be the Desdemonia you know, but something else, something…unnatural."

Conflicting thoughts collided in Kasai's mind. Of course, Gift was right. How could Des be alive? That's impossible. Wasn't it? But just as impossible was a diabolical portal that breached the Amaranthine Barrier and permitted angels and demons to bring their eternal war to the Mortal Realm.

Kasai searched the sky for answers and found none. Life seemed absurd at times, especially his. Not for the first time, he wondered why he had been chosen for such a fate. Worlds at war against one another, fighting over the souls of mortals, and the Ever Hero smack in the middle of it.

Just a stupid monk, he thought. Then, he noticed a winding trail of billowing smoke rising over the treetops.

"Look there," Kasai said.

"The wind brings the smell of magic and burning flesh," Gift said.

"The angels have found her. I have to go!"

"You'll never get there in time, and without the staff—"

"I'll find a way!" Kasai shot back.

He ignited his fire xindu and ran. *Des, I'm coming.*

Using his earth xindu, he communicated with the vibrations of the soil to give his steps a spring as they hit the ground, propelling him faster than the fastest deer. Using his air xindu, he channeled an open path before him to decrease wind resistance. The distant tree line came forward fast and soon trees were blurring past his eyes.

Aetenos, where are you when I need you? I could really use your help on this one. But Aetenos's no longer whispered his guidance in Kasai's ears. He was on his own and had been since the day Aetenos had declared him to be the next Divine Fist.

Kasai ran on. He knew he was burning through the precious energy he would need to fight against Sonnalle and his angels, but it didn't matter, he needed to get to her. Just to see her again would be enough.

Hold on, Des. I'm coming.

The forest thinned and a village took shape between tree trunks and low hanging branches. There was a loud commotion in the center square. Kasai saw scared people running, falling, and crying. At least one building was lost to fire, while smoke poured out of the shattered windows of smaller shops.

Kasai slowed to a stop. His chest heaved and his lungs burned. He wiped the sweat, leaves, and dirt from his face and saw a group of soldiers atop horses milling in a wide circle. Dust clouded around the horse's legs as they jostled close together.

Blue magic erupted from the center of the circle. Then, he saw someone trapped in the middle of the circling soldiers. It was Desdemonia! It had to be. There was no mistaking the raven hair and the fierce disposition. He quickly scanned the area, worried that something more dangerous would soon appear.

"No angels yet. I can handle this," he said between huffs with relief. He picked up his pace and ran into the village center.

"Stop!" he shouted. "Leave her alone!"

The soldiers glanced at Kasai angrily, but then turned their attention back to Desdemonia. They kicked their horses forward and raised their swords. With a command from their captain, they started hacking down.

"No!" Kasai yelled.

He lost her in a thick cloud of street dust and churning, black smoke. The soldiers were shouting out curses and swinging their swords repeatedly. Whatever he was going to do, he had to do it now or lose his love for the second time.

Kasai skidded to a stop. He ignited his fire xindu again and sparked his other xindu energies into action. He curled his hands into tight fists, summoning his air, water, and earth energy together. Raising his arms to the side, he opened his fists and let the combined energies manifest between his palms.

He felt a spark of the Boundless travel through him as thin lines of electricity danced over his hands and small rocks rose into the air at his feet. Water was drawn from the atmosphere and sloshed between his palms in a spinning vortex.

His air xindu twisted the collected energy into a thin spiral that stretched between his hands. He spread his arms until the connection snapped, leaving both hands charged with energy. Then he knelt and slammed both into the ground, sending a shockwave of energy toward the horsemen.

"Erupt!" he shouted, and the ground under the mounted soldiers heaved. The horses reared and two of the riders were thrown to the ground. Kasai watched them roll away before being trampled.

Kasai ignited his fire xindu and dashed forward, darting between the disoriented riders. His hands smoldered with residual energy, and he shoved them against the chest of a startled horse. The horse screamed and shied away. He then gathered the air xindu around him into a protective sphere and made his way to Desdemonia.

A tight ring of riders bore down on the center. Kasai could only hope Desdemonia was still alive. Then blue light flared, causing the men to shield their eyes. Kasai squeezed though a narrow opening between horses and stood by Desdemonia's side. He forcefully pushed the sphere of air xindu outward, creating space between him and the riders.

Kasai's hands burned with amber heat. "Leave her be! The next one to touch her will burn."

The captain barked out an order and the small group broke apart and galloped a safe distance away. When the dust and debris settled, Desdemonia stood unharmed. Her manner was aloof, as if nothing had occurred.

Kasai stared at her in disbelief. Then he looked to where the soldiers had gone. They gathered in a loose circle some fifty yards away. The surviving villagers had cleared the square.

"Oh, hello Kasai. I was coming to find you. But you've come to me instead. That was thoughtful of you. She was right. You're all grown up," Desdemonia said with an easy smile.

Kasai saw the horns and the glowing halo above her head, and so much black smoke. The soldiers had attacked her from all sides yet, she was somehow still alive. He stood breathless before her, trying to make sense of everything.

"I can't believe it,' he said at last.

"I know. You must think I'm a freak."

"You're alive. I can't believe you're alive!" He embraced her in a bear hug.

"Wha-what happened?" he said when he finally let her go.

"They made me into a monster. I'm sorry. I didn't mean or want any of this to happen. Why won't they leave me be, Kasai? What did I do that was so horrible?"

Kasai looked over his shoulder to the milling soldiers. They were arguing and the captain was pointing to one of them, but they hadn't made any other movements.

"I thought they had you for sure," Kasai said, turning back to Desdemonia.

"Some of them did, or they thought they did," Desdemonia said. She brushed herself off and stretched her back. "But the Great Balance would not allow it, and everything is as it should be."

Kasai was barely listening. "What do you mean a monster? You look wonderful. I've missed you more than you can imagine."

"Sweet Kasai. I've changed, far beyond the obvious," Desdemonia said. "Everything is a mess, especially me."

"It's not your fault, Des. We can fix it, somehow. I'll find a way. Maybe Illyria can help. I'll figure out how to contact her or Aetenos, or someone."

"If only it were that easy. But they cannot help me, not now," she said, then continued, but to Kasai it seemed like she was talking to herself. "I should be as dead as Sonnalle and his angels. But who am I to understand the ways of gods and devils?"

"Sonnalle is here, with angels?" Kasai searched the square. "Wait, he's dead?"

"Yes, Kasai and I killed him using a forbidden magic. It has always been in me, I think, and when it wanted to be released, I let it happen. It felt good to wield the sword of justice for once."

"Whatever happened, we can work this out. Trust me. I can fix it."

She looked at him and brought her hand to his face. "You must let me go, Kasai. I shouldn't be here, doing these things, but I'm not allowed to die. I have no connection to this place. You're the last fond memory I have here and that too is fading."

"Don't say that. We'll make more memories together."

"This world has gone all wrong. A paradise was created for us and the greed for power soured that beautiful gift. Look around, Kasai. Look at the real world. I see stealing, killing, and despair."

"There is good here too," Kasai said.

"You know as well as I that what we fought for was meaningless. After we die, we go to one Hell or another. There is no salvation."

"Des, we can get away. Let's go to your cottage where we can rest."

A look of calm came over Desdemonia's face. "Rest would be nice. Maybe."

Then Desdemonia's expression fell. She looked past Kasai to the burning buildings and dead littering the ground. "There is no rest for me now. I think I know why they did what they did to me, and why I am here. This world doesn't have to be such a terrible place. It can change and I can be the equalizer to bring back the balance."

"Des, just stay with me," Kasai pleaded.

"I'm sorry, Kasai. Desdemonia Mishi is gone. I have no name. I'm only a thing now; a harbinger of doom for those who seek to tip the balance."

"You are Manna'Desdevi Mishi," Kasai pleaded. "You just need to remember who you are."

"The potency of that name is gone for me. You keep it now and keep it safe. I am something altogether different, a nexus between order and chaos.

"There is a voice calling me to the North, beyond the lands of man and beast, whispering of answers that promise to remove the pain and suffering from this forsaken place. I will see to that. I'll do it for you, Kasai, and the memory of what we shared."

"Then, I'm going too."

"Do not follow me. It will end badly for you if you do. The Great Balance must be restored. Atonement is at hand."

Kasai looked puzzled by her comment, then heard a dull *thunk,* followed by a sharp pain in his gut. He took a stutter step forward, then saw the bright red arrowhead and sticking out of his midsection.

"I've been hit," he said, stunned. He looked at Desdemonia, confused, just as a second arrow hit him in the shoulder. His legs folded under him, and he collapsed to the ground.

Spots swam before Kasai's eyes as he tried to focus. Finally, he found Desdemonia's feet and looked up to see her face, shrouded by black, serpentine hair. The orbs of golden light spun faster, creating a halo band around the two horns, curling from her forehead.

"The price of death is the cost of life, when weighed on the scale of the Great Balance," she said as her expression darkened.

"This can't be happening. I can't die. I just...found you,"

he stammered and tried to get up, but fell back down to his side. "This isn't fair."

Inky vapor spilling from Desdemonia's back, eventually forming wispy batlike wings with long finger-tipped ends.

"Life was never meant to be fair, Kasai. But it can be balanced."

His head twisted awkwardly, trying to follow Desdemonia as she floated toward the soldiers. She threw her hands out with fingers spread wide. Thick strands of blackness grew from her nails and coiled in the air like a weird sea anemone, grasping for something to snare.

She swished her arms together and the tendrils shot in a crisscross pattern, wrapping around man and horse as if possessed of a singular mind. Kasai heard some of the soldiers shout in alarm, while others wailed like children babbling for their mothers in fear.

Then the screaming started, and he blacked out.

25

RAGUEL

Lord Raguel strolled leisurely through a tranquil garden grove of magnificent ancient olive trees at midnight. The branches and leaves were lit by a soft blue light, while a gentle mist rolled through the lanes. The half-light of the pale moon gave him peace away from the increasingly overbearing light of the sun, *her* sun.

He existed in worlds conceived by her and was made to follow rules dictated by her. But here, in *his* olive grove, under *his* moon, his mind was allowed to wander idly without care or concern of rules and laws. That was the lie he was fond of believing.

The time to spark his great work to life was drawing near. It would start slowly and gracefully like the rolling mist at his feet. He envisioned the inhabitants of the Seven Heavens cheering his name as he marched through the Gates of Elysian towards a glory not seen since the creation of the Three Worlds.

He imagined the multitudes of underworlds comprising the Layers of the Abyss, crumbling under the might of his

Heavenly Host. One by one they would fall like broken sandcastles against the unstoppable tide of his will. He could taste the sweet victories to come like honey drops tickling his tongue with savory flavor.

Lord Raguel picked up his pace and moved with the lean and hungry grace of a prowling wolf. Catching up to Lord Raguel's right was the herd master, Lord Malik. He was bent at the waist and had locked his calloused hands behind his back. His facial features were oddly shaggy, resembling the wartime manes of the mounts and magical beasts under his command.

Malik was a plodder and careful thinker with a keen memory of the smallest of details. The old general unwrapped each scenario of engagement carefully, spotting potential weaknesses in troop placements that could shift momentum to the enemy and lead to disastrous results.

Therefore, his ability to arrange the Heavenly Host in the most opportune formations was second to none. His battle strategies seemed almost rudimentary in their simplicity due to layers of astute observation, deciphering of enemy movements, and careful planning.

To Raguel's left was Metatron, the warrior poet who walked with the upright and pristine stature of one who knows no fault or error. His voice was a monotonous metronome of facts and figures as he read from a thick ledger, busily reciting allocation, and allotments of troops, ranging from the lofty seraphim to the lowest animal spirits.

"Every available warrior, steed, and beast has been accounted for and placed into balanced legions throughout each of the seven levels, my lord," Metatron said.

"Good, good," Raguel said, then he abruptly stopped

to prune away a misplaced bud, sprouting between two perfectly placed branches. "Everything is developing nicely."

"What is the percentage of unavailable assets to the whole?" Malik inquired.

"You will have more than you need for success, based on Metatron's calculations," Raguel said before Metatron could give an exact answer.

"I don't like variables," Malik said. "They have a way of creating unfavorable outcomes."

"Lord Raguel is correct. There is a 98.673333333 percent of achieving victory with the troops at your disposal," Metatron said. "Provided there are no other interruptions or diversions of troops "

"The Choir Council has not yet sanctioned your decree and trust me when I say, they are furious with your unilateral actions. My spies tell me they will vote against allowing this bold mobilization to continue. Getting their blessing would have gone a long way in securing more support from the city governors or level magistrates."

"The Choir Council has unwittingly and predictably maneuvered themselves into a bureaucratic impasse. The simplest of decisions cannot be made as they fight between themselves, looking for enemies and scapegoats, praying they are backing the right power to ensure their political survival.

"They have outlived their usefulness and will be disbanded once I have complete control."

"Disbanded? Is this the will of the Immortal Mother?" Malik asked.

"I am the first and the greatest of our kind. Are you doubting the rightful decree of my authority?"

Malik looked sideways at Raguel. "Of course not, lord. I am loyal and committed to the cause. The herds will muster at your call."

"See that they do," Raguel said. "The Immortal Mother understands she will lose the Three Worlds if changes are not made quickly. The scales have been allowed to tip disproportionally and a new hierarchy must be established to correct the imbalance. Metatron, please continue."

"In total—"

"Unless..." Malik interrupted.

"Unless, what?" Raguel said impatiently.

"You're assuming the able-bodied warriors and mystics not joining your rally will agree to follow your demands when the fighting starts. The Choir Council holds sway over the lower levels with powerful allies that influence their agendas.

"Don't think for a moment that your position of Chancellor Pinnacle has not been coveted by many elder True-borns among the Choir and their accompanying lackeys. The heads of that hidden hydra are many.

"Do you think they will sit idle while you move tens of millions of militias into battle groups across the Seven Heavens under the guise of invading the Abyss. We need their support to control their respective regions less a greater catastrophe will befall us."

"Metatron has the numbers of rebels you speak of, and they are too few to stop me," Raguel said.

"Quite right, my lord. Any who conspire against you will be imprisoned for treason and quietly banished long before that day," Metatron said. "The names of influencers who have demonstrated their lack of faith have been collected and a directive has been given for their arrest."

"Excellent. You see, Lord Malik. Everything is in place."

"But Lord Malik is not wrong in his summations. When you seize total control of the Seven Heavens, there will be consequences. I have calculated the outcome of the pending revolts, the damage to the infrastructure of the Seven Heavens, and casualties that will follow.

"What are the numbers?"

"There are still smaller percentages to calculate of souls lost from fringe battles and personal skirmishes and of course, the destruction of smaller towns and havens in the coming conflict."

"And?"

"Each Level will incur great loss. Elysian will suffer the most and will fall."

"Then I will make a point to rebuild the cities of fair Elysian first once the rebellion has been snuffed out. The newly arrived souls will join the Great Work or be condemned to haunt the void."

"You misunderstand, my lord. When momentum for victory shifts overwhelmingly to your advantage, which I predict will happen between thirty and thirty-three days from the first clash between loyalist troops and the fundamentalists holding to the old ways, my calculations conclude your enemies will seek to control the gateway into the Seven Heavens."

"And?" Raguel said.

"The dissidents will seek to stop you at all costs. They will have no other choice but to steal your strength by preventing fresh souls from replenishing your ranks,"

Metatron said, then paused for effect. "In their desperation, they will destroy the entire Heavenly Level of Elysian."

"They dare to stop the flow of souls? We will be weak and vulnerable to external attack," Malik said.

Metatron nodded his head. "The outcome of a war in Heaven will leave the Heavenly Host decimated. We should expect to lose an estimated third of the elite Seraphim Guard and an equal number of Principalite Mages. The foot soldiers of Arcadia will suffer the worst casualties at a conservative forty-eight percent. Lord Malik, your herds will be reduced by forty-two percent. This will, of course, impact the strength of the 777th Expedition before stepping one foot into the Abyss."

"Impossible," Raguel said confidently. "You both overestimate the reach of the Choir and their ability to orchestrate such a counter offensive. They are weak and do not have the stomach for a prolonged struggle. When the casualties mount, they will fold."

"The numbers align with my projected outcomes," Metatron said sounding annoyed at his calculations being questioned and then overruled. "Unless you have new data for me to process."

"Run them again with an additional buffer of fifteen percent to account for daily increases of support and latecomers joining the cause. I will initiate low-level martial law within the cities that are most likely to outwardly oppose me. It will be done quietly before the masses are aware they are being corralled.

"When the Seven Heavens are secured, we will establish operations in the Mortal Realm."

"As you wish, my lord," Metatron said.

"We will have everything we need when Sonnalle returns with the abomination. This will be a smooth transfer of power," Raguel said, and plucked a ripe olive from a nearby branch. He rattled it around in his partially closed palm, then turned to Malik.

"Nonetheless, to your earlier point, I will have the more vocal fundamentalist leaders removed immediately. Especially the animal spirits." Raguel tossed the olive in his mouth and bit down hard, cracking the pit between his teeth. "They have an uncanny knack of disrupting the best laid plans."

"And the Immortal Mother?" Malik asked hesitantly. "Her absence and input in this matter seems highly irregular, considering the scope of your plans."

"The Immortal Mother will not interfere. The pain and suffering caused by the lower realms must be yoked by whatever means necessary. She has left authority and responsibility of this task to me."

Malik grumbled something under his shaggy hair but nodded his agreement, nonetheless.

"Fine then. May I continue?" Metatron said.

"Please," Raguel said, pleasantly.

Metatron continued to read his report of the number of loyalist followers. He listed numerous generals and the staggering counts of angelic warriors under their command, and which garrisons were strategically occupied to control major cities should they rebel and block the passages between Heavenly Levels.

He looked to Malik to confirm the numbers of additional recruits of magical beasts and their handlers to his ranks of growing supporters. The coup for total control of the

Seven Heavens was a necessary step to securing the Three Worlds. It was time for the Great Balance to realign to the righteousness of Lawfulness.

"Tomorrow we shall meet in my chamber to finalize the details. Within the week, we will initiate the opening moves and take the leaders of the opposition off the table."

The following afternoon, Malik entered Raguel's Chamber of Reflections holding numerous scrolls and ledgers under his arms. The Chancellor Pinnacle was dressed in austere robes with multiple threads of gold and silver woven into the soft fabric. Attendants were placing uniquely shaped crowns, covered in priceless gems over his head.

"Ah, Lord Malik you've arrived. Perhaps you can help me chose which of these extravagant styles best suits me."

"Isn't it a bit too soon for a crown, Lord Raguel?" Malik said, glaring at the attendants who cowered in his presence. "Leave us. The Chancellor Pinnacle and I have much to discuss."

"It's a universal symbol of leadership, which all beings understand, even the devils in their sties."

"Apparently, you haven't been outside today. Groups are forming, filled with fundamentalists talking about challenging your authority."

"I have seen them. This is obviously a desperate attempt by the Choir Council to appear strong. It's nothing," Raguel said, dismissing the attendants.

"Are you enjoying the splendor of the high tower? Perhaps you should move to one of the upper apartments. The views are spectacular."

The old general's expression was grim. He walked to

a nearby table and dumped the contents in his arms on its surface. "There's much here that you have not shared," Malik said.

"It's more of the same. Small squabbles which fizzle out and die once the Protectorate arrive. I deemed it needless information."

"If you wish for me to conceive a strategy that assures victory, then I need every bit of information, not matter how trivial!"

"I said they are small squabbles," Raguel said, annoyed at Malik's harsh attitude.

"Squabbles, yes, but countless in number and occurring in every major city and town across the Seven Heavens. Are you convinced you have the backing of the masses for this crusade?"

"There must be a great culling in the Seven Heavens. We have become impure and are distracted by the unruly passions of emotion. Paradise is before us in the form of perfection, and yet we shun it, and give way to unlawfulness.

"Those who cannot see this, do not belong here, those who will not prescribe to my will, will be removed, never to be part of paradise again, they can live in squalor, in the Mortal Realm, or worse, in the putrid quagmire that is the Abyss," Raguel said.

"And the local unrest?"

"Yes, yes, I've noticed the small groups of activists pooling in the lobbies of the tower. Like a swarm of gnats, they hover and pester, but do nothing," Raguel said. "If one dares to bite, I send the Protectorate to remove them. There is a standing order to imprison any that resist."

Lord Raguel moved to the center of the chamber. The

sun was high overhead and the brightness outside the open windows made his eyes water.

She will see my worth again, he thought.

A clamor outside the chamber brought two Protectorate house guards and a battle-ready warrior to the doorway. He wore the insignia of Lord Sonnalle on his breast.

"What is it?" Raguel said mildly concerned.

"Chancellor Pinnacle, with sincere regret, we must inform you the equerry, Lord Sonnalle is dead," the captain of the guard said.

"Don't be absurd. Nothing can harm him in the Mortal Realm. Look to the waypoints. He may be there collecting the witch. Send him to me when you find him. I have important work for him to complete."

The two angles looked uncertainly at each other, and then to the third, who nodded solemnly. "Sire, this news is true. Protectorate Norad here was commanded by the equerry to return before he died," the captain said.

"You are mistaken. Aetenos's boy doesn't have the skill, or power to kill a True-born of the Seven Heavens. And that bothersome, one-eyed monk can no longer help him."

"It was not the one called Ever Hero, my lord. It was another; the wood witch, Desdemonia Mishi," Norad said. "The one Lord Sonnalle was instructed to bring back."

"Explain."

"I'm not sure I can, my lord. She wielded a power that shattered Lord Sonnalle's defenses as if he were a mere cherub instead of a True-born of the highest order."

"No."

"Sire?"

"Where is the body?"

"I believe it was obliterated, my lord. I escaped with my life to warn you, as was the last wish of Lord Sonnalle."

"Leave me. Gather more information. Go back if you must and confirm this outrageous report."

"Lord, it is confirmed."

"Just leave!"

Raguel heard the chamber door close. *No, not Sonnalle. Not him.* He moved to his desk. Absentmindedly, his hands curled into fists, and he slammed them both down hard on the surface. The white marble shattered under the force of his anger.

"So, the witch has found her way back home, and has grown powerful." He turned to Malik.

"I have a special mission for you. I will open a portal to the Mortal Realm big enough for one hundred of your elite warriors and their mounts. When you find the one called Desdemonia Mishi your will bring her to me, alive."

A messenger hurried into the room. "My lord, the rebels have overrun the lower levels and are now storming the tower. There are Protectorate Guards among their numbers."

"Perhaps quelling the coup at your doorstep would be a wiser first step." Malik said.

Thunderous claps boomed outside the walls of his chamber. Raguel moved to an arched window and saw a company of angels in full war gear materializing in the sky. Electricity bounced in twisting, orbital paths around their golden armor. Then, to Lord Raguel's amazement, the animal spirit, Zhao Houzi, appeared with a pop at their lead.

The monkey wore a black vest with cobalt blue runes of power etched in the material. His hairy arms were crossed over his small chest. Tucked under one arm was a small, orange and lime-green baton.

"Preposterous," Raguel said, and his anger rose. "What is that meddling monkey up to now?"

Then he saw hundreds of mounted lancers on griffons and hippogriffs appear, followed by thousands of winged warriors. No, not thousands but tens of thousands, who had come to stop him. Their teeming numbers packed the sky.

"Lord Raguel, surrender now and face the consequences of your actions. You have been charged with treason against the Laws of Heaven, set forth by the Immortal Mother," Zhao Houzi shouted over the din of the squawking flying beasts. "The Heavenly Host is here to bring you to justice!"

Epilogue

Kazumi Hime slashed her katana in a one-handed blur across the yanarothi's throat. The water demon's three eyes went wide in surprise. Green-grey blood flowed like a waterfall over the creature's boil-covered chest. A wet gurgle of what might be considered laughter came from its throat as blood spewed out in a fountain over the miller's floor.

Then, the demon's expression changed to outrage at being struck by one who appeared to be no more than a child. It lunged at her, and Kazumi side-stepped into a low crouch. She then thrust the sharp point of her sword upwards. It slid deeply into the demon's side as if it's skin and muscle were made of soft butter.

The yanarothi twisted and swiped a mucus-coated arm at her. Kazumi rammed the blade in deeper and the demon shrieked. She must have hit something important. Luckily for her, the water demons were less effective on dry land, or in this case, a house.

"Gotcha," Kazumi said.

The demon took two steps, then a third before toppling over into a mushy heap of gooey flesh. A terrible stench rose from the pile as the body decomposed into a wide puddle of demon death on the wood floor.

"Pugh. You stink," Kazumi said through a wrinkled nose.

Her acute senses listened for the next attack. Where there was one yanarothi, there was sure to be another. The minor demons preferred to hunt in groups, and she had been lucky to find this one alone.

Kazumi heard the creaking of the wooden mill outside, turning methodically, picking up and dumping water in a slow rhythm, and beyond that the lapping waves of the easy moving river.

"When engaging an unknown number of enemies, it is best to have a second sword at your side and a third to watch your back." Wise words from her mother. But today she was on her own. *This will prove to her that I am ready.*

She had found the bodies of the miller's family tossed haphazardly in the high reeds downstream. There hadn't been much left of them. She wondered if the villagers would be happy to know the old man was dead. He had a dishonest reputation of overcharging for crushing the local farmers' grain and then taking more than his cut of the final product.

But the children were innocent, and Kazumi would avenge them.

She slowly crossed the floor and paused sharply when her last step caused the dry wood to squeak in protest. Her eyes darted left and right, searching for movement, but the house was still.

"Two black marks for that blunder," she said in a cursed whisper.

She heard a rustling beneath the house, and then the thump and slurp of heavy steps on muddy ground. The floorboards ahead of her cracked and buckled in a line leading to the river outside. They were in the crawlspace under the house.

"Leaving so soon? I just got here," she said, trying to sound confident while running in the direction of the fleeing demons. *How many?* she wondered nervously.

Suddenly, the wood strips beneath her feet exploded upward and slimy hands grabbed her by the ankles and pulled her under. She clipped her wrist on a jagged piece of flooring and lost her grip on the sword.

Kazumi splashed into a muddy pool of water. The crawlspace was dimly lit by outside light coming in from an open door. She kicked and twisted, managing to free herself from the demon's hold. She leaped to her feet and shuffle-stepped back, glancing to the ground when she could, searching for the lost sword.

"Blood of the Abyss, where is it?"

There! It was half-covered in mud five feet to her left. Kazumi side-stepped toward the long, thin blade, keeping her eyes on the yanarothi before her. The water demon watched her with an amused expression but didn't bother to attack.

"What's so funny?" she said as she lowered herself to the sword.

Almost there. Her fingers could just touch the hilt. The yanarothi gave her a queer smile and turned away, just as a second demon shoved her face first into the mud. It grabbed her by the ankle and dragged her one-handed to the riverbank outside. If it reached the water, she was as good as dead.

Kazumi spat out the muck in her mouth and looked fleetingly at the distant katana. The enchanted blade was priceless and had been in their family since the First Frost War. Her mother was going to kill her if she lost that sword, but not before she was scolded for going on this mission alone.

Angrily, she snatched the wakizashi from the sash at her waist and curled her body forward. With a cruel smile she stabbed the short blade through the back of its neck and into the demon's skull. For good measure, she put the palm of her hand on the pommel and pushed it in deeper, forcing the blade's tip to come out its forehead.

Kazumi kicked off the backside of the demon and landed with a wet splatter on her back. A thick slurp followed when she dislodged herself from the muck. This time, she held onto her weapon.

"Well, this shozoku is ruined," Kazumi said, looking down at her clothing. She could feel the cold mud on her skin as it soaked through the fabric.

The remaining demon heard the death pang of its brethren and screamed in rage. It hunched its back and lumbered toward her. That was a mistake. Her small frame gave her room to swing her swords in the crawlspace, while its considerable bulk hampered its movement. The slick mud was nobody's friend, but her light weight made it easier for her to move quickly.

Kazumi shuffled backward and retrieved her katana, snapping it in a downward motion to remove the excessive mud. Then, she reached into a side pouch and deftly chucked six shuriken into the face of the oncoming demon, blinding its three eyes, and butchering its face. She appreciated the ensuing howl as it tried desperately to remove the sharp-edged stars.

Kazumi watched in dreadful amazement as two appendages tore through thin membranes at its sides. Needle-tipped barbs grew from the bulbous ends of the swaying arms.

"Oh, that's not pretty," she said and crouched into a ready position, holding the katana in one hand and the wakizashi in the other.

The yanarothi roared and threw its new arms forward, spraying the area with a barrage of thin projectiles. Her swords flashed in a whirlwind of motion, shattering, or deflecting the needles. It was a basic clan skill learned at an early age.

The demon roared in frustration and turned to flee to the river for safety. If it escaped, her mother would consider the mission to be a failure. Kazumi sprinted in a low run, careful not to slide in the slick mud. When she cleared the crawlspace, she leaped forward, tucking herself into a tight ball with her arms crisscrossed before her chest.

Her momentum carried her close enough to the demon for a deadly strike. She slashed out with both weapons. Each found their mark across the back of the yanarothi's neck. Its head dropped off its body and tumbled to the muddy ground.

Kazumi brought her feet up fast and kicked off the demon's back, somersaulting backward. She landed on her feet; thankful she had found solid ground. Then gagged violently as she mistakenly gulped in the reeking stink of the yanarothi's demon death.

When Kazumi recovered, she wiped the gooey blood

and muck from her katana, the edge of which never dulled, and sheathed it in the saya at her waist. She did the same for the smaller, wakizashi.

"Lose your sword, lose your life," her mother had chided her too many times to remember. But she was right, just like always.

Kazumi looked back to the mill house and frowned. The demon taint would remain in the floorboards and walls for years. The building would have to be burned and rebuilt, though she doubted anyone would want to purchase the property afterwards.

The locations of grisly deaths by demonkind tended to carry a stigma. But that wasn't her problem. She had done what she came to do.

"Three solo kills," she said, proudly. "The record was two."

Her body ached and was covered in mud and grime. She shivered. The sun was setting, and an orange glow was seen on the western horizon.

Kazumi was from an ancient, shizoku family, living on Yoru Island, which was part of the Archipelago of Mith. She was the newest member of the Yoru Ya-iba clan, the famed demon hunters, and the daughter of its clan leader.

She was rebellious, feisty, and stubborn. At seventeen, she felt she had mastered the craft of hunting and slaying demons. Convincing her mother was something entirely different.

Three solo kills! Her mother couldn't argue the facts any longer. She was ready to join the ranks of the Night Blades. Of course, she wouldn't bring up dropping the sword. That would be just the sort of thing her mother would hold against her.

Her clan had fought against the demon scourge since the time of Aetenos and the First Frost War. Even when the angels released their holy fires to cleanse the lands of the foul creatures after the Second Frost War, the demons somehow managed to persist. They were like roaches, multiplying in dark places, waiting for the call of a new master.

An Ever Hero had risen during this time, and if the rumors were true, he had blundered into a trap set by the enemy and opened a Chaos Gate. A Chaos Gate! Can you imagine the stupidity?

The Ever Hero was supposed to be the buffer between worlds; a safeguard to prevent full scale invasion. But six short years later, the land was dying, and demon-sightings were becoming common. Somehow, the demons had regrouped or possibly worse, found a way through the Amaranthine Barrier.

"Thank you, Immortal Mother, for sending us your Heavenly Host. And praise your first son, Lord Raguel, the true savior of the faithful for leading your armies to victory," Kazumi prayed. "May they forever protect us."

She then furrowed her brows. "And where is the Ever Hero now that the land bleeds and the people suffer? By the light of the Immortal Mother, I vow to find this false savior and make him answer for the damage and destruction he has caused. By all that is holy, I will not fail in my sacred mission."

She marched northwest where she would find a sea bearing vessel to ferry her across the Narrow Straits and drop her at one of the many port towns on the southern coast of Baroqia.

"I'm coming for you, Kasai Ch'ou," she said with lethal determination. "And you will pay dearly for your sins."

Also by Jeff Pantanella

Follow the adventures of Kasai, a young monk from the lost Monastery of Ordu and Desdemonia, an orphaned wood witch from the jungles of Sunne as they fight against the powers of chaos, and battle across worlds where the lines separating good and evil are constantly blurred.

The Three Kingdoms of Hanna are the initial backdrop to my new Ever Hero series which spans across the chaos of the Abyss, and the lawful order of the Seven Heavens. In all things, the Great Balance must remain!

AVAILABLE NOW

A HERO MUST RISE: The arrival of an unlikely traveler to the Abyssal ice world of Gathos creates a tear in the Amaranthine Barrier, allowing an unspeakable evil to enter the Mortal Realm and unleash a world of horror on humankind. Only one man can stop the madness, but the demigod, Aetenos, has vanished and hasn't been seen for over a hundred years.

Kasai Ch'ou and his mentor, blind Master Choejor, must flee the burning Monastery of Ordu in a desperate attempt to escape the wicked creatures of nightmare who have overrun the holy sanctuary. The two fugitives must reach the city of Gethem and warn the Grandmaster of the Seventh Heaven before the remaining monasteries of Aetenos fall to the same deadly fate.

But to reach Gethem, they must travel across the dangerous wilderness and through dark forests, prowled by preternatural beasts and haunted by witches. Meanwhile, other sinister forces vie for power to overthrow the king and plunge the land into darkness.

A new hero must rise, or all is lost.

The Chaos Gate is the first book in a dark fantasy series featuring unwilling heroes, crafty devils, capricious witches, and terrifying demons. If you like fast-paced, action adventures, with high court intrigue and highly imaginative worlds, you'll love the first installment in Jeff Pantanella's page-turning Ever Hero Saga.

Buy *The Chaos Gate* now to enjoy this exciting new series today!

https://www.amazon.com/dp/B08GPQ1557

Pantanella pours a dark, cinematic foundation in this first volume of his epic fantasy series as a singular hero rises to face both militaristic and demonic enemies. A propulsive fantasy that brings revenge, raunchiness, and heroism to the forefront.

"They were physically wrong as if their bodies had been stuffed into human skin a size too small."

~ Kirkus Reviews

AVAILABLE NOW

DARKNESS HAD TRIUMPHED: A diabolical portal connects the Abyss to the Mortal Realm, allowing hordes of demons to run amok across the lands of Baroqia, Sunne, and Trosk. One young monk may hold the key to the survival of the Three Kingdoms of Hanna, or he may lose his soul forever if he fails.

Sekka's Frost Legion now marches unchecked, harvesting human souls to fuel her diabolical war machine. Kasai and Desdemonia search for the demigod, Aetenos, but to find him, they must journey into the heart of the Abyss and the frozen world of Gathos. Can the newly proclaimed Ever Hero redeem himself and locate Aetenos before the archdevil has laid waste to the land and stolen the soul of every man, woman, and child?

The Foe Wars is the second book in the epic fantasy series The Ever Hero Saga. If you enjoy an engaging story that pits the underdog against overwhelming odds, where dark powers turn would-be heroes into unknowing puppets, and sinister plans that will throw worlds into conflict, then you'll love the second installment in Jeff Pantanella's page-turning series.

Buy **The Foe Wars** now and continue to enjoy this exciting new story today.

AVAILABLE NOW

THE SOUL HARVEST HAS BEGUN, and war rages across the Three Kingdoms. The smell of human souls seeping through the Chaos Gate awakens an ancient evil and destroyer of worlds. If the Ever Hero cannot close the portal in time, the Mortal Realm is doomed.

The lines between good and evil are blurred. Still, the harsh reality of the Great Balance is made clear when Kasai and Desdemonia travel to the Seven Heavens in hopes of salvation, only to be accused of consorting with evil and imprisoned.

Now, they must stand in judgment for treason before the Archangel, Raguel. If found guilty, the Chancellor Pinnacle will gladly sentence them to death.

There is but one way for Kasai to prove his innocence and save his soul, he must destroy Sekka. If he fails, his soul is lost, and he forfeits not only the lives of his friends but also countless souls of the Three Kingdoms.

The Divine Fist is the third book in the Ever Hero epic fantasy series. If you enjoy an engaging story, pitting the underdog against overwhelming odds, with dark powers turning would-be heroes into puppets, and sinister plans that will throw worlds into conflict, you'll love the third installment in Jeff Pantanella's page-turning Ever Hero Saga.

AVAILABLE NOW

THE ANCIENTS HAVE ARRIVED. Monstrous, cosmic beings, manifesting in the bodies of twin vampiric avatars, have established a foothold in the Mortal Realm. They race against angels and devils for a mythical being whose power can shatter the barrier protecting the Three Worlds and allow unfettered access to the souls of the Mortal Realm.

Six years have passed since the defeat of Sekka at the hands of the Ever Hero. The Heavenly Host has departed, leaving the lands a charred, ash-ladened dystopia. Kasai has returned to the ruins of Ordu, seeking solace. He is a broken man, without cause or purpose.

Enter Cyrus Wraith, a mysterious Master Monk of Symmetu who promises to guide the famed Ever Hero back to the elusive Boundless and help him rebuild the Four Orders of Aetenos. But Cyrus has a hidden agenda, and his obsession with the ancient staff, Ninziz-zida, quickly becomes evident.

The trials of the Ever Hero are not over as the stakes rise to world cataclysmic events. Kasai starts down a path that will force him to do the unthinkable to the one person he holds most dear or watch helplessly as the Three Worlds are consumed, literally.

If you are looking for a propulsive, epic fantasy series that brings intricate plots, revenge, forbidden attraction,

and heroism to the forefront, as unlikely companions rise to face both angelic and demonic adversaries, then this book is for you.

Buy, *The Forgotten Gods* now and enjoy the fourth installment in Jeff Pantanella's page-turning Ever Hero Saga.

AVAILABLE NOW

The Abyss is a world of chaos and conflict where weakness is purged, and failure equals death. Three Supreme Devils rule with uncontested might until a young, ambitious devil sets out on a path to overthrow them all.

Sekka of Nilas refuses to wait for the centuries it will take to amass the power she craves. She is cunning, manipulative, and willing to take risks a more prudent devil would never attempt. But ambition is a double-edged sword, and now she is bleeding out troops faster than she can replace them. Mistakes have been made, alliances broken, and she finds herself on the losing side of attrition against her enemies.

In a desperate gamble, the young devil launches a risky invasion to steal prized territory from a weakened foe, but one with ties to powerful allies. If the land grab is successful, it will catapult her over her enemies and into a higher echelon of power in the Abyss, but if she fails, she will lose everything; her land, her armies, and her life.

Sekka is a novella set in the epic fantasy series The Ever Hero Saga. Download Sekka now and read the origin story of the devil, Sekka, and her rise to power in the Abyss.

https://www.amazon.com/dp/B08D1W1NRY

If you have enjoyed this book, it would be tremendous if you were able to leave a review.

Reviews help me get noticed and they can bring my books to the attention of other readers who may enjoy them.

To leave a review, visit:

AMAZON UNITED STATES
https://www.amazon.com/review/create-review?&asin=B08JPVJGT7

AMAZON UNITED KINGDOM
https://www.amazon.co.uk/review/create-review?&asin=B08JPVJGT7

AMAZON CANADA
https://www.amazon.ca/review/create-review?&asin=B08JPVJGT7

Thank you!

Join my Band of Ever Heroes

Jeff Pantanella's Band of Ever Heroes members get free books, free behind the scenes photographs when you join his Advance Reader Team. You will always be the first to hear about his new books and publications.

Want to join this illustrious Band of Heroes? Then sign up for the Newsletter to be part of the Advanced Reader Team and help fine tune the books. Sign up below.

You can connect with me on:

🌐 https://www.everheroproductions.com

f https://www.facebook.com/Ever-Hero-Productions-2538551319505971

🔗 https://www.instagram.com/jeffpantanella

Subscribe to my newsletter:

✉ https://landing.mailerlite.com/webforms/landing/q6x9s8

About the Author

"I've always been drawn to the complexities confronted by being the hero in any story. Whom do you save, and what if you can't? The "Ever Hero Saga" is my debut series into the world of dark fantasy fiction, and I explore just how challenging it can be when you are indeed that hero or you're not and think you are."

Welcome to the Three Kingdoms of Hanna and your introduction to the life and times of the Ever Hero. Follow Kasai's adventures, spanning different lands, realms, and worlds as he does his best to fight the forces of evil, that unknowingly, he lets loose on the Mortal Realm.

I hope you have as much fun reading my novels as I had writing them.

Happy reading!
—Jeff

Made in the USA
Monee, IL
07 December 2021